Your Towns and Cities

Laindon

in the Great War

(including the old parishes of Basildon)

Your Towns and Cities in the Great War

Laindon
in the Great War

(including the old parishes of Basildon)

Ken Porter & Stephen Wynn

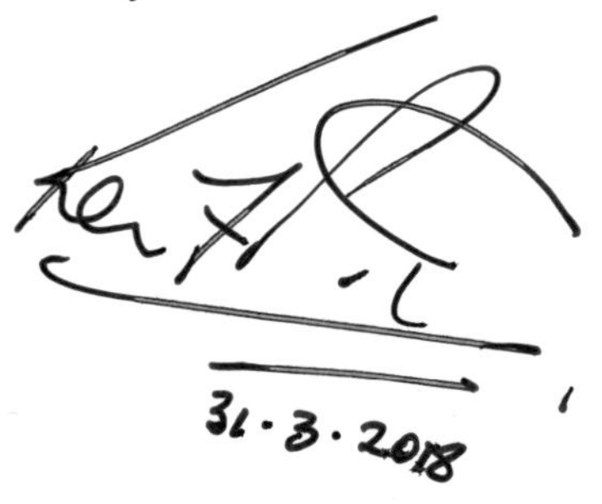

Pen & Sword
MILITARY

First published in Great Britain in 2014 by
PEN & SWORD MILITARY
an imprint of
Pen and Sword Books Ltd
47 Church Street
Barnsley
South Yorkshire S70 2AS

ISBN 978 1 78346 365 7

A CIP record for this book is available from the British Library.

Printed and bound in England
by Page Bros, Norwich

Typeset in Times New Roman

Pen & Sword Books Ltd incorporates the imprints of
Pen & Sword Archaeology, Atlas, Aviation, Battleground, Discovery,
Family History, History, Maritime, Military, Naval, Politics, Railways,
Select, Social History, Transport, True Crime, and Claymore Press,
Frontline Books, Leo Cooper, Praetorian Press, Remember When,
Seaforth Publishing and Wharncliffe.
For a complete list of Pen and Sword titles please contact
Pen and Sword Books Limited
47 Church Street, Barnsley, South Yorkshire, S70 2AS, England
E-mail: enquiries@pen-and-sword.co.uk
Website: **www.pen-and-sword.co.uk**

Contents

Foreword

I AM SO PROUD and honoured to be the first Mayor of Basildon. The Larkin family business has served the community in Laindon for over eighty years and is sited opposite one of the oldest schools in our borough, Laindon Park Primary School which originated from St Nicholas Church. Many of those who are named on the Church War Memorial attended this school. Here is where Annie Elizabeth Larkin was the school cook back in the Forties when the school was often referred to as 'Donaldson's' after the headmistress at the time, 'Miss Donaldson'. I have been the Chair of Governors at Laindon Park for over thirty years enjoying every pupil's success.

Our part of England (Laindon) made a large contribution to the Great War which sadly took the lives of so many brave men and women. The Laindon War Memorial has left a lasting testament to their courage. Ken Porter and Stephen Wynn deserve a huge 'thank you' for their commitment, dedication and enthusiasm in compiling this book.

May I leave you with my special thoughts, dedicated to the grandfather I never knew, who died delivering water to his brave men in the trenches. I have tried to capture his sacrifice in this poem:

POPPIES

A white feather falls on the poppies below
But these symbolic flowers will never grow
A field of red where winds doth blow
Ceramic poppies are there for show
For me to remember a feather that fell
My thoughts return to a living hell
Soldiers in trenches, bullets and shells
Mud, death and sacrifice for a soldier to tell
A soldier, a young man so special to me
A father, a grandad, whom I never did see
A grave, a tear in a foreign shore
A hero like thousands, who were loved and adored
So buy a poppy to remember them all
Without their brave stance our country would fall
Our freedom, their valour, a time to reflect
Whatever we do we will never forget.

Mo Larkin

Authors

KEN PORTER was born in Laindon in 1944; his passion has always been sport and history. At school he took an active part in athletics and football then in his early teens cricket took over and became his life's passion. Since retiring, history has taken precedence and, having lived in the area virtually all his life, his local knowledge is extensive. He became a leading enthusiast for the Basildon Heritage Group and Laindon and District Community Archive and gives talks to local societies. His enthusiasm for history inspires others to get involved and share their memories. His interest in the First World War stems from his maternal grandfather, James Frederick Pitts, who saw active service.

Ken has been married to Carol for forty-eight years. They have three children and five grandchildren.

STEPHEN WYNN has just retired having served with Essex Police as a constable for thirty years. He is married to Tanya and has two sons and a daughter.

His interest in history has been fuelled by the fact that both his grandfathers served in and survived the First World War, one with the Royal Irish Rifles, the other in the Merchant Navy, and his father was a member of the Royal Army Ordnance Corps during the Second World War. Both Stephen's sons, Luke and Ross, were members of the armed forces, serving five tours of Afghanistan between 2008 and 2013. Both were injured. This led to his first book, *Two Sons in a Warzone – Afghanistan: The True Story of a Father's Conflict* published in October 2010. He has also written three crime thrillers.

Ken and Stephen have collaborated on a previous book published in August 2012, *German POW Camp 266 – Langdon Hills*. It spent six weeks as the number one best-selling book in Waterstones, Basildon between March and April 2013.

Acknowledgements and Contributors

WRITING A BOOK of this nature requires a considerable amount of research and we could not have completed it without the help and co-operation of a large number of people and interested groups.

Our thanks must start with the individuals who have allowed us to write about their family experiences and reproduce their treasured photographs (see below). We hope we have rekindled their memories of their family heroes. We could not have produced the book without their stories, although we are aware there are many more out there just waiting to be unravelled.

We would also like to express our appreciation to those who helped us to verify information that we had sourced, members of the Essex Record Office and Basildon Heritage, in particular Jo Cullen and Eric Lamb, for access to their large catalogue of memories of local people taken in the 1970s; members of the Laindon and District Community Archive, in particular Denise Rowling, Sue Ranford and John Rugg; staff of Basildon Borough Council; Rod Cole of the Basildon Natural History Society; Chris Saltmarsh who has provided many postcards; Steve Newman; Karen Dennis; John Simpson, churchwarden of St Peters, Nevendon and Emma Thomas.

We have made every effort to contact the copyright holders of images and documents in this book. We apologise to anybody not properly acknowledged or whom we have not managed to trace.

Contributors
John Andrews, John Baker, Edna Baldes, Charlie Clarke, Janet Doughty, Ellen English, Albert French, Tony Hamilton, Roger Harris, Nina Humphrey, Edmund King, Gwen Lock, Peter Merten, Thomas Monk, Ivy Powell, Allen Seymour, Emma Thomas, Jan Watt, John Williams, Robbie Shields.

Introduction

WRITING THIS BOOK about Laindon and the surrounding district in the First World War was a labour of love for both Ken and Steve. Ken, because he was born in Laindon and has since spent most of his life living close by. Steve because he used to live but a mere stone's throw away, and as a young boy, spent most weekends and those never ending long summer evenings, playing nearby in the woods and fields when everything he did seemed like a new adventure.

In 2012 they had their first book published about a German prisoner of war (PoW) camp which was sited in the field at the end of Dry Street, Langdon Hills where it meets the junction with the High Road.

Langdon Hills have often played an important part in the history of the local area. There is a 10,000-year-old Mesolithic site on the south-eastern slopes and an Iron Age settlement, or possibly a fort, on the south-western slopes just east of the main road. The main road itself is fairly straight ending up at East Tilbury, where it is believed the Romans landed in Essex from Kent en route to Colchester.

Lord Fairfax and his Parliamentarian troops (Roundheads) travelled along the road to take part in the siege of Colchester during the second English Civil War in 1648.

Approximately 150 years later the hills were once again in the spotlight, this time because of the threat of a French invasion. Following the revolution in France, in 1793 the French declared war on both the British and the Dutch. The fighting took place in mainland Europe but Britain gradually became aware that Napoleon was considering an invasion and 105 defensive Martello Towers were built along the East Sussex, Kent, Essex and Suffolk coasts between 1805 and 1812. It was not only the coast which had to be defended; defences inland had to be considered as well in case the French did manage to invade. Various reports were commissioned and the following is what one of the reports had to say of the strategic position of Langdon Hills (referred to as Laindon Hills):

> 'Laindon Hills are situated near the lower Turnpike Road [current A13] leading from London to South Shoebury by Stifford & Stanford Le Hope and are about thirty miles distant from the former and fifteen from the latter Place.
>
> 'These hills stand upon a swell of ground that connects them with the Heights of Warley and Billericay and which circumvents the whole of the Flat Country to the westward, excepting at the narrow Gorge where the Mardike enters at Stifford Clays.
>
> 'They are esteemed as high if not the highest ground in the County. They have a bold and precipitate descent to the West and sink by more gentle Slopes to the East. That branch however that runs by Hawksbury Bush, Vange Hall, Basildon Church and Crays Hill, where it terminates entirely, commands the two Turnpike Roads.
>
> 'The soil on the sides of these hills is stiff clay which in wet weather is extremely heavy and impassable, towards the summit it partakes more of the Gravel. The enclosures are small with strong fences especially approaching the

The Crown Hotel, Langdon Hills – pre 1920. *Ken Porter's Collections*

Crown Public House situated near the top of the Hill.

'Four roads unite near the brow and are sheltered by thick woods. There is no reason to apprehend the supply of water would fail. Should those hills at any time be occupied by a large force there is a very good spring in the wood that constantly runs, a well at the Public House and ponds in the neighbourhood.'

Although there was a beacon position on the hill, the report was concerned that signalling from this elevated spot would be compromised by the woods. It was therefore felt that should it be necessary to communicate from the hill to the forces in the Southern District and at Warley and Danbury, scaffolding and a platform would have to be erected on the roof of the Crown Hotel and the branches of trees lopped.

The report concluded that Langdon Hills was a strategic position and if the area indeed fell into enemy hands, the whole of the low country to the west would be at Napoleon's disposal. All that could have then been done would have been to harass his army with light troops and riflemen.

In the end, Nelson and Wellington put paid to Napoleon's ambition to invade, a problem that was not going to rear its ugly head for another 100 years.

Leading up to the First World War Langdon Hills and the surrounding countryside was a favourite picnicking spot for the Victorians and Edwardians, who caught the train from London where they could marvel at views that had astounded historians over the centuries. For most it was pure escapism from the dirt and grime of the capital to the clean fresh air of the Essex countryside, only half an hour away.

This book will look at the small Essex towns of Laindon, Pitsea and the villages and hamlets of Langdon Hills, Dunton, Lee Chapel, Vange, Bowers Gifford, North Benfleet, Nevendon and Basildon, with the odd excursion into neighbouring Wickford, and consider how they were affected by the First World War going on just across the English Channel. So many men died that there were few families and communities who didn't experience the pain and suffering of losing a loved one.

Outside the big towns and cities, many of the communities were hamlets, small villages, or farms where everybody knew everybody else. The welfare state was in its infancy. Families looked after themselves the best way they could in a time where the man of the house was more often than not the only bread winner. Life was hard, there was a class system in place and many were at the wrong end of it, barely surviving day to day, where luxury was being able to put enough food on the table.

In these small communities farming was a big part of daily life, so many were dependent on it either as the farmer or a farm labourer, for work or for food, so having so many men away fighting in the war made life more difficult. When the men didn't come back many families were affected, and those who did come back were quite often different people from those who had left. Affected by the horrors of war, many never talked about what they had seen or done to survive, that was their way of coping; they simply got on with their lives.

The loss of every man normally meant devastation for the family back home, not only because of the emotional loss of a loved one, but it could mean several more years of hardship. This did not mean that those at home were passive, far from it, civilians played a vital role in the war effort.

View from the park at top of Langdon Hills, looking out towards the Thames.
Ken Porter's Collection – publication the 'County of Essex' Vol. 2 by Thomas Wright – 1835

Chapter One

The District Pre-War

THERE ARE MANY who can still remember the horrors and devastation of the Second World War and those of us who cannot, can appreciate what our parents or grandparents went through because of the advances in media broadcasting – newsreel reports, documentaries, etc. For the First World War the situation is different. There is now nobody around to tell us what it was like and filming was still in its infancy. There is, however, a considerable amount of historical data available, the only problem is that you will be lucky if it covers your local geographical area.

Today, news can be broadcast around the world in minutes which means that if any one of your loved ones is in trouble, you will hear of it in a very short period of time, but in the First World War it could be days, weeks, months or even years before families heard of what had happened.

Did our boys and their families realise what they were letting themselves into when they volunteered? The initial volunteers certainly did not as they thought it would all be over within the year. How wrong they were. As we now know millions of military personnel were killed on both sides of the conflict, but what about the civilians back home? In Britain they did not have to worry too much about the continuous bombing that was experienced in the Second World War, other than by the few Zeppelins that managed to get through our limited air cover. But how did they manage to get on with their daily lives thinking about their loved ones overseas and what did they do to help the war effort?

Laindon High Road – 1920s.
Ken Porter's Collection

Langdon Hills High Road – 1920s. *Ken Porter's Collection*

Pitsea High Street – 1920s.
Basildon Heritage Collection

Bowers Gifford, London Road – 1920s.

Basildon, Gardners' Lane.
Basildon Heritage Collection

Firstly we will look at what life was like in the years leading up to the declaration of war, focusing on the various parishes that border either side of the Southend and Fenchurch Street railway line between the two major parishes of Laindon and Pitsea.

To visualise what the Laindon/Pitsea area and Essex as a whole was like, take a trip to the farming villages of Suffolk and Norfolk with their local church, inn, general store and thatched cottages. Go for a walk, ignoring the motor car, and see how quiet and tranquil it is walking through the village to wander the lanes that run around the farmers' fields. This was our area one hundred years ago.

Then social changes happened very slowly; most men were still working a six-day week and Sunday was still church day so the chance of looking further afield to live or work was time restricted. There was no such thing as overtime, especially in the farming industry, if the weather was fine you worked. Despite the Education Acts of the 1870s with many new schools built, children were often called away from school to help, particularly during harvest times. The Bank Acts did, however, start to give people more

Vange, High Street.
Basildon Heritage Collection

Fortune of War – pre 1920s.
Ken Porter's Collection

holidays even if it was only longer weekends. Women still did not have the full vote and would not do so until 1928.

James Hissey in his publication of 1888 has this to say about the area…

> 'a glorious expanse of waving woods, green meadows and red tilled fields; miles of smiling verdure, dotted here and there with scattered farmsteads, red-roofed cottages, with ever and again a peep of a distant church tower or spire. All this goodly prospect, bounded only by the circling blue of the far-away horizon.'

The churches he was referring to would have been St Nicholas, Laindon; St Mary the Virgin, Little Burstead; Holy Cross, Basildon; St Michael, Pitsea; St Peter and St Paul's, Horndon-on-the-Hill, St Margaret's, Stanford-le-Hope which all stood on their own little hill top.

R.A. Beckett in his publication *Romantic Essex* published in 1901 had this to say when he visited the area:

> 'When last I visited the Fortune of War [Laindon], festivities were going on in a field near by and I was told that this was Fortune Fair, a yearly event since time immemorial. Like many of these old pleasure fairs, it has shrunk to very small dimensions and like many more it will doubtless soon disappear altogether. Only the slowness with which country people change their ideas and habits can explain the survival in our days of even a vestige of the simple modes of amusement which sufficed for their forefathers. In the lonely hills near Laindon the people are still very primitive. I remember once asking for a cup of water at a little cottage after dark. The kindly old mother and a daughter with a child in her arms seemed to think it strange that any one should choose to roam about the hills at night and

Laindon Blacksmith – 1990s. *Ken Porter's Collection*

> looked at me with open-eyed wonder, almost as at a being from another world.'

Perhaps we would find it strange or even suspicious, if people were walking the hills and knocking on doors at night for a glass of water! He goes on to say:

> 'Eastward, the land slopes downwards to Pitsea which lies at the head of the creek, with a massive church tower [St Michael's] standing boldly upon a bluff overlooking the innumerable channels that wind among the marshes.'

The main mode of transport other than the railway was still the horse and cart, all deliveries from shops were done by horse and cart. Farm produce was taken from the farms to the markets in large farm wagons. The reasonably well off would have had their own carriages but the rest, including children, had to walk though there might have been one or two bicycles around.

The horse was therefore dominant which accounts for the fact that there were a considerable number of roadside ponds and a blacksmith in every village. Laindon still has its blacksmith's shop in Dunton Road by the junction with Laindon High Road. It has been there since the early 1700s.

The motor car was just beginning to make an appearance. The *Laindon Recorder* of 1909 reported that a prominent local gentleman was going to make a trip from Southend to Billericay and to Laindon via the Fortune of War and thence to Laindon in a 'Motor Car'.

The roads were in a poor condition, full of ruts and mud in the winter and dust in the summer, as there was no such thing as Macadam surfaces.

In some respects it is a little surprising that the area was attracting the working man from the city of London, but on the other hand, understandable if they were looking for a retreat in the country. Only being twenty miles away from the city of London gave them the opportunity to live in a healthier environment and still travel back to the city for work.

So by 1914 it was an area in the early stages of a massive environmental change from rural farming to urban development. The change had in fact started thirty-odd years earlier in the 1880s when the country as a whole was going through an agricultural depression, brought on by several years of bad harvests and cheap imports from the prairies of North America. Essex was particularly hard hit and farmers started to go bankrupt and either sold up or just walked away. Farming at the time was a combination of crops such as wheat and livestock, mainly sheep. Land speculators moved in and purchased vast tracks of land that was gradually reverting to scrub. A few Scottish cattle farmers who were also having problems in Scotland moved in and bought up a number of farms cheaply.

Not too much happened until the railway (Southend and Fenchurch Street Line) linking Pitsea with Barking, running through Upminster, West Horndon, Laindon and Pitsea, was opened in 1888. Within three years entrepreneurs like Frederick Ramuz and Frank Steadman and others became involved in selling off small plots of land to pioneers from the East End of London, mainly for holiday accommodation. Pitsea saw the first plots of land put up for auction. The 'Plotland era', as it was to become known, had commenced; the following year in 1892 plots of land around Laindon Station went on the market.

The Laindon/Pitsea area was not the only location where this form of development was taking place. The Thames Valley – Henley-on-Thames, Surrey/Kent – Box Hill/North Downs, Isle of Sheppey, South East Coast – Camber Sands to Hayling Island, East Coast – Point Clear to Jaywick, along the river Crouch towards Maylandsea were also seeing similar developments. However the Laindon/Pitsea area had the greatest density of this type of development in the country. Some of the land here was very heavy clay and known to farmers as 'three horse land' as it required three horses to pull a plough, and this therefore was the first to go out of cultivation.

The original type of building would have been of wood, asbestos and probably self-built over a period of months. While the building was going on many families would have visited at the weekends and stayed in tents, old buses, train carriages, the last two often built onto the new wooden buildings which today would be considered no more than a shed. Facilities were non-existent – no gas, electricity, running water, sewage drainage and the roads impassable during the winter months, a situation that many were still experiencing into the 1960s.

Typical plotland building, Southview Avenue, Langdon Hills- pre 1920. *Ken Porter's Collection*

First shops built in Laindon by Elijah Collings – pre 1920. *Ken Porter's Collection*

The take up however was very slow. For example the population of the area in 1891 was as follows:

Laindon 321, Langdon Hills 213, Dunton 137, Lee Chapel 15, Vange 312, Pitsea 314, Bowers Gifford 201, North Benfleet 209, Nevendon 149, Basildon 179. Total 2,051.

The railways and land speculators worked together offering either cheap travel or the speculators offering to repay the fare if a plot was purchased. It took twenty years for the population to double to just over 4,000 though at weekends and holiday times these numbers swelled as city dwellers poured into the country. Because of this shops slowly started to get established and by the outset of the war Laindon and Pitsea were no longer hamlets but small villages. Occupations were also changing. The populace did not totally rely on farm or associated work. People were travelling back to the city and working in offices or factories, those that worked locally were finding employment in the shops and small local businesses that were starting up, house building contractors, for example. Elijah Collings, who had moved to Laindon prior to 1900, built shops near the station for his family. One such was a stationer's and post office run initially by Kate Collings who in 1911 was to marry Edwin Andrews. Read more about his war exploits in the chapter 'Our Heroes'. Farming however, was still prominent, in particular dairy farming. The Scottish farmers or 'invaders' as some would categorise them, were beginning to make an impact and change the farming environment away from arable and sheep to arable and cattle.

One such family were called Wilson. They moved down from Kilmarnock, Ayrshire, and took over Dunton Hall pre-1900 and a son William Walter was born at the hall in 1894. At the age of sixteen he emigrated to Australia as both his parents had died. He joined the Australian Expeditionary Force at the beginning of the war, saw action in the Dardanelles campaign before being killed on his way to France in September 1916.

Though farming was one of the largest employers, there was one large factory employer in the area, 'The Pitsea Explosive Factory', and many local men and women found employment there.

Religion still played an important part in many lives. When the first Plotland pioneers started to appear they would have only had the established parish church to attend (Church of England). A large proportion of these new settlers were Nonconformist and were rather shocked to find themselves in the country without a chapel, mission or Sunday school other than the parish churches.

One of the new settlers to the area of Langdon Hills was Jonas Charles Young and his second wife Johanna Wilhelmina (née Polenski). They moved around 1901/2 from St Pancras, London and the 1911 census has them living at 'Lyndhurst', High Road, Langdon Hills, his occupation being that of a coal merchant. Jonas was born in Germany in 1855, Jonas Karl Jung. The 1901 census informs us that he was a naturalised British subject and at some time anglicised the family name to Young.

Jonas was one who was concerned with the lack of alternative places of worship and in desperation approached Harry Foulger, a local entrepreneur, who had spotted the development opportunities available in Laindon and Langdon Hills. In the first two decades of the twentieth century Harry Foulger was not only selling homes, but also plots of land for self-build. He was obviously aware that with the influx of new people, there would be a requirement for a hall. So he had built The Nightingale Public Hall and offered to rent the place for divine worship. Jonas, with the help of Messrs Tatum, Diprose, Hayes and others, founded at the hall a non-sectarian mission, which was

J.C. Young on the left with his wife Marie at Laindon
Kind permission of Betty Telford

Nightingale Mission Church, built 1902.
Ken Porter's Collection

The new Nightingale Mission Hall built 1907.
Ken Porter's Collection

opened in December 1902, followed at once by the first Sunday school. Then in July 1903 Jonas, who was now secretary, gave notice to a meeting of an application to the Wesleyan, Congregational and non-sectarian churches to undertake the running of the mission and later in the year The Nightingale Mission Church was formed.

In 1907 a new site was secured on the opposite side of the High Road to the hall and on 1 April 1907, a stone-laying service took place during which the stone was laid by Isaac Levy. Then, in June, the New Nightingale Mission Church was dedicated by the Reverend W.S. Walsh and its first minister was the Reverend George Mitchell.

In the years that followed the First World War and up to the Second World War Langdon Hills and Laindon saw an even greater increase in the population. The church obviously grew at this time and by 1930 it was clear that an extension was necessary to cope with this growth. On Saturday, 19 June 1932, the service for the laying of the foundation stones for the new extension was conducted by the Reverend R. Whittaker, Superintendent of the East Ham Circuit. Nineteen stones were laid, the first being laid by Mrs Levy. Mr A.G. Scrivens, on behalf of Mrs Young, laid a stone in memory of

Extension built in 1902 – now Langdon Hills Methodist Church. *Ken Porter's Collection*

Mrs J.C. Young plaque.
Ken Porter's Collection

Thatched School, Langdon Hills -1860-1911. *Ken Porter's Collection*

Jonas Young who had died the previous year.

Whether locals at the time of the First World War were aware that he was German is unknown, but there does not seem to have been any attempt to report him to the authorities as an alien, perhaps because he had become a respected member of the community and accepted as one of them.

The church has since gone from strength to strength and in 1956 had a further extension added, this time opened by Her Royal Highness, Princess Alice, Countess of Athlone.

Jonas' daughter, Wilhelmina, from his first wife Annie (nee Hahn) married Jacob Jacobs Schlize, who was unfortunately interned at Frimley, then Knockaloe on the Isle of Man.

In the fifteen years since R.A. Beckett's visit the people of the area were no longer primitive but life did still appear to be slow and carefree compared with today.

Sometime in the mid 1970s Rod Cole, a member of the Basildon Natural History Society, interviewed George Siggers. He is referred to as George Junior in the chapter on 'Our Heroes' as he tells his father George's war story.

George Junior was born in Lee Chapel Lane, Langdon Hills in 1903 and when he was five he went to the local thatched school at the top of Crown Hill, now known as the Old School House. There were about twenty children from the ages of five to thirteen or fourteen years of age. Two teachers, Mrs Fothergill and Miss Burdon, taught the basic subjects of reading, writing, arithmetic with a little history and geography. The girls did some needlework. School hours were similar to today, 9am to 3pm and they had just over an hour for lunch for which they had to go home or take lunch with them. George Junior was now living in Dry Street in a small bungalow next to the Red Cow off licence which had previously been a beer house. George Junior had grandparents living down Old Church Hill near the Old Church of Langdon Hills, which was much closer than his bungalow in Dry Street, so he would go to them for a snack lunch and have his hot meal when he got home in the evening.

In 1911 the school was closed and a new board school was built closer to the railway station. George was unable to go to the school for at least three months because he and a friend had cattle ringworm in their hair. Mrs Fothergill transferred to the school as headmistress; one of the new teachers was Miss Tweet who came from East Ham. During the week she stayed at a bungalow in Dry Street and George junior used to call at the bungalow on Monday mornings on the way to school to collect her lunch then on the Friday take all the week's empties back while she caught a train back to East Ham. The lady who owned the bungalow in Dry Street kept chickens so would often give him an egg for his breakfast.

He left school when he was thirteen in 1916 and went to work for West Ham Council which owned a fruit farm in Dry Street, 'Wootton Farm' (see Appendix 1). West Ham Council had purchased the farm in the spring of 1914 with the intention of turning it into a home for those that suffered from smallpox, but the local parish would not allow it and the beginning of the war in August stopped any further suggestion for change of use.

George first worked for the West Ham Council at Harold Wood, Romford, but after a few months he was transferred back to Wootton Farm, where his main job was looking after the ponies and horses. He had worked there while at school, helping the previous owner Mr Bennett who used to take his fruit twice a week to York Road market in Southend. George Junior could only help out on Fridays because of school. He helped to get two wagons and horses ready, they would then leave around 5.30pm and reach Southend about 9.30pm. He would stable the horses with some hay while they went off and had some tea which was normally fish and chips. They would get back home around midnight and by the time he had helped put the horses away he would get home any time after 1am. Not bad for a child of eleven or twelve years of age! At the age of eight or nine, he often had to walk into Stanford-le-Hope some five miles away with a prescription from a visiting doctor, being told to hurry back by 8pm as it would be dark.

One of the old characters from Dry Street was Mr Tinworth who lived in an old shack.

Wooton Farm – pre 1920.
Ken Porter's Collection

Mr Tinworth the water carrier – pre 1920.
Ken Porter's Collection

His living was his allotment and being the local water carrier. He had a donkey and cart on which he had a large water barrel. He used to go out about three times a week often before people were up and they would leave out jugs and saucepans for him to fill up with water They would pay him when they next met him. He did this for many years right up to the end of the war when he went to work at the Wootton Fruit Farm.

Mr Tinworth was not the only person to have an allotment. Unlike today there was plenty of land available for allotments where locals could supplement their income by either selling their produce or keeping it for themselves, a luxury city folk did not have.

Frederick Jobson, also of Langdon Hills, in an interview with the local paper just before his death in 1963, gave a brief description of what the area was like in the years leading up to the war.

He moved to the area in 1906 because the land was very cheap and there was plenty of countryside although it was slowly being developed. He explained that there were no services; lighting was by paraffin and water from the wells. The last train from Fenchurch Street was the 8.41pm, so as Frederick said, it was difficult to go off the rails in London. The last train from Southend reached Laindon at 9pm. Social life centred on the church and when the church hall was built in 1907 all kinds of activities took place; plays, dances, concert parties, musical evenings, Shakespearian evenings, debating societies etc. When the war commenced the locals continued with these activities in support of the Red Cross.

One personal story was Frederick's wedding day, just preceding the declaration of war. Cars were non-existent in Laindon so he hired two from Billericay, a nearby town. One was to take him to St Mary's Church at the top of Crown Hill but at the bottom of the hill the driver turned the car round and went up backwards. Frederick was rather concerned but the driver explained that he always went up steep hills backwards and Crown Hill was a very steep hill, further explaining that his car could do anything in reverse, even climb a tree. Frederick explained that he had no wish to climb a tree. All he wanted was to get to the church on time. Fortunately the driver turned the car round and did the last hundred yards in a forward direction. Frederick's worry was that he would have ended walking up the aisle backwards and saying 'Will I' instead of 'I Will'.

He explained that it was a very law-abiding community. There was one policeman in Langdon Hills and he would have to take an offender to Grays, ten miles away (how he would have got them there he did not know). Laindon had one policeman and he had to take offenders to Billericay some six miles away but he said there was no crime as none of the folks had anything worth stealing.

Mr and Mrs Watson's bungalow, Honeypot, Lane, Basildon, a substantial building for its time, 1906. *Kind permission of the Essex Police Museum*

In general he was right but perhaps he had not heard of the 1906 murders, known locally as 'The Honeypot Murders'. Honeypot, was the name of the road where Mr and Mrs Watson were murdered, and was one of the boundaries between the old parishes of Laindon and Basildon. The accused were local neighbours Richard and Robert Buckham. Robert was acquitted but Richard was found guilty and hanged three months later on 4 December 1906. Robert was to join the army and serve throughout the war and return to Basildon in 1919.

The murders were a result of a lack of water. The Reverend Herbert Carpenter, rector of Laindon-cum-Basildon was one of the witnesses at the trial. In his statement he tried to paint a picture of what it was like in this part of Essex:

> 'We are used to the unkind vagaries of the weather in these parts. Water, both of its scarcity and its excess, is the problem. In winter, the ground is so waterlogged, its sticky yellow mass resembles the consistency of dirty treacle – or indeed, as local nomenclature testifies – it is like a monstrous honeypot. In summer, we are left to negotiate hardened ruts as best we can – the water deserts us for more friendly soils.
>
> 'This summer, more than any other I can recall, the dearth of rain hit the community hard. Ponds, rainwater-butts, ditches all dried up in a baking heat that has extended from late June to now. Even the mud in our dank cellars at the Rectory has dried to stone and our well has been uncommonly low. The drought has forced cows to be fed on turnips and there have been many haystack fires – the worst at Hanningfield where I understand nine stacks were consumed.'

He also made reference to a discussion he had with a local neighbour Mr Stevens who said: 'You would do this place a good turn if you could urge upon the Billericay Rural Council to act – firstly the need of a proper water supply…These people would not have lost their lives if they had had a water supply.'

The Reverend Carpenter, in his final comment went on to say:

> I do have sympathy with his views. Residents hereabouts have been much neglected as far as basic needs are concerned. People in the twentieth century should not have to drink untreated pond-water or struggle to keep clean without rainwater. Bishop Westcott wrote: "We must serve in order that we may understand. Sympathy, which is the strength of government, comes by service." We need more than sympathy in Laindon-cum-Basildon, however. This community certainly needs good water supplies and good roads but it also needs habitable houses rather than the proliferation of huts and sheds we have seen popping up hereabouts. Will further terrible acts need to take place for those in authority to take action?'

Very little action was taken and the situation had hardly changed by the start of the First World War other than that there was more shack-type housing and the population had swollen.

Miss Dorothy Gardner, born at Marsh Farm, Vange in 1904, related her memories of the lead up to war to the Basildon Heritage Group in 1985. She spoke of the nearby brickfields and said that her father had lots of horses and carts and used to cart the bricks for building local houses, including the farmhouse they lived in. Barges used to come up the nearby creeks to be loaded with bricks which were then taken to London. As a child she used to swim in the creeks. On the day war was declared she had returned home from the annual horticultural show held at All Saints Church, Vange to find her mother in tears. The War Office had taken several horses and her mother's mare that she used to drive her trap, for the war effort. During the war Dorothy, her sister and her younger brother used to do a milk round before going to school. Dorothy and her sister used to go to Pitsea station and put the milk churns on the 8.15 train for either Southend or Grays. This was followed with the milk round in the Bowers Gifford area. Near the Bowers Rectory was a gun site and her brother and another sister delivered milk to the troops there. They had been given one-hour morning session extension and did not have to be at school until 10am.

Today we are used to all forms of welfare benefits and though many people are still

Typical road of the area right up to the 1960s.
Ken Porter's Collection

considered poor, their situation is nowhere near what it was like prior to the First World War. The Poor Law acts were still in force and there were the dreaded workhouses if one was destitute. There were, however, welfare pioneers who were trying to find a way of solving the acute problem at the beginning of the twentieth century. One such was Joseph Fels, an American Jew. For some time he had been advocating the establishment of smallholdings and farm holdings to help relieve the problems of the poor. With the support of George Lansbury, who had become one of the most expert of Poor Law administrators in the country through his work with the Poplar Board of Guardians, where he endeavoured to improve the scope of poor relief, in 1904 Fels purchased 100-acre Sumpners Farm in Dunton, and created the first Farm Colony for the unemployed in England.

Lansbury's greatest concern was that of Poplar, one of the poorest of the East End districts, so because of his support, Fels lent the land to Poplar Board of Guardians on a three-year agreement at a peppercorn rent with the guardians having the option to purchase at any time during their tenancy for the original price.

The land was taken over in March 1904 and one hundred able-bodied paupers from Poplar were set to work. Temporary buildings for dormitories, kitchen, laundry, toilets and a reservoir for water was built. One of the major differences between a farm colony and the workhouse was the greater freedom. Papers, books, games and a piano were provided. Although there was a great amount of criticism of the scheme, a number of influential people visited and it was initially a great success. A large number of the men were old soldiers who had had at least ten years service but no pension.

In November 1904 a reporter on the Municipal Journal wrote:

> 'The first Poor Law Labour colony in England, run by the Poplar Board of Guardians, near Laindon, has now had a three month trial. It is quite easy to understand, when one has seen the working of this labour colony, why it should be considered the broad way out of the unemployment impasse. Sumpners Farm, acquired for the purpose of the colony, is completely isolated…'

The report went on to praise the new project in glowing terms and so did another report a month later. They were also impressed with the superintendent, Mr John Clark, who was to be in charge for the next thirty years until his death in 1933 at the aged of sixty-three. It was not always peaceful on the farm, however. The local papers had a field day over the next thirty years reporting various misdemeanours, such as drunkenness, stealing and assaults etc.

The Poplar Board of Guardians handed it over to the London County Council (LCC) in

Swimming in the creek at Pitsea – 1930s. *Basildon Heritage Collection*

1928 and they continued to run the self-contained community on similar lines until 1941.

The authorities certainly meant business and it could only be described as a small self-contained rural village. It comprised two large dormitory buildings (both 150ft x 50ft) and three smaller dormitories. There were workshops of all kinds, including tailors, cobblers, carpenters, plumbers. There were also stables, piggery, chicken and poultry houses, cow sheds, milking parlour, dairy, slaughterhouse, laundry, boiler house and a clinic, sick bay and dispensary. Doctor Henderson, whose surgery was at 'Hiawatha' in Laindon, used to attend two days a week during the 1930s.

It also had a dining hall with a large kitchen, several offices, cottages on or near the site for the permanent staff, its own sewage plant and of course there was a general store and clothing store. The general store supplied cigarettes and tobacco to the inmates. It also sold the fruit, vegetables and dairy produce etc produced on site to the inmates to take with them on the weekends when they were given passes and allowed to go home. Local residents could also purchase goods from the store.

At its height the inmates numbered between 200-300 and were housed in either the dormitories or in movable huts in and around the farm and orchard. They were employed either on the site farm or sent to other farms, hospitals or similar institutions in the locality. In 1941, owing to the hostilities, the colony was closed. The records show there were 175 inmates at the time, but not what happened to them. The permanent staff remained in occupation. The camp was immediately taken over by the Civil Defence and prepared and equipped as a hospital for local air raid and war casualties; fortunately the occasion to use it never arose.

In 1942 the Military Authorities took the whole camp over from the Civil Defence and every available building or accommodation was used to house troops and more camped out under canvas in the fields and orchard. Then in early 1943 they moved out and the Royal Air Force moved in and remained until the end of 1944.

During all this time the permanent staff of the LCC had remained in occupation and they did not leave until 1956. Early that year the main batch of permanent staff was transferred to various hospitals, leaving only Mr P. Hibbard, the gate keeper, and Mr Goldinggay, the accountant and superintendent, who both retired in June 1956 when Mr C. Gray acquired the colony and changed its name to Charles Caravan Park. It is still a private mobile home camp to this day.

Although this farm colony experiment was very successful, workhouses continued to flourish. There have been two types of workhouse, the parish workhouse which was run by overseers and church wardens of the parish, and the union workhouse, established in the 1830s by amalgamating a group of parishes which did away with parish workhouses and were run by a board of guardians. Their job was to see that the poor (paupers) were clothed and fed. The inmates were put to work on jobs that could be carried out within the workhouse or local vicinity.

To cover our area in question and other parishes there were two Union workhouses established at Billericay and Orsett. Billericay Union covered twenty six parishes: Laindon, Basildon, North Benfleet, Bowers Gifford, Dunton, Nevendon, Pitsea, Vange, Wickford, Little Burstead, Great Burstead, Ramsden Crays, South Benfleet, Brentwood, East and West Horndon, Ramsden Bellhouse, Shenfield, Thundersley, Little Warley, South Weald,

Childerditch, Downham, Mountnessing, Hutton and Ingrave.

Orsett Union covered another eighteen parishes: Langdon Hills, Fobbing, Bulphan, Aveley, Chadwell St Mary, Corringham, Horndon-on-the-Hill, Mucking, North Ockendon, South Ockendon, Orsett, Stanford-le-Hope, Stifford, Grays, Thurrock, Little Thurrock, West Thurrock, East Tibury and West Tilbury.

Percy and Beattie Monk have a clear recollection of inmates from these workhouses walking from one to the other doing work in the local area as they went, often stopping for a drink and a snack on their way from the locals. It would appear though that the majority of inmates were old or infirm. It was the last place anybody wanted to end up in.

During the First World War the Billericay workhouse was used to house German prisoners. Workhouses did not disappear until the late 1920s and early 1930s. Billericay eventually became St Andrew's Hospital and Orsett, Orsett Hospital.

In 1906 the Liberal Party swept to power and, though there were no promises of welfare reforms in their election campaign, it was not long before they started to introduce some limited welfare benefits that we take for granted today. The Old-Age Pensions Act 1908 was implemented in January 1909 for those over seventy years of age, but the criteria a claimant had to pass to obtain the pension of 5s week or 7s 6d for a married couple was very harsh. In order to be eligible, he or she had to be earning less than £31.10s per year, pass a 'character test', be a UK resident for at least twenty years and have worked throughout their life. The level of benefit was set low deliberately to encourage workers to make their own provision for retirement; no wonder only half a million were eligible.

Then in 1911 the first National Insurance Act was introduced and came into effect in July 1912. The intention was to create a national system of insurance for working people against illness and unemployment. Wage earners between the ages of sixteen and seventy contributed 4d per week, employers 3d and the state 2d. In return the workers were entitled to a level of free medical care and 7 shillings per week up to fifteen weeks per year in the event of unemployment. These two benefits were the start towards creating the welfare state as we know it today.

Another major difference is that today around seventy per cent of households own their own home; before the First World War the situation was totally the reverse with probably only about twenty per cent and this is possibly why our area is fairly unique. As stated earlier land was cheap, people wanted to get away from London so even with their low wages they were managing to buy a plot of land to build a small holiday home that in the decades to follow ended up being their permanent home. Until the war most property being built for sale was for renting but by 1914 tax relief on mortgage interest had been introduced to encourage home ownership, although in general this was cancelled out by other forms of taxation needed to pay for the forthcoming war.

So there we have it, our area was still mainly involved in farming but small businesses and industries were slowly moving in as the East End pioneers arrived and over the next forty years the area was going to change dramatically. The war helped speed up this change. There was a realisation that women could do as many jobs as the men and in some cases better, working in the munitions factories for example, and this helped them to eventually get the vote. The political scene was also beginning to change with politicians appreciating the effort and human sacrifice of the country's working families.

Chapter 2

Local explosives factories

Pitsea Explosive Factory

In 1891 the British Explosives Syndicate built a factory in Pitsea at what is now known as the Wat Tyler Country Park. Some of the original factory buildings survive to this day. The factory started out by producing all different kinds of explosives – dynamite, gelignite and others based on nitro-glycerine, for blasting rocks and mining. It also made nitro-glycerine as an ingredient part for the production of cordite, which was a smokeless propellant used in the manufacture of ammunition.

Extra Dynamite, which was also known as blasting gelantine or gelignite, had been introduced in 1875. Gelignite made for a more efficient way to mine the coal that fuelled the huge boom in Victorian industry and engineering. The new factory in Pitsea became very busy very quickly. They sent explosives as far afield as Australia where the demand for their products was high, mainly because people were mining everything from coal to gold.

In 1885, countries across Europe, including Britain, agreed on a 'Permitted List' of explosives for use in mining. These had chemicals added that would lower the temperature of their explosion and prevent the ignition of methane gas.

At first glance this might not sound a particularly interesting story, but there's more, much more. One of the partners in the British Explosives Syndicate was Alfred Nobel, who in 1863 had patented a new invention he had named 'Dynamite'. He had managed to develop a much safer way of handling the extremely dangerous and highly volatile explosive, nitro-glycerine. As a result of this success he went on to build an enormous business which stretched throughout Europe and to the United States. Nobel desperately wanted to expand his business and tap into the huge markets of the British Empire, but at the time regulations prevented him from doing so. Eventually he found a loophole in the law which allowed the factories in Scotland and then Pitsea to be built and begin their operations.

Initially Nobel had decided on being a sleeping partner but eventually he changed his mind and openly traded under his own name. He then decided that the way forward was in the world of chemicals and the company eventually became a household name as Imperial Chemical Industries (ICI).

Alfred Nobel.
Basildon Heritage collection

Alfred Nobel was of course the same man who was responsible for the invention of the Nobel Peace Prize, which is still awarded annually to the individual who has done the most or the best work for fraternity between nations, for the abolition or reduction of standing armies and for the holding and promotion of peace congresses. Besides his patent to make dynamite, Nobel also owned 350 different patents. Collectively they made him an extremely wealthy man.

Alfred Nobel's death in 1896 caused somewhat of a sensation, especially for his family, as he left none of them any money in his will. Instead he set up prizes for those 'making the greatest contribution to mankind'. The Nobel Prizes have been awarded every year since 1901.

There has always been some conjecture about why Alfred left his fortune as he did. Some say it was because of an article which appeared in a French newspaper after the death, in 1888, of his brother Ludvig whilst he was visiting Cannes. The article incorrectly believed it was Alfred who had died and in the obituary they wrote about him they condemned him for his invention of dynamite.

The obituary included, *'Le marchand de la mort est mort'* which translates to, 'The merchant of death is dead'. It went on to say, 'Dr Alfred Nobel, who became rich by finding ways to kill more people faster than ever before, died yesterday.'

He was said to have been greatly upset and angry about what he had read and was concerned about how he would be remembered after his death.

Alfred Bernhard Nobel died on 10 December 1896 aged 63, in San Remo, Italy. In his will he left £1,687,837 to cover the continued cost of the Nobel Prizes. That figure has now risen in value to approximately £300 million.

In 1902, with tensions increasing between Britain and The Netherlands over South Africa, the Pitsea factory added more buildings specifically for the manufacture of cordite, which was a smokeless explosive used as a propellant in military shells. Guncotton was a primary ingredient of cordite, which was a mix of waste from the Lancashire cotton mills and nitro-glycerine. It needed to be thoroughly 'picked' by hand to remove any impurities. Its manufacture was highly dangerous, as proven in the fatal 1913 guncotton explosion at Pitsea.

On 28 March 1913, three men died and many others were injured in an explosion in a guncotton drying stove at the Pitsea factory. The official government report that followed covered the incident in great detail and although it 'presumed' an element of some carelessness, it blamed no one individual. An alternative theory however suggests the explosion could have been caused by a faulty batch of guncotton delivered in from Ardeer in Scotland, which had only been part dried before being shipped down to Pitsea by sea.

Those that died were Arthur Cross, age 41, married with five children, Church Road, Pitsea, painter; Henry John Hanna, age 28, married, one child, Southend Terrace, Vange, foreman stove man and John Bayles, 21, single, Station Road, Pitsea, stove man. Two boys, who were outside the shed, were also slightly injured.

The shock of the explosion was felt for a radius of twenty miles and the damage to neighbouring property was considerable. A mess room, in which half an hour later some twenty-four girls would have been having dinner, was wrecked. People in the vicinity who heard the explosion saw immediately the whole of the 'store' rise into the air, enshrouded by a pall of thick yellow smoke and then fall in fragments to the ground. Ammunition was scattered in all directions. Windows were shattered in the villages of Vange, Pitsea and Laindon, Laindon being a distance of five miles away.

Bayles was blown into the air and landed ninety yards away, the impact of his body made a hole in the ground. Hanna was torn to pieces.

There were a number of lucky escapes. Mrs Davey of Pitsea Hall was lying seriously ill in the only room that did not have its windows blown in and her daughter, Mrs Solder, was nursing her four month old baby when a heavy horseshoe from the mantelpiece passed within an inch of the baby's head.

A worker, Mr Harrison, was wheeling the damp guncotton to the stove, when his trolley was wrenched from his hands and blown to pieces. He was knocked to the ground and had his trousers ripped from him.

Edward Adams, a member of the St John Ambulance and Dr Thompson of Laindon, entered the burning shed to find Hanna. As soon as they got inside they came across a bag of guncotton unexploded and rushed out again. The three men were beyond help.

The *Chelmsford Chronicle* reported that nothing like it had been known since the great Essex earthquake of 1884.

In May 1916, a chemist and his assistant were killed in a laboratory at the factory when one of the chemists dropped a small bottle of nitro-glycerine.

Every worker at the factory was searched on their way into work and once again when they finished for the day. Anything that could make a flame or spark had to be left at the gate and of course they didn't want any of their staff being tempted to take anything home with them. Throughout the factory there were wooden walkways, which stopped the workers' shoes from picking up stones from the pathways running the risk of the stones causing a life-threatening spark.

A lot of thought had gone into the working practices at the factory as just one mistake could have catastrophic consequences, not just for the person making it, but for everybody working there. The workers' overalls had no pockets, they wore different colours according to the particular job they were doing, so that they could only access areas they knew enough about to be able to work safely in. If there was an accident the colours helped the head count to discover quickly who was missing and in which area.

The factory thrived during the First World War, providing all kinds of explosives and munitions for the British war effort. It also provided much needed work for the local community and paid well, although the work was potentially very dangerous. With the end of

Uniform of 'cartridge girl' at the Pitsea Explosive factory

the First World War, the factory not surprisingly started to struggle, the need and high demand for munitions having plummeted. It closed for good in 1919.

Mrs Clara Gladding, a resident of Bowers Gifford, was 90 at the time she was interviewed in 1986 by John Williams on her memories of the time she worked at the Pitsea Explosive Factory. John went on to publish the history of the Explosive Factory – *From Corn to Cordite* – and dedicated the book to her. It is understood that Clara was the only person living in 1986 who had actually worked at the factory.

Clara was about sixteen when she found employment in the factory and at the time was living in Pound Lane, Bowers Gifford. She would walk from Pound Lane to the Pitsea Factory morning and night, her hours being 8am to 5pm. The men tended to work shifts but not the girls. She worked there from 1911 until just after the war in the munitions shed making and packing cartridges of all sizes into boxes. When these were filled they were placed on a trolley and taken away. John Simpson was one of the men that pulled the trolleys along a rail. The girls working there had to wear fireproof slip dresses and slippers and leave their own clothes outside in an undercover area. Their hair was in plaits, with no hair pins and every time they went out for meals etc. they were searched. There was a mess room on site, a long low building to the right, just after the entrance. The workers wore name tags to prove that they were allowed on the premises.

When Clara first started there she, like many of the girls, suffered from terrible headaches and many of them said they would not go there again but they did.

William Warburton was one of the foremen and John McDale was another. There were two sides to the factory, one working on the guncotton production and the others packing the cartridges. Men and women worked on both together and it was there that Clara met her future husband. Clara's future sister-in-law, Lilley, also worked at the factory in the guncotton department.

Clara married Alfred Stanley Gladding on 5 August 1919, the brother of Arthur, who later appears as one of our war heroes.

In 1985 Elsie Norman gave an interview to a member of the Basildon Heritage Group. Elsie was born in 'Hawthorn Cottage', North Benfleet in 1915. It was her grandparent's home. The family had moved there at the beginning of the First World War, after her grandfather had died. Her grandmother was fearful of the darkness in a land where there were more fields than neighbours.

This is her story about her father's involvement in the Pitsea Factory explosion:

> 'My father Herbert (Bert) Norman had worked for the old National Telephone Company in London for some time, when the Government seeing the potential, 'took over' the 'Old National' – "Everyone's job would be safe". In fact 2,000 men were put off including my father. No job, no money for London rent. My grandfather had died and my grandmother was in some fear of the lonely darkness on the Benfleet Park Estate. (Other houses had now been built but there was still far more open space than houses.) So the family went to live with her at Hawthorn Cottage.
>
> 'I was born there in 1915. Employment was limited, there were farms, but cows had neither wheels nor wires. The only place crying out for labour was Pitsea Explosives Factory on Pitsea Marsh. Dad went to work there. Mum was terrified.

'Dad learned a lot about the dangerous product and was therefore not very happy about being there. Seeing a group of men digging a trench one day he enquired and was told it was to take a telephone cable underground. He asked if there was any chance of a job. There was. He left the explosive factory and started digging with the Post Office contractors. A few days later a car drew up and a man got out. He took one look at Dad and said, "Bert! What are you doing here?" Dad explained. The man was an old London colleague. He was outraged. "You are digging trenches when we are very short of skilled maintenance staff. I'll report it."

'He did! Dad was returned to his previous category and was posted to maintenance at Stanford-le-Hope.

'At about the same time, the Explosive Company thought it would speed up their starting time if instead of waiting for the boy to come back with the clearance for starting work, they had a phone installed to ring and say, "OK". So the wheels of co-incidence revolved.

'A pole was put up outside the test shed and on that fatal morning, Dad with his co-worker were working at the top of the new pole and Dad was explaining what was made at the factory and why a boy was walking towards them with a carrier bag with two little jars in it. The boy was bringing the two jars with their ingredients up for testing at the shed. Dad's partner was very sceptical. "Not much stuff there!" "No, agreed Dad but if he drops them at the bottom of this pole we shall not be here any more."

'The boy went into the shed. In minutes he was out again – backwards through the window. Dad grabbed the 'tapper' and dialled Vange Exchange. "Ruby. Clear all lines and come back to me."

"Why Bert?"

"Pitsea factory is about to go up." There was a second whoop and the main factory exploded.

The operator at Vange came back. "All clear Bert."

"Get me Billericay Hospital quick and call Mr Cook and the police."

'His call came through. "This is urgent and important – Get two wards ready for injured patients and send all your ambulances and doctors, surgeons and nurses, everyone who can come. The Explosive Factory at Pitsea has gone up, if I can raise other help I will."

'He called soldiers in from Defence Positions, Mr Cook, the draper with his ex Boys' Brigade first aid training from the Men's Department staff, came running over the hill. The Fire Brigade and Police soon followed.

'Less than a quarter of a mile away, Mother stood still. I looked up from the pram. A woman walking towards us said: "What's that?" Mother said: "Pitsea Factory has gone up! Thank God my husband isn't still working there! He was working there until a few weeks ago."

'That evening, Dad came home. "Oh Bert!" Mother hugged him. "Thank God you weren't still at that factory today! It exploded."

'"No", he said, "Just thank God I was there, but I couldn't do much, I just did all I could – I don't want any tea, I'm going to bed." Mother sat down flummoxed.'

As stated the site closed in 1919 and in searching through the Basildon Heritage files we came across the following letter from the British Explosives Syndicate Limited dated 18 August 1919 to one of its employees.

To all whom it may concern.

We beg to certify that Miss P. Bibby was employed by us from 25 September 1918 to 16 August 1919 as a Cartridge Maker. We found her to be a good timekeeper and a very capable and willing worker and her services were in every way satisfactory. We dispensed with her services owing to the cessation of our manufacture.

For the British Explosives Syndicate Limited, Works Managers

Miss Bibby's Christian name was Prudence, she was born in 1902, married in 1925 and the 1911 census has her living with her family at Newark House, Vange.

In Wat Tyler Park today there are still a number of angular earthworks, which were purpose built blast mounds erected between and around the buildings of the factory to help contain any accidental explosion and stop it spreading from building to building.

A few of the buildings are still standing. The first one you come across as you enter Wat Tyler Park is the factory search hut. Workers were searched for any metal object that might cause a spark – matches, coins, watches, jewellery. A spark could easily ignite the volatile fumes and blow up the factory. The buildings opposite were the guard house and supervisor's house where trucks coming in and out would be stopped, searched and directed to various buildings around the site.

Concrete bowl used for washing guncotton
Ken Porter's Collection

The laboratory stands approximately a hundred yards away in front of the Green Centre. This building replaced the one that was destroyed in the 1916 accident and is possibly the one referred to by Elsie Norman. Laboratory staff tested the strength of incoming chemicals to guarantee uniformity and safety. Chemicals that fell below standards could lead to fatal

Pitsea Explosive search huts.
Ken Porter's Collection

The Laboratory.
Ken Porter's Collection

The earthworks in the distance.
Ken Porter's Collection

Explosive Factory. *Ken Porter's Collection*

Manmade ponds for washing the guncotton.
Ken Porter's Collection

accidents, like the one already mentioned in 1913. Finished explosives were also tested here by igniting a small amount of the explosives on a bench top.

Nearby, tucked away in the shrubs near the children's railway line, is the expense magazine. Work on the explosive factory was only carried out during daylight hours as electricity and gas were considered too dangerous as they might ignite the highly flammable fumes creating an explosion. If there were any unfinished batches of explosives at the end of the day they were stored in this building until morning. Also if any worker became unconscious because of the fumes, they would be dragged outside into the fresh air and once they recovered, they went straight back to work.

There are one or two natural looking ponds but in fact they are actually man made. They were designed to capture water waste from washing guncotton, an explosive made by mixing cotton waste from the Lancashire mills with nitro-glycerine. It was the most frighteningly unstable and powerful explosive. The guncotton was washed in the ponds to remove excess nitro-glycerine to make it stable enough to be handled and once a week a worker would throw a charge of dynamite into the ponds to get rid of any lingering traces of nitro-glycerine.

(Beginning to feel it might have been safer to be a soldier at the front?)

Down by the creek is a rather unusual concrete bowl, which it is believed was also used to wash or drain guncotton. On the other side of the bowl is a channel for draining its contents.

The Wat Tyler and the RSPB buildings were also part of the massive complex.

Edward Baker known affectionately by his family and friends as Ted was born in Bury, Lancashire in 1876. By 1901 he was living in Fobbing and working at the Vange brickworks as brick moulder. In 1904 he found employment with Pitsea Explosive factory working as a cordite blender and by 1911 his job had changed to that of a cordite packer and he was now living in Pitsea. He was one of the witnesses to the 1913 explosion and he placed flowers on the graves of those killed at the funeral. (Appendix 2).

On the closure of the factory in late 1919 he transferred to the HM Sea Transport depot that apparently took over part of the site. Unfortunately on 21 February 1921, Ted had a serious accident. It occurred while trying with a colleague to unload a horse trough off a barge moored on the wharf. The horse trough slipped off the end of the barge on to Ted, knocking him unconscious. He was initially taken to Southend Victoria Hospital where it was found that he had damaged his spinal cord and fractured his spine and was completely paralysed from the waist down. He was later transferred to Billericay Hospital. He was never to leave the hospital and died ten years later on 1 April 1931. He was buried in the graveyard of St Michael's Church, Pitsea.

The horse trough in question was the one that was situated next to the Vange war memorial.

Ted's story is like several others you will read about where individuals have lived through dangerous situations either at the front or on the home front, only to die through some unfortunate accident.

Edward Baker (Ted) in his factory clothing.
Kind permission of John Baker

Kynochtown

Around 1895 another high explosive factory was built close by at Shell Haven (now known as Coryton) by Kynoch & Co. It opened in 1897. The founder of the company was George Kynoch who was born at Peterhead, Aberdeenshire in 1834. Although he fell out with the board and resigned in 1888 and died in self-imposed exile in South Africa in 1891, the company has kept the name to this day.

The site – previously Borley Farm – covered 750 acres, included housing for many of its employees and was named 'Kynochtown'. Initial products made there were cordite, guncotton, gunpowder and cartridges. The company had other factories around the country but in the early years of the twentieth century began to struggle. However, within weeks of the outbreak of war the company obtained contracts to make an additional 3 million cartridges a week, which soon increased to 7.5 million. Other contracts followed for shell cases, detonators, cordite, acetone and other products. After the war things naturally slowed down again and by 1919 Kynochtown had closed down.

Kynoch's built the Corringham Light Railway (CLR) with a passenger branch line from its works to Corringham and a goods branch line to the LT&SR line at Thames Haven. The line eventually closed in 1952.

Percy Robert Chittock who lived in Vange prior to the war and who was later to join the Royal Horse Artillery, worked at Kynoch's as a charge hand. He travelled to the site on the Corringham Light Railway. It was on his travels back and forth to work that he met his future wife Clara who also worked at Kynoch's. She had to dress in an all-white uniform and white boots so that the various sparks did not catch her skin. They married at Holy Cross church in 1920 after Percy returned safely from the war. While at the front he suffered from the effects of a gas attack.

Clara was born in Bow in 1892 and went to Atley Road School which was renamed

Kynoch Hotel on Canvey Island.
Ken Porter's Collection

George Lansbury Primary School in 1951. George Lansbury was the person who supported Joseph Fels, the originator of the Dunton Farm Colony.

Either inside or outside, explosive factories appear to have been dangerous places to work. In October 1914 the local paper reported the drowning of George Henry Nash:

> 'An inquest was held at Kynoch Town and it was reported that on the previous Monday morning at about 11.16am the deceased was discovered lying face down in a ditch, dead.
>
> 'The ditch was about 8ft wide with approximately 2ft of water in the bottom. The deceased was covering in some hot air pipes that went over the ditch about 4ft above the water line. Across the middle of the ditch were two planks both about 9ins wide for Nash and another man, Mann to work on. Mann suddenly realised that Nash was missing and on looking, found him lying face down in the ditch. Mann ran about three quarters of a mile to inform the foreman. On returning they dragged Nash out of the ditch but they were unable to revive him. Nash was known to suffer from fits. Verdict – Found drowned.'

With the outbreak of war both explosive works had to expand to cope with the extra work. This meant that hundreds of women were employed on very long shifts, being paid 4d an hour. Many of these women came from the Pitsea and Vange areas. The factories were obviously vulnerable to air attacks. The wardens at Southend-on-Sea or Shoebury would send special telephone messages of an anticipated attack and the workers would shelter where they could or just watch the action. Being an essential part of the war effort Kynoch and Pitsea explosive factories were guarded by soldiers.

Life however had to go on and certainly at Kynoch various types of entertainment were organised and though sport, especially men's sport was restricted because of the lack of male personnel, Kynoch actually had a ladies' football team that played in a local female league.

Catherine Brown (nee McIntosh) started work at Kynock's in 1915 and eventually left two years later to take up other munitions work away from the danger and fumes.

She worked a two-week shift rota, Monday to Saturday from 6am to 6pm, switching to night duty from Monday night, finishing Sunday morning. Her rate of pay at the start was $4\frac{1}{2}$d an hour with time and half for Saturday night. By the time she left this had risen to $7\frac{1}{2}$d.

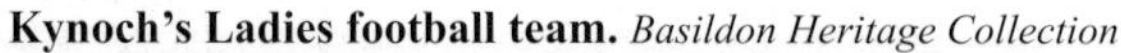

Kynoch's Ladies football team. *Basildon Heritage Collection*

Catherine found lodgings in Corringham and shared a room with two other girls. They would get to Kynocktown by the Corringham Light Railway, where they would check in and change into their safety clothes and when they reached their place of work slip into overshoes to avoid taking grit into the various workrooms. Many other company workers from surrounding villages were transported in by the company lorries – there were no buses.

Catherine was involved with making cordite. The fumes from cordite were very strong, so trays of cordite were moved out regularly and taken to a storeroom. Her sister joined her at the factory and on one occasion she was overcome by the fumes and became unconscious for a time. She spent the rest of the night in the first aid room.

As the war progressed, Kynock took on more and more employees so the company decided to build a colony. Catherine and her sister went to live there. They were supplied with individual lunches that could be heated in the factory canteen and on returning from work there was always a meal waiting for them, which, considering the rationing, was surprisingly good.

Catherine Brown standing with her sister, Dorothy, in their working clothes.
Basildon Heritage Collection

The colony had a large recreation room and many social events took place. Catherine and her sister once took part in an historical pageant dating back to the ancient Britons. Dances were held there regularly where friends could be invited.

During Catherine's time at the factory, she witnessed one or two nasty accidents. One

Kynoch workers' outing – 1918.
Kind permission of John Rugg

in particular was during the process of making cordite. There was an explosion that blew off the die (a heavy perforated metal plate which shaped the cordite as it was expressed from a cylinder of paste). There were two cylinders and while one discharged cordite, the other one would be filled by one of the workers, ready to swing round to replace the first one as soon as it became empty. As the cordite passed through the die a worker would catch it and pass it smoothly to another girl, who would feed it on to a long tray where it would be cut to the required length and then laid out very evenly on other trays. So when the die blew off, a young girl's right hand was underneath. Catherine said: 'It was all very tragic and it seemed extra sad as the girl was a keen pianist.' The explosion also caused a fire and everybody had to vacate the factory.

Whenever there was a Zeppelin air raid they had to take refuge out on the marsh. Catherine was there and saw the Zeppelin which was brought down over Great Burstead. But in spite of the danger and long hours she enjoyed her stay there, singing as they worked.

Kynoch's finally closed in January 1919 and in November 1919 a sale took place which continued for four days. Items for sale included portable buildings, plant, machinery, tramlines etc. Some of the huts from the women's colony were purchased by locals and re-erected as private dwellings. One such building, bought by Frederick Jobson of Langdon Hills for £100 and re-erected in Samuel Road, Langdon Hills by volunteer labour, has been known as the Hut ever since. Initially it had two billiard tables, a table tennis table and a stage to provide a centre for general entertainment. The hut is now the home of the Langdon Hills Women's Institute.

Kynochtown

In 1890 from Birmingham the firm of Messrs Kynoch
Came to Thames Haven where their ships could dock.
They had a wide ranging armaments business to extend
Including smokeless powder at the lower end.

To support the new factory a new town was born
With houses, a shop, a club and a brand new lawn.
There was a school, a cricket and a football team
And a new hotel on Canvey, just across the stream.

With the start of the Great War, a hospital came
And a fire and police station to great acclaim.
But the factory was subject to floods from the river
And danger from bombs that aircraft could now deliver.

1919 cutbacks closed the factory and oil became the theme.
Cory Brothers from Cardiff were the new owners on the scene.
Kynochtown was renamed as old patrons had gone,
And the new site for oil refining was renamed Coryton.

Andrew Summers.

The question now is why and how did we get involved in such a terrible war, a war the world had never experienced before.

Chapter 3

The Road to War

EVER SINCE WILLIAM the Conqueror, the English pastime seems to be fighting or trying to get one over on the French, but by the middle of the 1800s we found ourselves on the side of the French and the Ottoman Empire (Turkey) fighting the Russians in the Crimean War. From then onwards we seem to have been on their side with the exception of the Franco-German War of 1870/71 in which we did not participate. While they were involved with this conflict in which the French were heavily defeated, Britain was more concerned with consolidating its overseas Empire outside Europe. Afghanistan, India, China, the Middle East, and South Africa were just a few of the conflicts that Britain, up to the turn of the twentieth century, was involved in.

Following the turbulence of the Napoleonic era, in 1817 the Serbians gained independence from the Ottoman Empire and became a principality within the growing Austrian Empire. Then in 1829 Greeks gained independence from the Ottoman Empire.

In 1830 the United Kingdom of Netherlands split and Belgium and Luxembourg gained independence, although Luxembourg lost half of its territory. Then came the Crimean War of 1853-56 where the Russians were heavily beaten.

Romania was formed in 1859 from the provinces of Moldavia and Wallachia but remained within the Ottoman Empire.

Then following several years of the Italian War of Independence in 1860 came the unification of Italy. In 1866 the Austro-Prussian War was won by Prussia which became the dominant German state. This resulted in the formation of the Austria-Hungary Empire in 1867.

During the Franco-Prussian War of 1870 several of the German states joined the Prussians in defeating France and united together to form the German Empire in 1871.

In the Russian-Turkish war of 1878, which Russia won, there was a considerable change in the Balkan region of Europe. The Russians wanted to bring Serbia, Montenegro, Romania and Bulgaria out of the Ottoman Empire's area of control into theirs. However Britain was concerned about the growing power of the Russians so through a show of force managed to maintain a balance of power. As a result most of the Balkan nations gained independence. This was the real beginning of the fall of the Ottoman Empire. Other changes took place, Austria gained Bosnia and Herzegovina from the Ottoman Empire, the only problem here was that the Bosnians were Muslim and preferred to stay within the Ottoman Empire. Austria officially annexed Bosnia in 1908.

Of all the Balkan nations only Albania elected to stay within the Ottoman Empire. In 1881 Romania gained independence from the Ottoman Empire. A year later in 1882 Serbia gained independence from the growing Austrian Empire.

Britain then became involved with the proceedings by seizing control of the Suez Canal at the same time assuming control of Egypt, as the area was becoming turbulent and Britain wanted to protect its investment in the Suez Canal which was important in administering our Asian and African possessions.

Russia then lost a war to Japan in 1905, resulting in the Russian Revolution of the same year culminating in the civil war of 1917. Norway gained independence from Sweden in 1905 and in 1912 Italy took Libya away from the Ottoman Empire.

There were many other side conflicts going on that helped to increase distrust amongst the European nations, who all appeared to be trying to control or influence each other – real power games, that could only end in war

Then in 1912-13 the Balkan wars changed the face of the area yet again. There is no doubt that these wars and the previous century of conflicts set the scene for the First World War. Austria-Hungary was concerned by the growing strength of Serbia, who had now allied itself with its former enemy Russia. The Ottoman Empire was concerned with its lost territory and eager to get some of it back, so was more than happy to fall in with Austria-Hungary and the growing strength of Germany. Bulgaria also joined in with them in the hope of regaining lost territory.

What about Britain? We were concerned with the German aggression that was helping to foster even greater distrust among the various European powers.

The German Emperor (Kaiser) William II set Germany on a course to compete with Britain to become the world's dominant super power. He wanted an overseas empire like Britain and France and within Europe he wanted to expand into the east at the expense of Russia.

Britain and Prussia had traditionally been allies, since the days of Napoleon, and both being Protestant had a common interest in keeping France in check. However, the aggressive approach by Germany pushed Britain into an alliance first with France and then with Russia as she had also became distrustful of Germany's ambitions, resulting in the three countries forming alliances against it. All this resulted in four main reasons for the outbreak of war.

Nationalism – the various countries and states of Europe were flourishing in national pride and many ethnic groups craved for independent nations.

Imperialism – The major countries within Europe held many colonies abroad and new lands were being contested by them.

Militarism – As nationalism and imperialism took hold so the need for greater military strength to defend their possessions became necessary.

Lack of international organization – There was no international governing body to help solve the various problems. The League of Nations was not established until after the First World War.

It is not surprising therefore that the countries of Europe were increasingly hostile to each other. Russia and Austria-Hungary wanting to dominate Balkan states and Britain, France and Germany jostling for world trade dominance, led to the formation of powerful military alliances. By 1914 the political situation in Europe was very tense indeed.

All it needed was a spark to ignite the First World War and they did not have to wait long for that. Serbia was angry by the annexation of Bosnia by Austria and with Archduke Franz Ferdinand, heir to the throne of Austria-Hungary, visiting Sarajevo in Bosnia with his wife, Sophie, to observe military manoeuvres. This gave the Bosnian Serbs the opportunity they had been waiting for.

The Serbian Military Intelligence planned an assassination attempt and helped train six young Bosnian Serbs, arming them with bombs and pistols. The political objective of the assassination was to break off Austria-Hungary's south Slav provinces so they could establish a Greater Serbia.

So on 28 June 1914 these young assassins waited for the Archduke's car as it drove along the main road towards Sarajevo. The first conspirator threw a bomb at the car but missed and was arrested. The Archduke decided to cancel the visit and return home by a different route. Unfortunately nobody told the driver and when he realised he stopped the car to turn round. The car stopped in front of Gavrilo Princip, one of the conspirators, who was on his way home thinking they had failed. He immediately pulled out his pistol and shot the Archduke and in the following tussle he also shot and killed Sophie.

A chain reaction followed with Austria-Hungary initially demanding Serbia to investigate and implement harsh punishment against the suspected assassins, with close inspection by Austria. Serbia was on the verge of complying but Russia offered support. This resulted in Austria declaring war on Serbia on 28 July 1914 and invading on 12 August. Russia immediately invaded Austria-Hungary. The First World War had started.

Germany invaded Belgium on 4 August on the way to invading France. This was all part of Germany's Schlieffen Plan that had been devised by General Count Alfred Von Schlieffen in December 1905. He believed that any future war was going to be initially on the Western Front and that France posed more of a military threat to Germany than Russia. His intention was then to attack and defeat France believing it would deter Britain from getting involved. He would then turn his attention to Russia.

Germany's mistake was to attack Belgium first with whom Britain had formed an alliance. When they then refused to withdraw their troops under the threat of an ultimatum, Britain declared war.

The 'war that will end war' (according to H.G. Wells) had begun. The players were made up of the Central Powers: German Empire, Austro-Hungarian Empire, Ottoman Empire, Bulgaria, and Finland, Azerbaijan and Lithuania who were to join later in 1918 once Russia had dropped out. Italy, just before the start of the war, was in an alliance with Germany but refused to participate and in fact later joined the Allies.

The Allies included France, Russia, British Empire, Serbia and later USA, Romania and Italy.

It was soon realised that it was not going to be the war to end all war. So what possessed some of the soldiers of the opposing armies, with all the carnage going on around them, to hold an unofficial ceasefire at Christmas 1914 and celebrate it together by singing seasonal songs, walking between the trenches, talking to their opposite numbers and exchanging gifts with games of football being played between them? It was as if the war was just another game, but this game included killing each other.

On another occasion during the battle of the Loos (September/October 1915), men of the London Irish Rifles dribbled a football through no man's land while under fire with the intention of kicking it into the German lines. In the end it just got tangled up in the barbed wire. It would appear that the soldiers had at least six footballs they intended to try and kick into the German lines, but just before they went over the top one of the platoon commanders became aware of what they were up to and did not think it was a good idea so he went round puncturing the balls. Sergeant Frank Edwards, however, kept one tucked under his tunic and it is said he dribbled the ball twenty metres before he was wounded.

In the battalion's records, it is noted that the men were seen to pass and re-pass the ball until they disappeared in a smoke cloud close to the German front line. Another soldier wrote that the men were crying out 'On the Ball, London Irish', as they advanced.

The ball was retrieved from the barbed wire and for a time displayed in the regimental museum, then stored in a container and forgotten. It eventually came to light in 2011. It has been restored to the delight of Edwards' granddaughter who says, 'I remember very well and remember his love of football. His story is one that had been forgotten.'

The various infantry units and formations that went to make up the British Army of the First World War were fourteen men to a section commanded by a corporal; four sections plus one officer, sergeant, runner and batman to a platoon; four platoons to a company, usually commanded by a captain; four companies to a battalion; four battalions to an infantry brigade; three infantry brigades to a division and normally three divisions to a corps.

According to one British historian, the British Army in 1914 was the best equipped, trained and organised that had ever been sent to war. Unlike the French, who in the early months of the war wore highly visible blue coats and red trousers, the British wore a form of camouflage uniform first adopted in the Indian and Colonial wars and improved during the Second Boer War, and by 1902 dark khaki serge was adopted. The weakness in the uniform was the peaked cloth cap, which gave very little protection and is one of the reasons that so many men were killed in the early months of the war. Fortunately in 1915 the Brodie or Tommy helmet was designed. It was made of heavy steel and initially there were insufficient so they were only issued to those in the front line. It was not until the spring of 1916 that large quantities of the helmets became available for all military personnel.

The war had started and the underlying question was whether we or any of the parties were ready for such a war. Germany probably was, France should have been. We certainly were not.

Chapter 4

Your Country Needs You

ON THE DECLARATION of war the British Army consisted of 710,000 men including reserves but only 80,000 regular troops were ready for war. There were six divisions and one cavalry division in the United Kingdom and four divisions overseas. In addition there were fourteen Territorial Divisions. Secretary of State, Lord Kitchener considered the Territorial Army untrained and therefore not very effective. His view was that the regular army should not be wasted in the forthcoming battles but used to train up to seventy new divisions to match the size of the French and German armies. He was one of the few who believed it would be a long war.

Most people are aware of Lord Kitchener's campaign and his famous poster, 'Your Country Needs You'. This very successful campaign encouraged over a million men to enlist in the first five months of the war. At the outbreak of war the government issued a call for an extra 100,000 men and recruitment in the first few weeks of the war was high, peaking in the first week of September, when the news filtered through of the British retreat following the Battle of Mons.

Today one wonders why so many volunteered; enthusiasm and a war spirit was certainly the initial pulling power but there is no doubt that unemployment helped. Poor Law Guardians refused to support those fit for duty. There was also a concern that their homes, district and country were under threat. One of the calls to arms advertisements in a local paper read:

> '500 Wanted at Once – If you want to help your country at this critical moment you must COME FORWARD NOW and be trained as a soldier. You will not be sent to the front till you are trained and fit to take the field against the enemy. As soon as you are trained you will be given your chance to show your stuff that is in you. As soon as the war is over every facility will be given you to secure your discharge and get back to your ordinary work.'

Unfortunately many did not return.
Ken Porter's Collection

Recruiting propaganda. *Ken Porter's Collection*

Stirring stuff. No wonder the young initially volunteered in their thousands. This advertisement was aimed at those aged 19-35, although perhaps the older element were not so enthusiastic. Did those that survived the war find that the authorities kept their promise to help them back to work?

However even with all this rhetoric going on, it soon became obvious that the war was not going to reach a successful conclusion within the year as many thought and with the mounting casualties, it was becoming obvious that it was not possible to continue fighting by relying on voluntary recruits.

Although the government was divided on the question of conscription (compulsory active service), it soon realised that with the possible collapse of morale in the French Army there was no alternative and Prime Minister H.H. Asquith introduced the Military Service Act in January 1916 which came into force on 2 March 1916. It was the first time in British history that legislation had been passed introducing conscription. It was not very popular and the following month over 200,000 demonstrated against it in Trafalgar Square.

Then in other quarters we see the formation of groups of men from the same factories and businesses joining up together. These were known as 'Pals battalions'. The idea was first suggested by Lord Derby and was reasonably successful with a number of battalions being formed across the country. The major drawback though was that many towns lost its entire military-age menfolk in one stroke. This did not seem to affect our area to any degree, as there was no large employer other than the explosive factories which needed their workforce.

The act imposed conscription on all single men aged between 18 and 41, exempting those not medically fit, clergymen, teachers, widowed with children or those working in reserve occupations such as war industries. Two months later in May 1916 married men were included and in 1918 the age limit was raised to 51.

Men called up were able to appeal against the conscription and they or their employers could appeal to a local Military Service Tribunal in the town or district. Any applicant refused exemption by the Local Tribunal or dissatisfied with the type of exemption given, had the right of appeal. Conversely military representatives or recruiting officers could appeal against the exemption granted to an applicant. If either party was still dissatisfied they could appeal to a Central Tribunal but only if allowed by the Appeals Tribunal.

There were also Conscientious Objectors (COs) who claimed the right to refuse to perform military service on the grounds of freedom of thought, conscience and religion. They also had the right to go through the procedure as laid out above. By the end of the war around 7,000 men had been granted non-combatant duties, 3,000 were sent to special work camps, 6,000 were imprisoned and forty-two were sent to the front to face a firing squad. The sentences were immediately reprieved but many of them faced ten years in penal servitude.

The *Chelmsford Chronicle* on 30 June 1916 reported a speech by the Prime Minister, Mr Asquith that a Home Office committee had been appointed to determine what kind of work the genuine conscientious objector could be put to. He went on to say: 'All men who honestly objected to military service ought to be able to avail themselves of Parliamentary exemption, but those guilty of the double offence of cowardice and hypocrisy would be treated with the utmost rigour.' Men held to be genuine conscientious objectors would be released from civil prisons on condition of their performing work of national importance.

The local papers were full of those applying for exemption:

> 'Conscientious Objector Arthur Robert Murray, a roadman, of Nevendon, applied for exemption on conscientious grounds and said he would do service in any way except the shedding of blood. The chairman (Mr Collingwood Hope KC), after reading applicant's statement of grounds of appeal, said, "I am not going to ask any more questions on this subject of conscientious objection. I am going to take the advice of the *Essex County Chronicle* and keep quiet. Captain Howard, you can ask questions." Captain Howard: "It is very difficult – may I do the same?" Eventually Captain Howard asked the applicant to explain how it was that he a married man, could be a conscientious objector. Applicant: "That is all right, I would protect my family but I would not slay". Applicant was ordered to take non-combatant service.'

The advice of the *Essex County Chronicle* referred to by the chairman was conveyed in the following paragraph in the previous week's issue:

'No body of men not possessing the judicial mind could sit and hear, with any degree of patience, the sentiments and principles expounded by many of the objectors to military service. But it is a question to my mind whether the Tribunals would not do better if they ceased from questioning objectors on their peculiar tenets. Let them have their say by all means but why lengthen the proceedings by questions which only elicit probably ridiculous answers? In nine cases out of ten the objector wants to save his skin. That is Alpha and Omega of the objection and though it is questionable whether so-called conscientious objectors would be any good as fighting men, there is work in the Army eminently fitted for such and they should be sent forthwith to do it.'

Imagine a chairman of a tribunal today taking any notice of a newspaper article, though the advice does appear to be sensible.

'THE FORGETFUL FARMER (*Chelmsford Chronicle* 5 August 1916.)

'Mr A.B. Markham, farmer of Laindon, asked for leave to be allowed to apply for exemption. He stated that he had applied for the exemption of a number of his men but had acted under the impression that he himself was 41 last December but he now received notice calling him up for Army service and he found that he was only 40. Of course, if they took him, they might as well take all his men and close the farm.

The Chairman: It seems an extraordinary thing to forget one's self in this way. A member stated that he understood Mr Markham had lost his registration card. (Laughter). The Chairman said that Mr Markham was a month over the date in which he should have applied. His carelessness had put the Tribunal in a very difficult position. They realised that it was necessary for a man like Mr Markham to claim the exemption to which he was entitled. Leave would be given to apply.'

Essex Newsman 21 October 1916. Mr A.B. Markham found himself back at the tribunal again:

Laindon Hotel – 1930s. *Ken Porter's Collection*

Edmund J. King Butcher's shop Pitsea – pre 1920. *Kind permission of Edmund King*

'Exemption to 31 December, not renewable was given to Wm Bull, 38, thatcher's mate and hay binder, in the employ of Mr A.B. Markham, farmer. Mr Markham stated that one of the men for whom he had previously obtained exemption on condition that women were brought in to help, had refused to work with women and had left him. He had not been able to get another man and had therefore given up one milk round. If the people wanted the milk they must now come and fetch it.'

Chelmsford Chronicle 22 December 1916.

'Mr A.W Garrod, Brentwood appealed for Lewis S. Letch, 29, a stockman on a farm at Nevendon. This man was indispensable as he was the only all-round man there. A conditional exemption was granted on the basis that if he left the farm he would go.

'An appeal was made for Ernest John Wager, 27, horseman and Wm. G. Hazell, 31, cowman engaged on a farm at Bowers Gifford. Mr G.E. Fennell who appealed on their behalf said "machines had solved the difficulty of milking but it was necessary to have men to look after the feeding stock. They also did some colt breaking". Conditional exemption was granted to Hazell but the appeal was dismissed in the case of Wager but it was recommended that he would not be called up until 31 January 1917.'

Edmund J. King butcher's cart. *Kind permission of Edmund King*

*Chelmsford Chronicle*19 January 1917.

> 'The Military appeal was allowed in the case of W. Gardiner, 21, cowman, Marsh Farm, Vange. George A. Stammer, 24, single, horse man, Dunton. Percy H Beale, 25, single, farmer, Nevendon. George Rolando, 28, baker, Vange.'

John Holman, the publican of the Laindon Hotel, was well known but he was not exempted from going to war unless he could find a way to obtain exemption.

> 'John Holman, 31, of the Railway Hotel Laindon whose case was adjourned at the last Tribunal to enable him to find work in munitions, he being a trained engineer, now presented a certificate showing that he was being taken on as a toolmaker for a munitions firm. The Chairman said these men were wanted, and they would give conditional exemption so long as he remained at this work. The Tribunal thought, however, that a young man with his experience should not have waited till he was forced into this work. He should have taken it up long ago.'

No doubt John could continue his publican work in between shifts, enabling the people of Laindon to still get their daily pint.

> '*Essex Newsman* 21 April 1917. Edmund J. King, 34, butcher, Pitsea, appealed for exemption on business grounds. He was the only butcher at Pitsea. Applicant gave details of the business he was doing and the Chairman said this amounted to nearly £6,000 a year but appellant paid no income-tax. The Tribunal gave exemption to 30 June and the Chairman said the difficulty of taking him for the army was that there was no other butcher in Pitsea and the workers must have

meat. It was hardly fair that he should be reaping all the benefit and not even paying income tax.

J.W. Lagden, 33, master butcher, Laindon also appealed for exemption on business grounds and gave details of his business. He did not pay income tax – Conditional exemption to 30 June was given. The opinion was expressed that the authorities should consider the positions of butchers and income tax generally.

Application was made for Wm. J. Brittain, 29, married, foreman bread baker for Mr Cottis, baker, Laindon. Mr Cottis said he was the only resident baker at Laindon and he did not overlap any other district baker. This was the only man now baking for him in place of four formerly and unfortunately people had not got any potatoes and were eating more bread. The chairman said it was a difficult case but Mr Cottis must realise that this was a young man whom the tribunal ought really not to exempt. Exemption would be given to 30 June but Mr Cottis must make every effort to replace him.'

We know that King and Lagden did not join up so they must have obtained further exemptions.

In September 1915 Edmund Joseph King was advertising for a slaughter man who will also do a delivery round. The advertisement also stated that he would prefer a man who was not eligible for the army.

At that time butchers, like bakers and milkmen had delivery rounds. With very little transport about it was simpler for shopkeepers supplying food products to have delivery rounds as the majority of them would have had a horse and cart. Peacheys, today a successful family business, started back in the 1950s pulling a greengrocer's cart around the streets of Laindon.

Edmund Joseph came unstuck on at least one occasion when delivering meat. The *Essex Newsman* of 5 September 1914 reported that 'Frederick Reeves of Langdon Hills, labourer and Charles Vinn of Basildon, labourer, were charged on remand with stealing 6½lb of pork and 4½lb of mutton, value 6s.10d in Vange, the property of Edmund Joseph King of Pitsea, butcher.' Reeves was fined £1 and £1 costs and Vinn 10s and £1 costs.

Edmund Joseph's grandson, another Edmund, said that his grandfather, on one of his long rounds, delivered to Henry Ubele, an old German who lived at Oliphants Farm and who appears later in the story. Although Edmund Joseph was a little nervous of him he got on well with him and Ubele referred to Edmund Joseph's son, Frank, as 'Frankie boy'. On one occasion Ubele gave Frankie a pocket knife but insisted that he gave him a farthing for it as it was unlucky to give somebody a knife as a present.

The delivery round took in Pitsea, Vange, Basildon, North Benfleet and Nevendon. On the route there was an anti-aircraft battery at the top of Gun Hill and on one occasion during a raid the soldiers threw Frank into a trench near the gun and covered him over to protect him from shrapnel. Frank would have been five or six at the time.

Frank also remembers that one Christmas the family were having a day out at One Tree Hill (now a country park) and they believe they could hear the guns in France.

In 1920 Edmund Joseph had a meeting with other local tradesmen to discuss the possibility of getting together and buying a van to deliver bread, meat and groceries but unfortunately nothing came of it.

Edmund says that his grandfather had a nodding acquaintance with the law, or should we say with the bits he did not think were very important, such as paying income tax. For example in 1922 he was prosecuted at Billericay Magistrates court for obstructing the highway in Pitsea. Edmund believes he was fined but it did not stop him sending the policeman who brought the prosecution a crate of brown ale.

Chelmsford Chronicle 21 September 1917:

> 'An appeal was made for Barnett Ruskin, 24, single, White House Farm, Laindon – agricultural worker for his father, Morris Ruskin. The local tribunal had refused the appeal because the man was really a carpenter and joiner. In answer to the chairman, the father said he was a naturalised Russian. He had been at the farm for two years. Mr Copland Gray: "What were you in London?" Mr Ruskin: "Wool Merchant and job iron." The Chairman, "Job iron?" Mr Copland Gray: "He means rag and bone merchant (laughter). In answer to Capt. Howard, the young man said he was a carpenter and joiner and held a protection certificate in London. Mr Ruskin senior said he wanted to get the hay crop in. The appeal was dismissed.'

Chelmsford Chronicle 2 August 1918:

> 'Thomas M. Endean, 47, married, Grade 1, boot finisher, Laindon was given six months conditional exemption and exempted from the Volunteers. Mr Endean complained of the perfunctory character of his examination. Mr T. Healop said many men stated that they were examined with great thoroughness. Mr Endean said he was graded before he was examined. It was decided to make arrangements for Mr Endean to go before the medical board.'

These are just a small sample of the thousands of people who tried to get out of going to war, either because they did not want to fight or because their business needed them to help the local economy and many went to quite some lengths to convince the tribunals that they were needed at home – people had to be fed to survive.

Chapter 5

Home Front

WHAT WAS CIVILIAN life like during the war years? We have a fairly good understanding of what civilian life was like during the Second World War because there are still a huge number of people around to tell us but with the Great War a hundred years ago it's very difficult to get a real feel of what it was like. Unlike wars and skirmishes over the previous centuries the First World War was going to have a devastating effect and the term Home Front appeared for the first time.

Zeppelins were attacking civilian targets, U-boats affected our imports and there was rationing. Women had to take over many of the men's jobs, entertainment and sport changed and there was hardly a family that was not changed by this uncompromising war. By 1918 a great number of families had lost a loved one or had one return home wounded.

Initially the main concern was the pending food shortages, especially as prior to the war over seventy-five per cent of butter, cheese, eggs and bacon consumed in the UK came from overseas. To save foreign currency and to reallocate shipping for the war effort there was an urgent need to cut down on imports. Panic buying soon appeared with queues forming as worried customers tried to stockpile basic commodities. This caused prices to rise and regulations were therefore soon put in place. Shops were instructed to restrict sales to no more than 2lbs of sugar to anyone. Larger retailers campaigned for customers to purchase only own-brand or home produced commodities, though this again had an effect on prices.

Horses were being requisitioned for the army and so distribution was seriously affected, especially in areas where there was a home delivery service. As in all the previous wars, horses were in great demand. At the outset of the war the military only had 26,000 horses but within two weeks they had requisitioned 140,000 horses. They were able to do this because over the previous two years the military had been carrying out a census of horses, ponies and mules and knew where every one was. Of course they had to pay for them but when one considers that they were more common on the roads than the motor car it was a tremendous loss to the local economy and the country as a whole. Ken's ancestor, Fred Hinton, started up the first motorised buses in Laindon in the early 1920s but prior to that their buses were horse drawn. The farmers relied heavily on the horse to pull the plough and other farm equipment.

Food problems were felt more severely in the cities and towns than in the countryside because in the rural areas a large number of families grew their own vegetables, had chickens, ducks, geese, rabbits, and goats etc. and of course there was the local farmer with his cattle and sheep. After the initial panic buying people settled down and it was not a problem until late 1916 when the German U-boat attacks on merchant shipping were having a dramatic impact on our food supply.

By April 1916 it was estimated that Britain only had six weeks of wheat left. Suddenly the war was brought home to most people. So in 1917 the government took over 2.5 million acres of land for farming, resulting in the Women's Land Army being established. The government also tried to introduce a voluntary code of rationing but this did not work and by the winter of 1917 food queues were beginning to appear again so eventually in February 1918 rationing was brought in.

The things that were rationed at its height were: bacon and ham 4oz, margarine 4oz, butter 2oz, sugar 8oz, 1lb jam every two months, tea 2oz, one fresh egg each week, one packet of dried egg every four weeks, 12oz sweets every four weeks. Meat and coal was also rationed. In early 1918 in Essex there was an appeal for every man who had a farm, a garden or an allotment to plant more potatoes to help make the county self supporting. Although things were beginning to get really bad, surprisingly rationing did have a bright side; malnutrition almost disappeared among the poor and nobody truly starved. It makes us begin to understand why our grandparents and parents, following the First and Second World Wars, were far more frugal than we are today.

The Defence of the Realm Act of 1914 (DORA) was intended to govern the lives of the civilian population and if any laws were broken they could be prosecuted. The original list of do's and don'ts etc were as follows:

no-one was allowed to talk about naval or military matters in public places
no-one was allowed to spread rumours about military matters
no-one was allowed to buy binoculars
no-one was allowed to trespass on railway lines or bridges
no-one was allowed to melt down gold or silver
no-one was allowed to light bonfires or fireworks
no-one was allowed to give bread to horses or chickens
no-one was allowed to use invisible ink when writing abroad
no-one was allowed to buy brandy or whisky in a railway refreshment room
no-one was allowed to ring church bells
the government could take over any factory or workshop
the government could try any civilian breaking these laws
the government could take over any land it wanted
the government could censor newspapers

As the war continued and evolved, the government introduced more acts to DORA.

the government introduced British Summer Time to give more daylight for extra work
opening hours in pubs were cut
beer was watered down
customers in pubs were not allowed to buy a round of drinks or 'treat' servicemen.

Today some these don'ts seem very strange and some totally unacceptable. Another change, and one that still causes arguments today, was the introduction of 'Summer Time', the changing of clocks to create more daylight hours. Although it had been suggested several times previously it was the Germans and their allies who first implemented the change on 30 April 1916, soon followed by Britain on 21 May 1916. The idea was that creating longer daylight hours would help businesses preserve fuel.

Every parish or district had in place a Local Emergency Committee which would carry out instructions given to them by the government or military authorities. One of their responsibilities was to collate a Domesday survey which was sent to every estate holder, farmer and probably smallholders requesting the following information for the military.

Number of horses? Riding, light draught, heavy draught.

Number of stock? Cattle, sheep, pigs.

Quantity of forage? Grain (threshed), grain (in stack), hay, straw, flour.

Number of vehicles? Wagons, farm carts, other horsed vehicles. motor cars, motor bicycles, pedal bicycles. If you keep a motor car or motor cycle, state 1. horsepower, 2. identification number, 3. maximum number of gallons of petrol you store.

How many implements? Picks, shovels, spades, felling axes, hand saws.

How many male employees? Cattlemen or drovers, labourers, motor or traction engine drivers, foresters, carpenters, furriers, men accustomed to use of explosives.

Has your farm or estate a telephone; if so, what is your telephone number?

Would the destruction by fire of stacks in your yard involve the destruction of buildings (yes or no)?

A further document was sent to the various committees informing them what their duties were in the event of an invasion. The opening paragraphs of the leaflet read as follows:

> 'An invasion is improbable. But an invasion is not impossible and hence the civil population must be prepared and organised for it. In case of an invasion in the district the business of the civil population will be:
>
> '1.To destroy everything that might be of service to the enemy.
>
> '2. To evacuate the district entirely.
>
> 'If an invasion occurs, the civil population will know for the first time what war really means. All conditions will be altered; things which previously had great importance will suddenly have to cease promptly, obediently and with the utmost goodwill, to do their share in the general scheme of operations. Citizens who lose their heads, or refuse to obey instructions, even though such instructions may seem harsh, will be helping the enemy and endangering not only the lives of their fellow citizens but the safety of the Empire.'

Strong words! How many people were aware of the various procedures that were in place? The farmers probably but the memories we have found of ordinary people do not mention any such requirements in case of an invasion. Elsewhere in the document it explains how to go about destroying all livestock:

> 'All livestock must be destroyed. The best way to kill cattle is to shoot them. Carcasses should not be bled, nor disembowelled. It is absolutely forbidden to use poison.'

Then there were instructions on the evacuation of the population and the route to take. Civilians on the continent, in particular Germany, were to experience such a thing but the last time Britain experienced anything like this being suggested might have been the invasion of William the Conqueror in 1066.

Surprisingly in the local stories that have been passed down there has been no mention of fear of an invasion and the action needed to be taken if there was one. The fact that our area is close to the coast you would have thought it would have been at the forefront of their minds but it seems not.

What is also strange considering the fuss made in the early months of 2013 following horsemeat appearing in the food chain, was a report in the *Chelmsford Chronicle* in March 1918. Mr E. Palmer had written to the Chelmsford Borough Food Centre Committee claiming that because of the rationing scheme, the demand for horse flesh had fallen off dramatically and unless he were allowed to sell horse meat without coupons he must close down. The chairman said that he had eaten a horse steak and never wanted to eat anything nicer. However all the time one was eating it, one would think of the horse, but that would be sentiment. The meat was wholesome, sweet and exceedingly tender. One of the members of the committee moved that horse flesh should be outside the meat scheme and that permission be given to sell it without coupons for three months. The proposal was seconded and the chairman explained that one having meat which was likely to turn (go off) within a certain time could get permission from the committee for it to be sold without coupons.

One of the other areas causing real concern was the number of emigrant Germans that had settled in Britain over the past two or three decades. The papers did not help the situation, some of them had pages entirely devoted to belittling the Germans and stirring up hatred; the government did not help either. Just before war broke out *The Times* placed a front page advertisement from the German and Austrian embassies suggesting that all nationals eligible for service return home. Because of all this anti-German feeling in the country gaining momentum, there were many stories of shops owned by Germans having their windows smashed or graffiti painted all over them. Many German families did go back home but others rapidly anglicized their names in an attempt to remain in the country unmolested.

German phobia soon became a national obsession and any German was automatically deemed to be a spy. Because of all this scaremongering on 5 August 1914 the government introduced the Aliens Registration Act. The act required all those of enemy nationality to travel with a permit and register at the local police station. It was not long before internment was introduced.

Herman Alwin Gleissner.
Kind permission of the Essex Record Office

Hermann Alwin Gleissner was born in Germany on 26 September 1878 and came to England sometime between 1901 and 1911. The 1911 census has him living with his wife Bertha at Nelson House, Fairhouse Estate, Vange. He had married Bertha Amalie Weitz, a widow who was nine years older, at the parish church, St John's the Baptist, Hoxton, Hackney on 5 January 1908. At the time of his marriage and the census his occupation is recorded as being that of a carpenter. At some date after his marriage he moved to Vange and on the declaration of war it would appear that he owned and was living at Basildon Hall. He must have had farming in his blood because his father back in Germany was a farmer. He continued to

Basildon Hall – pre 1920. *Kind permission of the Essex Record Office*

farm at the Hall until 1937 when he moved to Hill Road. He still owned the property and he rented it out.

At the outbreak of war he was interned at Frimley Internment Camp in Suffolk for the duration of the war returning to Basildon Hall in 1919. In his absence the house was ransacked so it would appear that Bertha either went with him or moved elsewhere for the time being. Following his return to the area in September 1919 he was issued with a new identity card which states that he had been in the German army from October 1898 to September 1900 and had reached the rank of corporal.

Hermann died on 11 August 1956 and a newspaper cutting reporting his death states that the reason he had stayed in England is because he missed his ship at the London Docks.

Conditions in internment camps in Britain in the First World War were far from good so it is a little surprising that he returned to Basildon and settled into the community and became a well respected member of it. When the New Town of Basildon was mooted he helped to form the Basildon branch of the Residents' Protection Society and for five years he was chairman of the branch and a member of the Association's Executive Council. He was already Vice-President of the St Alban's Mission Boys' Club and later became a member of the Basildon branch of the Conservative Association. The newspaper report stated that 'Basildon lost an old pioneer on Saturday but the story of his struggle through life without giving in is a lesson to us all.'

There were a number of rumours about spies in the area. It was understood by the locals that in the First World War a German spy by the name of Shroeder used the skylight in the roof of the Basildon Rectory

Oliphants – pre 1920 – later became Laindon-cum-Basildon Rectory
Ken Porter's Collection

'Oliphants' to signal to the Zeppelins en route to bomb London. He was allegedly caught and interned. It was believed that this was the reason that the house was bombed so many times in the Second World War as the Germans knew of its location.

Police records lodged with the Essex Record Office reveal a number of reports where locals had reported neighbours of German extraction. One of the reports confirmed that a German naturalized in 1887 purchased 'Oliphants' and 47 acres of land around it in 1900. He rented it out initially until he took up residence in 1911 after retiring from his chop butchers business in West Ham. His name was Henry Ernest Ubele. Shortly after taking up residence the house was destroyed by fire while he was in London. He had it rebuilt of hollow concrete blocks with a slate roof by John Schroeder, a German who at the time of the report was in internment. The local residents could not speak of any suspicious acts but felt uneasy about having a German in their midst even though he had been a naturalized British subject for twenty-five years.

Further checks revealed that he had a drink problem and on one occasion had been summoned for being drunk in charge of a pony and cart. He had also been arrested for releasing a pigeon from his premises but was discharged on 18 April 1915. Deferred internment was recommended.

What is pleasing about this report is that it confirms the presence at the house of a Mr Schroeder (slight difference in spelling). It is not often one can confirm rumours many years after the alleged event.

There is also a police report that confirms a Carl Anton Hugo Johnnes Schroder (different spelling again) who came to England in 1882 and was naturalized on 18 May 1888. His occupation was Optical Glass Grinder and Mathematical Instrument Maker. Described as being a little eccentric, that is possibly why people became suspicious of him. It appears he moved around the area, Wickford, Hockley, North Benfleet and on one occasion he was living for a short time at Kingswood Hall, Vange. There is no mention of his being a builder or being involved with 'Oliphants'. He was detained in July 1917 by the police under the Aliens Restriction Order but, after proving his nationality, was released and he left the area. Was he our man?

Another report proved just how nervous and suspicious people were in the early days of the war. They did not trust anybody and the papers and the government certainly did a good job in stirring people up as this report shows:

'Mrs Longmuir, Summerhill, Basildon.

> 'On 18 November 1914, an anonymous letter is received through the Metropolitan Police alleging that Mrs Longmuir was keeping two German boys in her house and was driving her motor car about amongst the troops daily.
>
> 'Enquiries were made by the Police on 23 November 1914, who reported having interviewed Mrs Longmuir who resides with her husband at Summerhill, Basildon. She is a member of the Relief Committee of the District and during the last ten days has only on one occasion driven her car to Billericay. She denies the allegation of her having German boys in her house. She has taken her son for a drive in the car and on one occasion when returning from Billericay gave two men a ride in her car.

> 'Mrs Longmuir is a very respectable person well known to the Justices at Billericay and is certainly above harbouring German Aliens – Mrs Longmuir is a friend of Lord Kitchener.'

Motor car, friend of Lord Kitchener – it sounds like it was a bit of sour grapes by the locals.

Percy Monk who was born in the Railway Cottages at Laindon Station in 1897 in an interview given to Rodney Cole in the mid 1970s, was of the opinion that a German by the name of Kuhrt, who lived in a large red brick house in the area now known as Marks Hill Nature Reserve, Langdon Hills was a spy and would signal to the Zeppelins as they flew over on their way to London. Percy said that one day he just disappeared and the locals believe he was interned. As far as Percy was concerned the house was never lived in again.

It is possible that the locals thought that Kuhrt was a German, to them he was definitely a foreigner, but the 1901 and 1911 census states he was born in 'Walston Holsten', Denmark around 1845. He became a naturalized British subject in 1894. He married Annie White who was from Chipping Ongar in 1880. The 1901 census has them living at Mount Pleasant, Langdon Hills, but if we look at the 1891 census it states he was born in Holstein, Germany. Today we know that Holstein is in Germany but was it back in 1845? The problem was that the states of Schleswig and Holstein had a mixed population of Germans and Danes and the area had been disputed over for generations, various wars had taken place to settle the problem and it was not until 1865 that it eventually came under the control of Germany.

After the First World War various referendums were held and the outcome was that the majority wanted to stay with Germany. This still begs the question though. Was Kuhrt Danish or German? But does it really matter because by 1914 he was 69, nationalised British and a retired police officer with an English family. We believe he was Danish and moved and settled in England because of the conflicts back home.

The other question that Percy poses from his memory is whether Kuhrt and family left the area. It would appear that he had got his timing a little mixed up. The Electoral Registers have the family living there in 1918 and when Kuhrt dies in 1927 he was still living at Mount Pleasant.

Further police reports proved that if you had a foreign name or accent you came under suspicion even if you were not German.

Joseph Hector Negrotto was reported while living in Billericay. He was a British subject born in Gibraltar and his father was Vice Consul there. Even being in Holy Orders did not exempt some from suspicion. Mr Harry Glehn was a clerk in Holy Orders and assisted the rector at Nevendon. Harry was born in Sydenham Kent on 3 May 1852 and was chaplain at Bremen, Germany until 1913. He came under suspicion as it was believed he was German. In fact his father was a naturalized Russian. Both Joseph and Harry were deemed not to be covered by the Aliens Restriction Act.

Mr Cushman was a British subject born in St James, Westminster on 16 December 1859 who had resided in Vange for fifteen years. He changed his name from 'Kuchemann' to 'Cushman' on 24 August 1914 so that his child who attended school at Grays should not be called German.

One of the more amusing reports was that of local military officers surveying the surrounding countryside from the top of the Crown Hotel, Langdon Hills. This followed a letter from Mrs White of 11 Porchester Terrace, Hyde Park, London suggesting that the hotel and a bungalow at Langdon Hills should be searched as they held a very commanding position for spying and signalling and that one of the bungalows was formerly occupied by a German. It turned out that the bungalows were occupied by an Englishman and the licensee was Scottish and beyond suspicion.

What people seem to have forgotten in their state of panic is that there was a blackout so the opening and closing of doors for example could throw out a light that could resemble a signal.

There were many more: George Heinemann of Wickford, Anton Busser of Vange, Frederick Schuch of Crays Hill, Walter Reeks of Vange, Arbuthnot John Sloper of Billericay, Luding Mallinckrodt (Dutch) of Vange, Mrs Giddings of Pitsea, Johannes Neervoot (Dutch) of Wickford and James Harris (American) of Little Burstead.

Opposite what is now Nevendon Fire Station in Nevendon Road there was a German PoW or internment camp. After the war the huts were used to house the homeless and the last remaining hut became a clinic. Just before D-Day in 1944 Allied soldiers were billeted at the site and on a Friday and Saturday evenings would attract many a young lady.

Nearby Chelmsford Prison was used as a detention camp for German prisoners. The *Essex Newsman* on 2 June 1917 reported that there was considerable excitement around Chelmsford as two German prisoners had escaped.

They were Lieutenant Otto Thelen, aged 32, of the Imperial Military Air Service who had already escaped from three previous prisons and Lieutenant Lehmann, aged 24. They managed to avoid recapture for twenty-four hours, before being caught by the Army Cyclist Corps in the neighbourhood of Basildon.

Their escape plan had been clever as well as daring. Somehow they had managed to get hold of keys and tamper with the various locks. They just walked out the front gate, leaving behind dummies in their beds. Their clothing was made to look like civilian clothes.

Thelen said: 'We were confident that we could get out of the country. Our plan was to hide by day and travel by night. We were making for the sea and once there we were sure of getting on board ship.'

How did the children of the district fare? Hunger was probably not too much of a problem especially around the farming communities other than for the very poor and that would have always been a problem. Although the very young would have missed members of the family who had gone off to war – especially if it was their father – they would not have understood the consequences. Children of school age would have had a much better idea of what was going on especially as some of the schools would have been involved with various activities to help the war effort. For example we know that in addition to the adults, local schools were set to work knitting socks, mittens and handkerchiefs for the soldiers at the front. Also they helped out in fund raising for the various relief funds to provide gifts for the soldiers and sailors overseas.

Socks

Shining pins that dart and click
In the fireside's sheltered peace
Check the thoughts that cluster thick –
20 plain and then decrease.

He was brave – well, so was I –
Keen and merry, but his lip
quivered when he said good-bye-
Purl the seam-stitch, purl and slip.

Never used to living rough,
Lots of things he'd got to learn;
Wonder if he's warm enough –
Knit 2, catch 2, knit 1, turn.

Hark! The paper-boys again!
Wish that shout could be suppressed;
Keeps one always on the strain –
Knit off 9, and slip the rest.

Wonder if he's fighting now,
What he's done and where he's been;
He'll come out on top, somehow –
Slip 1, knit 2 purl 14.

Jessie Pope

The *Southend Standard* 11 February 1915 reported that the rector of North Benfleet had received two letters from the front, thanking the community for the parcels sent to those enrolled with colours either in the Army or Navy. One was from Driver E.J. Alliston who was in the Army Service Corps with the Indian Contingent in France.

> 'I received the parcel quite safely and I thank you very much. The shirt and socks came very handy for I had not got any shirts or socks and I have a rest today to go and have a bath; so it came just right and I thank you a hundred times for it was a godsend. I shall now be able to pull off my jacket and show a nice clean shirt. Till now I have been ashamed to pull it off. We are getting on well and if things go on as well it won't last long but we are having some very rough weather, up to our knees in mud and water. It is just like a pond along the roads but never mind, we shall get through it all right and if God gives us luck, that's all we want. I wish you a happy new year and to all my mates about there.'

Another was from Leading Stoker W. Heard whose serious illness had caused so much concern in the village. A previous report has him on HMS *Boadicea*:

> 'The shirt is nice and warm and the plum pudding went down quite all right. We are having a very nice time out here and should like to see you all again but am

afraid it won't be yet but we are trusting to God to bring us all back safe.'

Throughout time sports have had a great impact on the world in many different ways, bringing different countries and cultures together. It also helps people through difficult times and no doubt through all the bad times at war, sports and the thought of families back home were two of the things that soldiers relied upon to get them through.

Soldiers were required to be in good physical and mental shape so if they had previously been a sports person this was a great advantage. Soccer players were particular sought after. Arthur Conan Doyle, author of the Sherlock Holmes detective stories, made a direct appeal for football players to volunteer for service.

Sports were obviously curtailed during the war years not only due to military action but also due to the flu pandemic that swept the world in 1918. Various professional and amateur sports completely ceased, for example:

Oxford and Cambridge boat race.
Tour de France
Rugby League
Wimbledon
British Open
Motor racing
First Class Cricket

One of the greatest cricketers of the nineteenth and early twentieth century was W.G. Grace (WG). Not only was he one of the greatest but he also had a tremendous influence on the game and on the 27 August 1914 with the County Championship still in progress he wrote a letter to *The Sportsman*:

> 'Sir, There are many cricketers who are already doing their duty but there are many more who do seem to realise that in all probability they will have to serve either at home or abroad before the war is brought to a conclusion. The fighting on the Continent is very severe and will probably be prolonged.
>
> 'I think the time has arrived when the county cricket season should be closed for it is not fitting at a time like the present that able bodied men should play day after day and pleasure seekers look on. There are so many who are young and able and yet are hanging back.
>
> 'I should like to see all first class cricketers of suitable age, etc, set a good example and come to the help of their country without delay in its hour of need.
>
> – Yours etc. W.G. Grace.'

It is interesting to note that WG felt that it would be a prolonged war and not over by Christmas as many were predicting.

The letter had great effect and the county championship came to a premature end with club players also heeding the letter. Looking back it is obvious that the game could not have continued for long because of the lack of men and women available to play, but at the time with the war just starting it is amazing that one letter should stop what at the time was the country's national game.

As usual a poem soon appeared:

The Sterner Game

Manhood of Britain, our Country is calling,
Put by your toys, for no longer 'tis play.
Ours be shirking while comrades are falling,
Rally we now and let ours be "The Day."

Prove we the lessons our clean sports have taught us,
The pluck that endures and the scorning to yield,
No matter the strength of the foemen who fought us –
That was the spirit that won us the field.

That was the object of sporting as a training,
Each for his side, none for personal fame,
Prove now its value, give all uncomplaining,
Give for your country, though sterner the game.

Leo Munro 1914.

The game resumed in 1919. Unfortunately WG was not to participate or watch another game as he died just over a year later in October 1915 at the age of 68. However his appeal obviously had a tremendous effect on local clubs. For example, at least seventeen members of Wickford Cricket Club were killed.

Although the previous two decades have been described as the 'Golden Age of Cricket', there were not too many local clubs around. Langdon Hills Cricket Club was founded at least a decade earlier. Wickford and Billericay were thriving clubs, formed back in the 1880s and North Benfleet had a side. Further afield there were teams from East Hanningfield, Southminster, Rettendon, Hawkwell, Woodham Ferrers, Danbury, Maldon, Brentwood, Southend and various company teams.

Availability of players all depended on the agricultural demands and the fields they played on would certainly not have been the neat cut grounds and well prepared wickets of today, but more likely farmers' fields with the outfields long and cropped by livestock and the wicket mowed in the centre just before the start of the game. Although village cricket ceased during the war in some cases the grounds, such as the one at Wickford, were kept in reasonable condition mainly by volunteer labour to enable different battalions stationed in the neighbourhood to have a game. Wickford Cricket Club's first casualty was Lieutenant C.G.B. Loos, aged 30, killed in action on 12 March 1915. He was shortly followed by P.C. George Burnett (see the chapter on 'Our Heroes').

A members' Roll of Honour was commissioned and retained for many years in the Wickford pavilion but unfortunately it has been lost. On the memorial was a short poem, reflecting a mixture of feelings of tragedy and patriotism.

'No ear was deaf to the trumpet's call,
T'was not for prize nor fame,
Unselfishly they gave their aid,
And nobly played the game.'

Over 200 First Class cricketers from Britain and its Empire were killed during the war on active service (five from Essex) including many Test players.

Fox hunting is not a sport that has a great following today. Like all sporting activities it was affected by the war but surprisingly, given the opportunity, some enthusiasts participated even at the front. Amongst the family records of Colonel Whitmore of Orsett Hall, Orsett, which are in the Essex Record Office, Chelmsford, is the story of a foxhunt at the front told by Mr. J.K. Swine of the Essex Yeomanry in a letter to his father:

> 'FOX HUNT AT THE FRONT. Whole Squadron Joins In The Chase.
>
> 'Guy brought the squadron home after the battle and on the way we put up a fox, this was too much for Guy and me and off we went followed by Edward and Jolliffe and had the best ten minutes of my life. I caught him up and kept right on his brush for about half a minute and ran right across the front of the squadron.
>
> 'This was too much for them and the whole lot broke loose and amid a perfect inferno of hunting noises they all joined in the chase. About another five minutes he was so cooked that I managed to do the true jorrocks touch and leapt from Old Tim and lifted the fox over my head by his brush and the scruff of his neck. We gave him five minutes breather and then let him scuffle off quickly on his way.'

What is astonishing is that the squadron had just returned from engaging the enemy in the Second Battle of Ypres (13 July 1915) and still had the energy to engage in a sporting activity they loved.

It was not long after the war that sport was again high on the popular agenda. For example: in 1914 there were forty clubs registered with the Football Association and by the end of 1919 this had risen to eighty-six.

Zeppelins

Although the people of our island did not experience the devastating bombing that occurred in the Second World War, Germany tried her hardest to demoralise Britain's civilian population by sending over her frightening airships, known as Zeppelins.

The first Zeppelin airship raid on London was in September 1915 and it killed thirteen people and injured eighty-seven, making it clear that some form of air defence was necessary. Most Royal Flying Corps forces were in France but the Home Defence Network was quickly organised by using squadrons of fighters such as BE2s and Avro 5045s which were not considered suitable for front line service.

Eastern England took the brunt of Zeppelin attacks. Although airships were costly to build and vulnerable to attacks, the Germans used them whenever possible because they were aware that the rattling roar of the Zeppelin was feared as much as the whine of the V1 in the Second World War.

One of the contributors to this book, Ivy Powell (née Hymas), who was only about six at the time, remembers quite clearly sitting next to the window of her classroom at Langdon Hills School and hearing the local policeman ringing a bell to let people know that there was a Zeppelin

Zeppelin flying over Laindon.
Kind permission of Tom Monk

raid on. There was no air raid warning system in place like there was in the Second World War, and people had to rely on the local 'bobby' to let them know. Looking out of the window she could clearly see the Zeppelin on its way to bomb London. This was a little time after the Zeppelin (L32) that was brought down in the Great Burstead area.

It was at night, however, when they were most frightening, especially if they were caught in the light of a full moon or by searchlight. The Zeppelins used the railway line to navigate to London.

L32 that crashed at Great Burstead had commenced its journey on 23 September 1916 along with eleven others. Eight made their way from Germany to the Midlands and Northern England and the other four, which included L32, made their way to Southern England. These four were the latest super-Zeppelin and Germany believed that they would leave London in ruins. These airships were 650ft in length, 78ft in diameter and around 92ft in height including the gondolas of which there were four. They required 2,000,000 cubic feet of high volatile hydrogen gas. Their bomb capacity was approximately five tons and they had four machine-guns. Their three engines could drive the airship between forty-five and sixty-five miles per hour.

L32 had a crew of twenty-two and their commander was Oberleutnant-zur-See Werner Peterson of the German Naval Airship Service, an experienced Zeppelin captain. It is interesting to note that they did not have any parachutes.

It was well turned midnight when Peterson decided, because of the probing searchlights and heavy gunfire, to abandon his attack on London and so he dropped his bombs in the Purfleet area and turned eastward and headed for the coast and home. The

L32 Zeppelin Crash at Great Burstead.
Ken Porter's Collection

Ken Porter's Collection

Ken Porter's Collection

Imprint of one of the German bodies from Zeppelin L32. *Ken Porter's Collection*

airship was then attacked by Second Lieutenant Frederick Sowrey in his BE2c biplane. The doomed airship, blazing from end to end, crashed to earth about a mile from Billericay town at 1.30am.

Lieutenant F. Sowrey who attacked the Zeppelin L32.
Ken Porter's Collection

As normal the population of East London and South East Essex were woken from their beds by the policeman's whistle. A few took shelter but others, few in number to start with but soon joined by thousands in the towns, villages and hamlets, watched the duel in the sky.

One of the first on the scene was the Billericay Fire Brigade under Ted Wheeler, followed by the Police and a detachment of troops who were soon joined by Second Lieutenant Sowrey.

The following morning word soon spread of where the wreckage was and, as it was a Sunday, thousands of sightseers descended on the scene. They came on foot, bicycle, trap, car and train. Cockle stalls were set up and pieces of the Zeppelin were being sold. It was like a bank holiday on Southend beach.

All the crew were killed and buried in Great Burstead churchyard with full military honours but later in 1966 were exhumed and reburied at the military cemetery at Cannock Chase. Second Lieutenant Frederick Sowrey was awarded the Distinguished Service Order for conspicuous gallantry.

The intensified and determined Zeppelin offensives had led the civilian population in England to demand greater protection. The result was the introduction of a network of anti-aircraft gun batteries and searchlights together with small airfields around the perimeter of the capital. Laindon and district was only twenty miles from the capital with a railway and the River Thames to help the Germans to navigate into the city, meaning that any action in the air would often be witnessed by the population of the area. Fortunately, due to the large number of Zeppelin disasters like that of the L32, raids were reduced but they still carried on virtually to the end of the war.

It is understood that near Sadler's farm, Bowers Gifford there was a First World War Aerodrome but unfortunately the authors have not been able to find out much information on it. A visit to the First World War Aerodrome museum at Stow Maries, Essex (see appendix 3) confirmed that under the name of North Benfleet it was registered as a Landing Ground, in other words it was an emergency landing spot. Whether any aircraft landed there we have not been able to establish.

Britain and France only used their airships as lookouts for submarines during convoy operations or occasionally employed them on

Graves of the Germans from Zeppelin L32 at Great Burstead Church.
Basildon Heritage collection

Army observations duties. The dictionary describes an airship as 'any self-propelled aircraft that is lighter than air and can be steered – sometimes called dirigible'.

Although the population initially were concerned about Zeppelin attacks, they had very little effect on morale; in fact they increased the popular hatred of the Germans as 'baby killers'.

By mid 1916 Germany realised that the Zeppelins were not going to achieve the success they expected so they began to equip their Gotha twin-engine bomber with a bomb load of 1,100lbs. These aircraft could fly at 15,000ft and had a range of 500 miles. Their first attack on England was on 25 May 1917 and was aimed at London but due to poor weather they were forced to target the Channel port of Folkestone. There were several other raids during the year but as Britain's air defences improved the Germans were force to switch from daylight raids to night raids.

The raids continued throughout 1918 with the last attack in October. Earlier in the year, on the night of 7 March, Captain Alexander Bruce Kynoch (no apparent connection to the Kynoch factory owners) of 37 Squadron took off from Stow Maries in a BE12 C3208 and Captain Henry Stroud of 61 Squadron took off from Rochford at the same time in SE5a B679, both in search of a reported lone raider heading for London.

It would appear that they collided with each other as they came out of a cloud over Shotgate, Wickford. The aircraft crashed in a field on Dollymans Farm, Wickford, killing both pilots. The local farmer, Mr. W. Wilson, had two memorials in the form of two 9ft crosses placed at the site. Later an officer from 37 Squadron flew down and landed at the farm and placed a small memorial at the base of Kynoch's memorial. It is believed this was later removed and placed at the base of Stroud's memorial.

Both parents visited the site and thanked Mr Wilson for his kindness and consideration. He subsequently had a clause written into the deeds of the farm, that if sold the two pieces of land where the memorials stood, would forever remain his property. The parents of the two airmen paid for more permanent memorials which are still there to this day.

Captain Kynoch had joined the army in 1914 and was wounded at Gallipoli. Then in 1916 he joined the Royal Flying Corps (RFC). He is buried in the Victorian part of North Finchley cemetery, London and Captain Stroud in the churchyard of St Andrew's Church in Rochford, Essex.

Captain Stroud Memorial at Dollymans Farm, Wickford.
Basildon Heritage collection

Captain Kynoch Memorial at Dollymans Farm, Wickford.
Basildon Heritage collection

Captain Alexander Bruce Kynoch.
Kind permission of Stow Maries WW1 Aerodrome Museum

There was further excitement over the Wickford airspace on 28 January 1918, when a Gotha GV heavy bomber was shot down and crashed in a field at Hospital Farm just off London Road, Wickford (near Victoria Avenue). The following is an extract from the *Southend Standard*, of 31 January 1918:

'For five hours on Monday people again experienced the perils of an air raid, this being the first one which has materialised since the dawn of the New Year. London was reached by some of the Hun machines and the casualties were forty-seven killed and 164 injured. On the way home the Germans were subjected to heavy bombardment from the anti-aircraft batteries and in some districts shrapnel fell in showers.

'Soon the good news spread that to Essex again had fallen the distinction of having accounted for one of the raiders. In an Essex village not far from the railway station, about ten o'clock there were unmistakable signs that a fight was in progress at a great height, residents could hear the rat-tat-tat of machine-guns, this continued for some minutes, the forks of flame leaping forward and seeming to cross one another in the most erratic manner.

'Then something strangely alarming happened, as one eye-witness put it, there was a peculiar sound high above as of a thousand grandfather clocks running down together and he saw a machine was falling, falling, falling quite close by, it came to the ground burning and as it struck the earth it burst into flames and a shower of sparks and smoke drove upwards.

'Two corpses could be seen in the flames and also the fragments of another, the machine continued to burn for over an hour, the three German airmen were apparently quite young and later were removed to an adjacent barn.'

The three airmen were buried at Downham Church, Essex and in 1933 a memorial in oak was erected over their graves. (It is no longer there)

The bombing by the Zeppelins and bombers resulted in 2,000 civilian deaths, a small number compared with the 66,000 killed in the Second World War. As far as we can establish there were no civilian deaths in our area of Laindon to Pitsea.

RFC MESS SONG

(To the Tune – My Bonnie lies over the ocean)

A poor aviator lay dying
At the end of a bright summer's day
His comrades had gathered about him
To carry his fragments away.

The airplane was piled on his wishbone
His hotchkiss was wrapped round his head
He wore a spark-plug on each elbow
'Twas plain he would shortly be dead.

He spit out a valve and a gasket
And stirred in the sump where he lay
And then to his wondering comrades
These brave parting words he did say.

"Take the magneto out of my stomach
And the butterfly valve off my neck
Extract from my liver the crankshaft
There are lots of good parts in the wreck.

"Take the manifold out of my larynx
And the cylinders out of my brain
Take the piston rods out of my kidneys
And assemble the engine again.

Pull the longeron out of my backbone
The turnbuckle out of my ear (my ear)
From the small of my back take the rudder
There's all of your aeroplane here.

I'll be riding a cloud in the morning
With no rotary before me to cuss (to cuss)
Take the lead from your feet and get busy
Here's another lad needing the bus!"

Author – anonymous – by kind permission of Stow Maries WWI Aerodrome Museum.

Princess Mary

Not only was the Great War going to end all wars, it was going to be over very quickly, but by the autumn two opposing armies were facing each other in trenches stretching from northern France to Belgium. It quickly became obvious that the war was going to go on for a long time and our troops would not be back for Christmas. So with Christmas fast approaching families back home started to send messages of love and support. Seventeen-year-old Princess Mary, daughter of King George V and Queen Mary, approached the British Government with a suggestion to create 'Her Royal Highness the Princess Mary's Sailors and Soldiers' Fund'. The aim was to gather donations from the general public with the idea of sending every sailor afloat and every soldier at the front a Christmas present from 'home' on 25 December 1914.

A committee was formed and agreed that the gift would take the form of an embossed brass box containing a number of small items. Princess Mary published the following letter in the British and Colonial newspapers in early November 1914: 'I want you all to help me send a Christmas present from the whole nation to every sailor afloat and every soldier at the Front.' Another of her letters read:

> 'For many weeks we have all been greatly concerned for the welfare of the soldiers and sailors who are so valiantly fighting our battles by land and sea. Our first consideration has been to meet their more pressing needs and I have delayed making known a wish that has long been in my heart, for fear of encroaching on other funds, the claims of which have been more urgent. I want you all to help me send a Christmas present from the whole nation to every sailor afloat and every soldier at the Front. On Christmas Eve, when, like shepherds of old, they will want to hang out their stockings, wondering what the morrow had in store. I'm sure that we should all be happier to feel that we had helped to send our little token of love and sympathy on Christmas morning, something that would be of useful and permanent value and the making of which may be the means of providing employment for trades adversely affected by the war. Could there be anything more likely to hearten them in their struggle than a present received straight from home on Christmas Day? Please will you help me? Mary.'

The response from the public was overwhelming and approximately £170,000 was raised which meant that an estimated 2,620,019 service men and women would qualify for the gift. The only problem was that there was no way that they would be able to get them to everybody by Christmas Day. It was therefore decided to deliver in order of priority:

Class 'A' Naval personnel and troops at the front, as well as the wounded; Class 'B' British, colonial and Indian troops serving outside the British Isles; Class 'C' troops stationed in Britain. Gifts for those that were prisoners of war were held in reserve and those in class 'B' and 'C' would receive a Happy New Year card instead of a Christmas greeting sometime in the New Year.

The gifts consisted of an 'embossed brass box' in which gifts would be packaged. The front and the centre of the box contained Princess Mary's silhouette and monogram, with the words 'Christmas 1914' embossed below. Smokers received one ounce of tobacco and twenty cigarettes, non smokers received a packet of acid tablets, a khaki writing case and a lead bullet pencil, while nurses received chocolates. A picture of Princess Mary and a greetings card were included.

Princess Mary's Christmas box to the troops, Christmas 1914.
Kind permission of Bill Diment

The considerable number of problems that the committee faced in getting the presents out to everybody resulted in many personnel not receiving their gifts until the summer of 1916. In total 2,500,000 gift boxes were distributed during and after the war.

The Sailors' and Soldiers' Christmas Fund continued throughout the war and in fact did not cease until 1920. The remaining money was transferred to Queen Mary's Maternity Home, an establishment founded to support the wives and children of sailors, soldiers and airmen.

The photograph (left) displaying the items mentioned above was given to the Basildon Heritage by William Diment of Laindon. He had acquired it from his father who had been given it by his brother, Jack.

National Relief Fund

A few days after the outbreak of war, on 7 August 1914, the Prince of Wales made an urgent appeal.

> 'Buckingham Palace – all must realise that the present time of deep anxiety will be followed by one of considerable distress among the people of this country least able to bear it. We must earnestly pray that their suffering may be neither long nor bitter but we cannot wait until the need presses heavily upon us. The means of relief must be ready in our hands. To allay anxiety will go some way to save any distress. A National Fund has been founded and I am proud to act as its Treasurer. My first duty is to ask for generous and ready support and I know that I shall not ask in vain. At such a moment we all stand by one another and it is to the heart of the British people that I confidently make this appeal. Edward.'

Why was this appeal made so quickly after the outbreak of war? Unlike the Second World War where there was a period after the declaration of war before any troops went into action, a period known as the phoney war, the army of the Great War was mobilised immediately and sent off to France. It was so quick that it caused considerable confusion, many families did not know how or where to apply for their separation allowances which must have caused considerable hardship.

On 6 August following a question on what provision was being made for the wives and children of Reserve men, the Prime Minster replied that the matter would be given full consideration. However, it would seem that very little was done and it was left to the public via the Prince of Wales's appeal. By the end of the week the fund had reached a massive £1,000,000. In today's money that is £54,000,000. To help the appeal fund-raising postcards were produced and these helped in providing large sums of money for some of the 18,000 charity and relief organisations that had sprung up. One such appeal was set up at the Kynoch factory and within four weeks collected £67.6s.3d.

In early September 1914 a house-to-house collection in the Laindon and Basildon area raised £18 for the fund. There were several types of appeal, this was just one of them.

Chapter 6

Women's Land Army

War Girls

There's the girl who clips your ticket for the train,
And the girl who speeds the lift from floor to floor,
There's the girl who does a milk-round in the rain,
And the girl who calls for orders at your door,
Strong, sensible and fit,
They're out to show their grit,
And tackle jobs with energy and knack,
No longer caged and penned up,
They're going to keep their end up
Till the khaki soldier boys come marching back.

There's the motor girl who drives a heavy van,
There's the butcher girl who brings your joint of meat,
There's the girl who cries 'All fares, please!' like a man,
And the girl who whistles taxis up the street,
Beneath each uniform
Beats a heart that's soft and warm,
Though of canny mother-wit they show no lack;
But a solemn statement this is,
They've no time for love and kisses
Till the khaki soldier boys come marching back.

Jessie Pope

WHEN WAR BROKE out in 1914 although there were many women in the workforce, many jobs and professions were still closed to them. Most women tended to work in traditional female categories such as nursing, teaching, dressmaking, social and secretarial work and domestic service. Very few married women went out to work as it was deemed unacceptable.

Initially women's unemployment went up due to the middle classes wanting to economise, therefore laying off their servants. However this soon changed with the need for increased military material and with so many men being called up, women were recognised as a valuable resource; they also demanded to be allowed to help with the war effort. It was not long therefore before women were being employed in a variety of jobs they would never have dreamt of before the war.

Between 1914 and 1918 the female work-force increased by 1,600,000 in government departments, public transport, post offices, clerks in industry, land workers (known as the Women's Land Army) and in factories, in particular in dangerous munitions factories – which employed 950,000.

However the entrance of women into the work-force was at first met with some hostility, mainly because male workers were worried that the women would work for lower wages and eventually put them out of work. With six million men away at the front, the government persevered and it was not long before they were accepted and appreciated for their hard work and efficiency and were soon regarded as indispensable to the war effort.

Those working in the munitions factories were known as munitionettes and were soon producing up to eighty per cent of the weapons and shells used by the British Army. It was dangerous work and they were daily risking their lives working with poisonous substances without adequate protective clothing. Health and Safety measures as we know them today were non-existent.

It was the responsibility of the Board of Agriculture to get women working on the land and by the end of 1917 there were between 250,000 - 260,000 women working as farm labourers. This was the beginning of the Women's Land Army but again many traditional farmers were against this, so the Board of Trade sent agricultural organisers to speak with farmers to encourage them to accept women's work on the farms.

Wallington, Alice

Alice was born in Fulham, London in 1901. Soon after the outbreak of War, Alice was called up to work in a blanket factory. Her job was to collect woven wool pieces cut to blanket size and place them in boiling vats. This gave off a considerable amount of heat and steam (the health and safety of the workers was not a consideration), which resulted in the blankets shrinking, making them thicker. The blankets were then sent off to the troops in the trenches.

Alice Wallington.
Kind permission of Gwyn Lock

'Lyndhurst', Leinster Road. Laindon-early 1920s. *Kind permission of Gwyn Lock*

Due to the conditions Alice contacted tuberculosis (TB) and soon after the end of the war she went into an isolation sanatorium, but after a period of time the doctors spoke to her father and told him that there wasn't anything further they could do for her and that she was slowly dying. It was suggested that they moved her to the country.

Her boyfriend at the time was Len Newman who was living in Ulster Road, Laindon. He suggested to the family that they considered moving down to Laindon where the air was healthier than the smog of London. Her father, on his advice, purchased a piece of land in Leinster Road, Laindon from the owner (Alfred John Markham) of the local farm 'Blue House'. He had a small wooden bungalow built for them of two rooms. One a bedroom the other a kitchen, there was no gas, electricity or water laid on. Water was from the roof into a well, no sewer, the toilet was the 'bucket and chuckit' arrangement in a small shed at the bottom of the garden. It was called 'Lyndhurst'.

It was even difficult to call the road a road, the bungalow was more or less in a field with no other buildings around. In 1922 Alice's sister, Elizabeth, and her two-month-old daughter, Gwendoline, moved in. Gwendoline's father Fred Charles Churchill stayed in London with her grandparents. Fred eventually moved down to Laindon in the late 1920s and in the early 1930s had a more substantial bungalow built next door, which they called 'Wallington'. Alice had died in April 1927 aged 26 and was buried at St Nicholas Church, Laindon.

Churchill, Frederick Charles was born 21 February 1893 in North Kensington. He enlisted on 24 October 1915 at Harrowby Camp, Grantham, why so far from home is unknown. He initially joined the Army Ordnance Corps, service number 013132 before transferring to the 11th Training Reserve Battalion probably attached to the 7th (Service) Lincolnshire Regiment, service number 32769 where it is believed

Frederick Charles Churchill.
Kind permission of Gwyn Lock

he became an officer's servant (batman). It would appear that he saw a considerable amount of front line action. The list of battles his regiment was in is endless, including the first and second battles at Passchendaele and at some point he was caught up in a gas attack. He was awarded the Victory and British Medal. The extremely unpleasant sights he saw were to stay with him for the rest of his life. He married Elizabeth Wallington sister of Alice on 13 November 1920. During the war Elizabeth worked in the War Office.

Fred's elder brother **Philip Llewellyn Churchill**, who was born in 1892, joined the Royal Flying Corps on 27 June 1916 as a fitter on 5 shillings a week, service number 34920. He rose to the rank of Corporal Mechanic and was awarded the Victory and British medals. After the war he worked as a bus driver for the London General Bus Company. A women walked out under his bus, he never got over the shock and died shortly afterwards on 17 March 1936.

Incidently, Fred and Philip's father, Frederick Charles worked at the Tower of London as a Foreman Decorator. On one occasion when painting in the Crown Jewels house he accidentally set off the alarm. This caused the drawbridge to come down and the beefeaters and the army to be called out.

Philip Llewellyn Churchill.
Kind permission of Gwyn Lock

Ashley, Lynette

Lynette's experiences in the Land Army at Blue House Farm in Laindon first appeared in the *Essex Countryside* in the late 1960s. Alfred John Markham was the tenant of the farm at the time and though the farm is no longer there, disappearing under the development of the Basildon New Town, descendants of the family are still farming in the Laindon and Billericay area.

There were others on the farm with her and they were billeted some distance away and had to walk across the fields, not so pleasant in the winter months although hurricane lights could be seen from all directions lighting up others on their way to work. They started work at 4.30am and the girls walked across the fields in single file, eating large slices of bread and jam; as Lynette says they needed the strength of youth, as the work was heavy and continual.

Her main task was getting the herd of cattle in for milking as the milk had to be ready to catch the 7am train for London and as she says: 'I doubt whether Blue House Farm any longer sends a horse and cart racing along the road at breakneck speed in order to catch the train at Laindon as it makes its way in the distance from Pitsea.'

In the summer months she was given the task of minding the herd.

> 'I got to know the cows' gentle art of relaxing when chewing the cud as one by one, they rested. I generally sat down too and very soon was stretched out fast asleep. I always woke to find myself alone, with no sign of the herd anywhere

and panic seized me. Any onlooker would have seen a frantic figure flying round in circles in a vain search for the cows. I would feel quite sick with guilt that any minute they could get on the road and I had failed in my duty to look after them.'

Although it was quite unheard of to have a day off, they still seemed to make time to go to St Nicholas Church to sing in the choir on Sundays. Lynette would often drop off to sleep during the sermon and dream that she was not milking as many cows as she should. However, a quick nudge by the person next to her would wake her up to her great embarrassment, being in full view of the congregation. The Rector at the time was the Reverend Herbert Carpenter.

During Lynette's time on the farm there was an article in the daily papers stating that the world was coming to an end. The girls were filled with alarm and believed it to be inevitable. Strangely enough on the morning in question it was very foggy and as they walked to work in stunned silence everything seemed different. Lynette takes up the story again:

'We assumed that there had been some kind of earthquake. As we came to an unusually tall shadow in the fog, we both stopped in consternation but on closer observation it was found to be only an extra tall hedge. With some relief we started to walk again, only to find ourselves before another strange shadow in the fog. After a time it cleared slightly and we found we were merely walking round in circles and our usual stile was visible; the world was with us after all!'

Though Lynette never returned to Laindon after the war she remembered her time there with affection.

Stenning, Alice

Alice was born in Surrey. The 1901 census has her and parents living in cottages at Dunton Wayletts, Dunton and in 1911 working nearby at Langdon Hall as a domestic servant. During the war she had signed on as a Land Army Girl working at Blue House Farm, Laindon, probably alongside Lynette. She must have taken a liking to the farming environment because on 21 April 1919 she marries George Edward Walker, a dairy farmer, at St Nicholas Church. They lived and farmed out of Rose Farm, Basildon. Both are buried at St Nicholas. Two of Alice's brothers, Harold Ernest and Walter Frederick Stenning, joined the Navy and survived the war.

Agriculture was one of the industries for which a stable work-force was needed and many farmers were often able to obtain exemption for some of their men,

Alice Stenning in her Women's Land Army clothing – note the hare in her right hand. The family were not going to go hungry..
Kind permission of Edmund King

although it would appear that some businessmen might have exploited the employment of women to reduce their wage bill.

The following article appeared in the *Chelmsford Chronicle*

'The Chairman said the Tribunal would remember a case in which Mr Alfred John Markham, a farmer at Laindon, informed them that one of his men, for whom he had obtained exemption, had thrown in his job and gone into the Army because he said he would not have a woman working there. This man, Brockwell, had now written to him, the chairman, as follows:

"I am taking pleasure of writing a few lines as I have just read in the *Essex County Chronicle* that Mr Markham had been trying to get one of his men exempted and he said a man had left him because he got a woman to help in the milk round. I am the man in question. Mr Markham got me exemption from June to December. The very next week he said I should have to let a women do my rounds on the weekdays and I on Sundays and I should have to do work for less money but more than that, I am not the only one he has done it to. He said if I did not like it I could join the Army or accept less money. Knowing I could not live on the money, I joined the Army. I had worked for Mr Markham for eleven years."

'The Chairman: "If it is true it is a very mean trick." Mr W. Dalton: "This shows what good the press do by being here." '

To All Land Girls

I saw a Land Girl working
Alone in an open field.
Her hard, once elegant, hand
A stalwart hoe did wield.
Her back was bent as she slew the weeds
That spoiled the potatoes' growth;
She never wilted, she never paused,
She had taken her silent oath.

At last the day was nearly done,
The sun was sinking low;
She gathered up her jacket
Then slowly cleaned her hoe.
She passed the chair where I sat
(I am feeble in body and sight)
She smiled at me as she said:
'Been hot to-day. Good-night.'

We hear the valiant deeds of our men in 'furrin' parts',
Deeds which bring the tears to our eyes, a glow
of pride to our hearts -
But when the war is over and peace at last restored,
I shall always remember the Land Girl, who made her hoe a sword.

From an admirer of their work.

Chapter 7

Our Heroes

The Medal

Tis not the bit of bronze and metal,
That tells the time-worn tale,
Of some act of heroism
Where bullets whine and wail.

Nor are the coloured ribbons,
Pinned on some strutting chest,
Always truthful indicators,
Of the men who fought the best.

Nor do gold stripes upon the arm
Always tell the story,
Of men who have seen action
Or fought their way to glory.

These are outward indications
Made by the hand of man,
Why they're sometimes passed about,
Is hard to understand.

They will tarnish with the weather,
In the plush or on the shelf,
For the real and lasting medal,
Is the soul within yourself.

Did you do your best when called on,
In the air or torn shell-hole,
You've got some real satisfaction,
Buried deep within your soul.

No bit of bronze or ribbon bright,
Or words of praise high spoken,
Can change the thoughts that lie within,
They are the genuine token.

Telling the tale as long as you live,
And the truth of how you fought,
If you played the game with all you had,
You've the medal that can't be bought.

From Rhymes of a Lost Battalion Doughboy

Great War Campaign Medals and Gallantry awards

It was after the Battle of Waterloo in 1815 that the issuing of campaign medals was regularised with the Waterloo Medal, even though the issuing of war medals can be traced back many hundreds of years previously. Campaign medals are awards for service within a particular campaign without regards to the recipient's rank or achievement.

The Great War saw some of the most appalling fighting in history, earlier campaigns like the Crimean, Zulu, India, and Boer wars fade into insignificance when compared to millions who died on both sides in the Great War in conditions that we can barely comprehend. The following is a brief description of these medals:

Campaign Medals

The 1914 Star. This medal was awarded to the initial British Expeditionary Force (BEF) or the 'Old Contemptibles' as they were known, along with their immediate reinforcements, who crossed over into Belgium and France following the declaration of war. It was awarded to British Soldiers, Royal Marines, Imperial forces and Sailors if they served on land. Approximately 378,000 were awarded to those that served between 4 August 1914 and 22 November. The main campaigns of this period were the Retreat from Mons which is why sometimes it is incorrectly referred to as the 'Mons Star' and the fighting around Ypres.

1914 Star.
Ken Porter's Collection

To distinguish between those who had been in action and those who worked behind the lines the former were awarded a clasp but this had to be personally claimed and is probably why there were far fewer clasps than the actual medal.

The authorisation of the medal came in April 1917 and was a simple bronze star bearing the date 'Aug-Nov 1914'. On the flat reverse it bore the recipient's name. The clasp read '5th Aug – 22nd Nov. 1914' and was normally stitched directly onto the ribbon and not attached to the medal.

All recipients of this medal also qualified for the British War Medal and Victory Medal.

The 1914-15 Star. This was one of the most common of the campaign medals awarded to some 2,360,000 members of the British and Imperial forces that served around the world in any theatre of war, either on land, sea or in the air. Although common it must be remembered that the recipients would have been involved in some of the fiercest fighting of the war. Similar to the 1914 Star, it was flat on the reverse with the recipient's name and details. The colour of its ribbon was also the same as the 1914 star. This sometimes caused resentment. Recipients could not receive both but they could receive both the British War Medal and Victory Medal.

1914-1915 Star – Private W.G. Lamb.
Kind permission of Eric Lamb

The British War Medal 1914-1918. This medal was awarded

British War Medal – Private John Clark.
Kind permission of Charlie Clark

to all forces of the Empire, foreign citizens who rendered service to Allied causes and to British forces that were involved in the Allied intervention in the Russian Civil War between 1918-1920. It was also awarded to the support services, nurses, ambulance units and transport personnel. It was silver in appearance, unlike the previous two that were bronze, and approximately 6,500,000 were awarded making it the commonest of British Campaign medals. On the front is the head of George V and on the back a design depicting a naked warrior, possibly St George on horseback, trampling the Central Powers and the emblem of death. It is believed it was to symbolise man's control over nature and the forces of destruction.

There was also a bronze version and these were awarded to non-combatant units such as the Chinese Labour Corp, India, Maltese and the Macedonian Mule Corps but only 110,000 were awarded.

The Victory Medal – Private John Clark
Kind permission of Charlie Clark

The Victory Medal. Approximately 5,725,000 of these bronze gilt-washed medals were awarded. It is also known as the Allied Victory Medal as the various Allied countries decided to issue a standardised medal and ribbon. So the Victory medal of Great Britain is very similar to that of France, Belgium, USA, Japan etc. Similar to the British War Medal, the reverse dates are '1914-1919' to include the post-war intervention in the Russian Civil War. On the reverse of the South African medal the wording is in both English and Afrikaans.

The medal is never seen worn by itself but is worn in conjunction with at least the British War medal or other 1914-18 awards.

Anyone awarded the 1914 Star or the 1914-15 Star was automatically entitled to the British War Medal and the Victory Medal.

These three medals, 1914 Star or 1914-15 Star, British War Medal and Victory Medal were often referred to as Pip, Squeak and Wilfred.

Why? Well, it would appear that when they were being issued in the 1920s, it coincided with a popular comic strip published by the *Daily Mirror* newspaper. Pip was a dog, Squeak a penguin and Wilfred a rabbit, the author was Bertram Lamb and the cartoonist Austin Payne. For some unexplainable reason the three names of the characters became associated with the three campaign medals.

In the same vein if the British War Medal and Victory Medal are worn together they are often referred to as 'Mutt and Jeff.'

The Territorial Force War Medal, 1914-1919. Only 34,000 of these were awarded and are therefore the rarest of the general series for the Great War. It is a bronze medal and was granted to members of the Territorial Force serving before August 1914 or who had four years service. It was not possible to receive this award and the 1914 Star or 1914-1915 Star; it is usually seen with British War Medal and Victory Medal.

The Mercantile Marine Medal 1914-1918. As its name indicates it was an award given for vital services performed by the Merchant Navy and just over 133,000 were issued. Again it was a bronze medal with George V's head on the front and the reverse has a rather dramatic scene of a merchant ship ploughing through heavy seas with a sinking submarine in the foreground. Its colourful ribbon shows the port and starboard lights of a merchant ship.

Gallantry Awards

Victoria Cross. The Victoria Cross is our highest military decoration awarded for valour 'in the face of the enemy'. It was introduced by Queen Victoria in January 1856 to honour acts of valour during the Crimean War and can be awarded to a military person of any rank in the British Forces (all services), British Empire countries and civilians under military command. It is usually presented to a recipient or to next-of-kin by the monarch at an investiture at Buckingham Palace. Since its inception 1,357 have been awarded, 627 to recipients during the Great War which is the largest number for any campaign to date. The medal is a Bronze Cross pattée (with arms narrow at the centre and broad at the perimeter) with Crown and Lion superimposed and the motto; 'For Valour'. Originally it was thought that the medal was cast of gunmetal from a Russian cannon captured at the siege of Sebastopol during the Crimean War. It is now believed that many of the medals have been made from Chinese cannons that may have been captured from the Russians in 1855.

Distinguished Service Order (DSO). The DSO is one level down from the Victoria Cross. It was instituted in September 1886 by Queen Victoria for distinguished service by officers of the armed forces during wartime. Although normally for officers ranked major (or its equivalent) or higher, it has also been awarded to junior officers. During the Great War 8,981 were awarded and all announced in the *London Gazette*. The medal is a gold (silver-gilt) cross, enamelled white and edged in gold. In the centre, within a wreath of laurel, enamelled green, is the Imperial Crown in gold upon a red enamelled background. On the reverse is the Royal Cypher in gold upon a red enamelled background, within a wreath of laurel, enamelled green. A ring at top of the medal attaches to a ring at the bottom of a gold suspension bar, ornamented with laurel. At the top of the ribbon is a second gold bar ornamented with laurel.

Distinguished Conduct Medal (DCM). This was until 1993 an extremely high level award for bravery. It was awarded to other ranks below commissioned officers and was established in 1854 during the Crimean War. It is a silver medal, since 1902 the front face bears the effigy of the reigning monarch. The reverse bears the inscription 'For Distinguished Conduct in the Field'. The suspender is of an ornate scroll type. The ribbon is of three parts crimson, dark blue and crimson. In 1993 it was replaced by the Conspicuous Gallantry Cross.

Military Cross (MC) – Distinguished Service Cross (DSC) – Distinguished Flying Cross (DFC). These three were the next level up, level three and represented the various armed forces. The Military Cross was awarded to officers of the British land forces in recognition of 'an act or acts of exemplary gallantry during active operations against the enemy on land'. It was created in 1914 for commissioned officers of the rank of captain and below. In 1931 it was extended to majors and also members of the Royal Air Force for actions on the ground. Then in 1993 it was extended to all ranks in the British armed forces on the ground. It is a silver cross with straight arms with a Royal Cypher in the centre and plain on the reverse.

The Distinguished Service Cross (DSC) - Was first established in June 1901 as the Conspicuous Service Cross, an award for Navy warrant and junior officers who were not eligible for the DSO (Distinguished Service Order) in recognition of 'gallantry during active operations against the enemy at sea'. It was renamed in October 1914 and its eligibility extended to all naval officers below the rank of lieutenant. During the Great War 1,193 were awarded. It is a plain silver cross with rounded ends, the Royal Cypher in the centre surrounded by a ring and the reverse being plain.

The Distinguished Flying Cross (DFC). This is a military decoration awarded to commissioned officers and warrant officers of the Royal Air Force. It was established on 3 June 1918 shortly after formation of the Royal Air Force for 'an act or acts of valour, courage or devotion to duty whilst flying in active operations against the enemy'. In the Great War approximately 1,100 were awarded.

Military Medal (MM). This was established on 25 March 1916 for other ranks below commissioned officers who would normally receive the Military Cross. The MM ranked below the MC and DCM. It is a silver medal and the front face bears the effigy of the reigning monarch. The reverse has the inscription 'For Bravery in the Field' surrounded by a laurel wreath, surmounted by the Royal Cypher and Imperial Crown. The suspender is of an ornate scroll type. The ribbon is dark blue, with five equal centre stripes of white, red, white, red and white. In 1993 the MM was discontinued and since then the MC has been awarded to personnel of all ranks.

Mention in Dispatches. Although it had been customary to mention in official reports by senior officers the names of officers and men who had distinguished themselves in action but who were not necessarily recommended for a decoration, it was not until the end of the Great War that it was agreed that those recognised in dispatches could wear a bronze oak leaf spray pin on the ribbon of the appropriate campaign medal. For the Great War it was the ribbon of the Victory Medal, also only one pin would be issued irrespective of the number of times the individual was mentioned. There was not normally any citation only the mention of the name. It is classified as level four, the lowest level of gallantry awards.

As with all these campaign and gallantry medals additional bars or clasps can be added.

The Call

Who's for the trench –
Are you, my laddie?
Who'll follow French –
Will you, my laddie?
Who's fretting to begin,
Who's going out to win?
And who wants to save his skin –
Do you, my laddie?

Who's for the khaki suit –
Are you, my laddie?
Who longs to charge and shoot –
Do you, my laddie?
Who's keen on getting fit,
Who means to show his grit,
And who'd rather wait a bit –
Would you, my laddie?

Who'll earn the Empire's thanks –
Will you, my laddie?
Who'll swell the victor's ranks –
Will you, my laddie?
When that procession comes,
Banners and rolling drums –
Who'll stand and bite his thumbs –
Will you, my laddie?

Jessie Pope

One of the most enjoyable aspects of writing a book of this nature is the research, delving through the various archives, surfing the internet, interviewing people and watching old documentaries. However, we still found it difficult to get into the minds of those that went to war, until we watched the two-part documentary on Channel 5 – 'WWI's Tunnels of Death: The Big Dig'. At last it really got home to us just how brave these men were. The following are some of their stories. They do not all originate from the area but at some stage have a connection to it.

Pitts, James Frederick

Although Ken's grandfather and family did not move to Laindon until 1928, his story is worth a mention. His maternal great-great-grandparents, Nathan and Rosetta Beardwell, moved to the Basildon area in 1883 and his great-grandmother, Annie Beardwell, worked in service at Goldsmith Manor, Langdon Hills in the 1890s.

His grandfather's story came to light when Ken was researching his family tree. He

YMCA at Le Havre, France where many of the soldiers rested. *Ken Porter's Collection*

met his great uncle, Wally Cooper, who informed him that his grandfather, Fred, and he were in the same regiment, Wally being attached to the Medical Corps. Following one of the battles of the Somme, Wally had become concerned that he had not seen Fred for a few days, so he decided to go and look for him. He found him injured a few yards from the German lines where he had lain for three days.

A family story, it needed checking out, so with the help of a researcher Ken was able to locate his grandfather's war records. Fred was a volunteer, enlisting in the Territorial Army on 2 September 1914 for a period of four years with the 6th Battalion, City of London Rifles. His service number was 320566, his age 21 years 6 months and he was living at 28 Glenister Road, East Greenwich.

On 17 February 1915 he signed up for overseas service, as a Rifleman, Unit 2/6th Battalion, London Rifles, service number 2205. It would appear that he was then transferred to the 1/6th Battalion because a month later on 17 March 1915 at 7pm he embarked at Southampton and sailed on the SS *Marguerite* to Le Havre, France. The previous twelve hours the battalion had waited on the quayside more or less in silence while the Navy carried out a sweep of the seas to ensure there were no enemy submarines present. Then just as they were beginning to board voices could be heard singing and very soon a thousand voices were singing the following hymn.

Eternal Father, strong to save,
Whose arm hath bound the restless wave,
Who bidd'st the mighty ocean deep,
Its own appointed limits keep;
O hear us when we cry to Thee,
For those in peril on the sea.

As Fred would become involved with the Laindon and District Operatic Society after the war, he would surely have been in good voice that day.

They disembarked the following day 18 March and fortunately it was an uneventful crossing, no submarines to be seen. The bell of the SS *Marguerite* stands in the church of the Holy Sepulchre, Holborn, near the war memorial.

On disembarkation the battalion marched to Camp No 6. The following day the battalion took a twenty-hour train journey to Berguette, this was followed by a nine-mile march to billets in the small mining town of Raimbert. There they had a few days rest before moving on to Béthune, another nine miles away where they were billeted in an orphanage, and by this time men and horses were extremely tired. Over the next few days all the various units received some training in modern trench warfare.

Although it is possible that they were involved in a few skirmishes with the enemy, the first major battle the battalion was involved in was for the village of Festubert. It started on 15 May 1915 and was preceded by a sixty-hour bombardment by 433 artillery pieces that fired about 100,000 shells, the idea being to blow gaps in the German lines through which the infantry could pour through. The attack went on and off over the next ten days until 25 May when the village was captured. More than 16,000 casualties were sustained in the attack, which was in support of a much larger French offensive to the south at Vimy Ridge. French losses were over 102,000, against German losses of about 50,000 which included those at Festubert. The conditions at the front were so bad that food rations were delivered by the quartermaster in a wheel barrow.

The 6th London Rifles had taken over the front line on the 20th and remained there for ten days. One German assault across their front presented them with excellent targets to fire at from about 500 yards. The enemy was forced to retire on two occasions waving white flags. There was some concern later that their fire may have caused casualties in other units. So friendly fire as we know it today is nothing new.

The following is the type of wounds they suffered:

Smashed Jaw bones
Legs missing
Foot missing
Arm missing
Hand missing
Eyes shot away
Mouths battered to pulp

Gashes to heads, sides, backs, thighs, stomachs and buttocks
Crushed feet, hands, arms and legs
Shell shock

Many were dead, others were dying; some managed to survive. It must have been a dreadful sight. It is very difficult for us to understand what it must have been like for the stretcher bearers, the medics and those that had survived without injury and had to go and fight another day knowing that it could happen to them next time – what heroes!

After the Battle of Festubert the 6th London Rifles remained in the battle area at Noyelles and Vermelles until 12 June when they were relieved, though still involved in a number of small skirmishes. Their next involvement was the Battle of Loos in September 1915 which was one of the major British offensives on the Western Front in 1915. It marked the first time the British used poison gas during the war, along with the specialist Royal Engineer tunnelling companies, who deployed mines underground to disrupt enemy defence lines through the use of tunnels and the detonation of large amounts of explosives. It was considered a British victory, although our casualties were 50,000 compared to the Germans 25,000. The Germans named the battle 'the corpse field of Loos' (see Herbert Samuel Grant story on p.90).

At Festubert the 6th had shown its ability in defence; now, at Loos, it had proved its worth in offensive action.

Vimy Ridge was their next major area of activity where the battalion settled down to three months of trench warfare. There were short breaks behind lines but they were kept busy training and in their few leisure hours there was very little to do other than to visit shops and estaminets (small cafés that supplied drinks and food). Even this was of little use if their pay had not got through which was often the situation. Much of their time was taken up in keeping clean, freeing themselves from lice and other vermin.

The Somme river source starts at Saint Quentin and travels 152 miles to the Bay of the Somme at the English Channel. It is interesting to note that the word Somme is of Celtic origin meaning tranquillity. Its history and surrounding area has proved that it is far from an area of tranquillity.

In 1066 the invasion fleet of William the Conqueror was assembled in the bay at Saint-Valery-sur-Somme. Edward III in 1346 forded the river at the Battle of Blanchetaque, culminating in the Battle of Crécy and then again it played an important part in the Battle of Agincourt. Tranquil? Do not think so.

The Battle of the Somme commenced on 1 July 1916. The 6th London Rifles had

Explosion of a big tunnel mine.
Ken Porter's Collection

Walter William Cooper – James Frederick's future brother-in-law. *Ken Porter's Collection*

British Mark I tank. *Ken Porter's Collection*

stayed behind near Vimy Ridge but by September they were in the Somme area getting ready for the forthcoming Battle of Flers-Courcelette which began on 15 September 1916 and went on for a week. The general plan was to cut a hole in the German line by using massed artillery and infantry attacks. It was in one of these attacks on High Wood that Fred was badly injured and his record shows that he lay on the battlefield only metres away from the German line and for three days. The only question outstanding is, was he really found by his future brother-in-law, Wally. Ken has no reason to doubt it.

One of the major events of this particular battle was the introduction by the British of tanks. All of the forty-nine tanks that the British had were used. However seventeen were unable to make it as far as the front line, a further seven failed to work at the start of the attack but the remaining fifteen managed to roll slowly into no man's land. Although their effectiveness was limited, the initial surprise had a devastating effect upon German morale, probably similar to the fear the civilian population back home suffered upon a Zeppelin attack. Although the tanks did not lead to the anticipated breakthrough, they so impressed General Haig that he requested another 1,000 to be constructed.

Fred's injury was a compound fracture of the right leg, tibia and fibula, and by 29 September he was back in England at a hospital in Sheffield. He had an operation on the leg on 26 January 1917 and was eventually discharged from hospital on 22 September 1917 (360 days in hospital – one year). He was discharged from the Army on the grounds of his injury on 5 November 1917. His discharge papers stated that his military character was very good, steady and well conducted.

On returning from the war he rejoined the South Metropolitan Gas Company as a Mechanic (fitter and turner). In 1918 he married Beatrice May Cooper and they moved to Laindon in 1928.

In the Second World War their house at Greenwich was bombed and compensation of £300 helped to pay off the mortgage on their bungalow in Laindon.

Fred got home safely and so did Wally but Fred's brother, Herbert Ernest Pitts, a gunner with the Royal Horse Artillery and Royal Field Artillery was killed on 6 November 1917.

In the Second World War Fred enlisted with 5th Battalion Essex (Brentwood) Home Guard on 27 March 1942 and was discharged on 31 December 1944 when the Home Guard was stood down. He failed to get a defence medal by sixty-nine days non service. For the Great War he received all three medals, the 1914-1915 Star, The British War Medal 1914-1918 and the Victory Medal.

Just to complete the Somme story, poor weather brought a halt to the offensive on 18 November 1916. Although the Allies gained an area of about a hundred square miles, this increased to a thousand when the Germans later retired. The Allies also captured about 38,000 prisoners and 125 guns but in doing so British casualties amounted to 22,923 officers and 476,553 other ranks. French casualties were about 200,000 with German casualties estimated at 500,000.

Fred died on 17 February 1955 at the age of sixty-one and is buried at St Nicholas Church, Laindon.

James Frederick Pitts in his Home Guard Uniform (Second World War) and his wife, Beatrice.
Ken Porter's Collection

Herbert Samuel Grant

It is assumed he enlisted in London, joining the 6th Battalion London Regiment (London Rifle Brigade) as a rifleman; service number 2477.

He was the son of Samuel Henry and Alice Grant of 'Midhurst', High Road, Laindon. The area at the time was part of the Laindon Station Estate and was in the parish of Little Burstead. He died on 20 May 1916.

The family were living there at the time of the 1911 census and Herbert's occupation is stated as 'booking clerk'. It is not clear when he enlisted or he arrived in France but we believe he saw some early action.

The 6th was formed in August 1914 at Farringdon Road and was part of 2 London Brigade, 1st London Division. On mobilisation they went to Bisley then in September to Crowborough. In November they moved to Watford and transferred to 4 London Brigade in the 2nd London Division.

Five months later on 18 March 1915 they landed at Le Havre. It is assumed that he went over on the SS *Marguerite*, the same vessel that Fred Pitts was on. Perhaps they knew each other. The first battle Herbert was involved in was the battle of Festubert

Herbert Samuel Grant.
Steve Newman Collection

(See Fred Pitts' story on P.84) that commenced on 15 May 1915.

The next major offensive was the Battle of Loos. It was the third time that the British used the tactic of tunnelling underground and getting as close to the German lines or beneath them to detonate large amounts of explosives in an attempt to disrupt the enemy defences.

They also used chlorine gas but it was not that successful (140 tons) as in some places the gas was blown back into the British trenches. The gas masks were very primitive and many soldiers removed them because they could not see through the fogged up eye-pieces or breathe properly. This meant that many of the British soldiers were badly affected by their own gas.

The battle started on 25 September 1915 and mainly through superior numbers the British managed to capture the town of Loos, but due to the considerable number of casualties the fighting subsided on 28 September with the British having retreated to their original positions. Although there were a number of skirmishes by both sides in the following days, the fighting ceased on 13 October.

Although described as a British victory, the British did not gain any ground and their losses were similar to the Germans. There were a number of notable deaths, two in particular being: Captain Fergus Bowes-Lyon, an older brother of Queen Elizabeth the Queen Mother and uncle of Her Majesty Queen Elizabeth II and Lieutenant John 'Jack' Kipling only son of the writer, Rudyard Kipling.

The Loos memorial commemorates over 20,000 officers and men who fell in the battle and have no known grave.

As Herbert had died at home our first reaction is that he had died from wounds received in the battle for Loos or through effects of the gas but this was not the case. A report in the *Essex Newsman* reveals that Private Herbert Samuel Grant, London Rifles, the 22-year-old son of Mr S.H. Grant formerly of Valetta, Belle Vue Road, Southchurch and now of 'Midhurst', High Road, Laindon, while boating in the River Gripping at Ipswich, was thrown from a canoe and drowned on Saturday, 20 May 1916.

Then in the 3 June addition of the *Essex Newsma*n and the *Chelmsford Chronicle* we find the following report of his funeral at St Mary and All Saints, Langdon Hills:

'The funeral of Pt. Herbert S. Grant, 21, of the 2/6th City of London Rifles, took place at Laindon Hills on Saturday, with full military honours. The remains were taken from Ipswich Barracks, on a gun-carriage, by an escort, with regimental band and conveyed to Billericay.

Herbert Samuel Grant CWWG at St Mary's and All Saints, Langdon Hills. *Ken Porter's Collection*

'There the cortege was met by Mr W. Grant (Uncle) of Lovelace Gardens, Southend and proceeded to 'Midhurst' Laindon, the residence of the deceased's father Mr Henry Grant, under the charge of Lieutenant Lathbury and an escort of sixty NCOs and men. At 'Midhurst' the procession was joined by detachments of the Essex Volunteer Regiment, the Special Constables and Royal Berkshire Yeomanry. The service at the Church of St Mary and All Saints, Laindon, was conducted by the Rector, the Reverend G.J.H. LLewellyn, assisted by the Reverend J.W. Lindsay DD, vicar of St Erkenwald, Southend. Mr Joliffe Pawley was at the organ and the choir was augmented for the occasion. The service throughout was of the most impressive character.

Dr Lindsay spoke of the qualities of the deceased which had endeared him to so many in Laindon as well as Southend and in Ipswich. At the graveside the committal was read by the Rector; three volleys were fired and 'The Last Post' was sounded.'

Harry Ernest Collett

Harry was not initially from the area but when he got married in 1922 at All Saints Church, Vange to Violet Weaver he moved in with his in-laws at 13 Vange Cottage, Paynters Hill, Vange.

Harry Ernest Collett.
Kind permission of Peter Merten

It is interesting to note that he was born at Warley Barracks, Brentwood, to William and Margaret Collett in 1896. William at the time was in the Army in the 56th Foot. The 1911 census has William's occupation as an Army Pensioner. The 1901 census however has William as a 'patrol man' at the explosive works, presumably the Kynoch Explosive factory, Stanford-le-Hope. Being a patrol man would probably mean he was a security guard, an obvious occupation for somebody with army experience. Harry's elder sister Jessie also worked at the explosive factory. At the time of the 1911 census they were living at Mill Cottage, Fobbing near the church, a neighbouring parish to Vange.

Perhaps because of his father's army service, Harry signed up for an Army career although why the 1st Battalion Queen's Own Royal West Kent Regiment (service number 10024) is not known, because at the time war broke out the battalion was in Dublin. Harry's initial training took place at Maidstone, Kent. The orders were received to mobilize on 4 August 1914 and embarkation took place on 13 August 1914 on HMS *Gloucestershire* amid scenes of much enthusiasm. They disembarked on 15 August at Le Havre. The battalion was under the command of 13 Brigade in the 5th Division.

We have not been able to find Harry's war records, other than his medal record, which shows that he was awarded the 1914 Star and that his date of entry into the theatre of war was 15 August 1914 which clearly establishes that he was in one of the first units of the British Expeditionary Force (BEF) to land in France.

On arrival at Le Havre they were met with tremendous enthusiasm and many of the locals wanted them to part with their cap badges etc. They then took a sixteen-hour train journey to Landrecies reaching the destination early on 18 August which was followed by a four-mile march to Maroilles. At every station and on the march were enthusiastic people offering cigarettes, sweets, handshakes and every now and again the shout 'Guillaume', meaning the German Emperor, and then pretending to cut their throats.

The next few days were spent route marching and musketry and then on 23 August the first major action the BEF encountered was at the Battle of Mons. The British were to hold the line of the Mons-Condé Canal and although they fought well, the numerical strength of the Germans forced them to retreat. The Queen's Own in fact had spent the early stages of the battle lying inactive in the second line but by the 26th started to come under heavy fire, especially at Le Cateau, as they retreated.

The retreat lasted for two weeks and covered 250 miles and, although a tactical victory for the Germans, it was a moral victory for the British as they had achieved the main objective of protecting the French Fifth Army from being outflanked. The British commanders were not dissatisfied with the outcome and the men were also in high spirits for they had met a superior number of the most highly renowned army in the world and had given a good account of themselves. The Battle of Mons was a small affair compared with what was to follow and British casualties amounted to just over 1,600 of all ranks. German losses were in excess of 5,000. At Le Cateau the situation was slightly different with British and French losses amounting to nearly 8,000, killed, wounded or missing (this included 2,600 prisoners) but German losses were again high in excess of 5,000.

It is interesting to note what Walter Bloem, Reserve Captain 12th Brandenburg Grenadier Regiment had to say in his autobiographical work *Vormarsch*:

> 'Our first battle is a heavy, unheard of heavy, defeat and against the English, the English we laughed at.'

Later he goes on to say:

> 'The men all chilled to the bone, almost exhausted to move with depressing consciousness of defeat weighing heavily upon them. A bad defeat, there can be no gainsaying it – we had been beaten and by the English – by the English we had so laughed at a few hours before.'

Ypres after two years of war.
Ken Porter's Collection

What an opener for Harry; he was one of the original 80,000 British Expeditionary Force made up of an entirely professional force of long-service volunteer soldiers and as a result it was probably the best trained and most experienced of European armies of 1914. It was an exceedingly small army compared to the Germans and French who each had forces exceeding a million men.

In October 1914 the battalion made a heroic stand at Neuve Chapelle being the only unit not to fall back. Out of 750 men only 300, commanded by a lieutenant and a second lieutenant, survived.

There were plenty more battles but we do not know what Harry was subsequently involved in. But the following are a few where he might have seen action:

First Battle of Ypres
Second battle of Ypres
Battle of Festubert
Battle of Loos
Battle of the Somme
Battle of Messines
Battle of Passchendaele
Second Battle of the Somme

On 1 April 1918 the 1st Queen's Own Royal West Kents were on their way 'to war' after a short time of quiet on the Italian Front. It was therefore ready for immediate deployment. They did not have to wait long as the second of the German offensives of the year broke through the Portuguese near Neuve Chapelle in what became known as the Battle of the Lys. The 1st Queen's Own did not have a particularly prominent part to play in stopping the German advance. However the nearby forest of Nieppe was to become very familiar to them and from the middle of April until the beginning of August the 5th Division with the 1st held this important sector.

On 28 June the battalion was given the objective to take over and control the line leading down to Plate Becque. To ensure a surprise attack it was decided that there would be no preliminary bombardment. At 6am a heavy barrage was suddenly put down with the British infantry coming crashing down on the Germans who offered stiff resistance which was overcome by hand to hand fighting. The bayonet was used very effectively by one of the platoons (perhaps Harry's) and it accounted for thirty-six of the enemy.

Harry, who had been promoted to corporal, won the Military Medal for the attack on Plate Becque. It was one of the first successful counter-strokes of the summer and a reversal of the roles of attacker and defender. It was the beginning of the end of the war for Germany. The Germans suffered heavily, over 500 prisoners were captured and thirty machine-guns plus 6,000 yards of German line was taken. Although only a minor operation, it was a worthy episode and gave the troops renewed confidence. The 1st Royal West Kents had carried out to the letter its share of the plan, the battalion then took a short break but by 4 July they were back in the line. The rest of the month saw heavy fighting with the German aircraft being very active and their guns maintained a harassing fire, although the British guns replied with aggression. By the end of July they had secured the line and the battalion took a well-earned rest until the middle of August.

There were still three months of fighting left but when firing ceased on 11 November

Harry Ernest Collett, grave at All Saints Church Vange.
Ken Porter's Collection

1918 there was hardly a man and not one officer present who had heard the first shots fired on 23 August 1914. Harry was one of them.

So Harry had survived the war but only to die in 1928 from injuries received in a fire at Coryton oil foundry. He was dipping the tanks when the fuel ignited, Cory Works did not have any ambulances so they had to get an ambulance from Shell Mex. He was taken to Tilbury Hospital, his boots had burnt to his feet and he died five hours later. He was buried on the 22 November 1928 at All Saints Church Vange and given a full military funeral.

The following report appeared in the *Essex Newspaper* Saturday, 24 November 1928:

> 'FIREMAN'S SAD DEATH. Harry Ernest Collett, 3 of Vange Hall Cottages, Vange, a fireman employed by Messrs. Cory Bros of Coryton, died in Tilbury Hospital from burns received in a fire at the oil refinery of his employers. Deceased was enveloped in flames and another employee, Thos. C. Thorpe, rushed to his assistance, wrapping an overcoat around him and rolling him on the ground. Mr Collett, however was badly burned. At the inquest on Tuesday Mr Deputy Coroner H.J. Jefferies complimented Mr Thorpe on his plucky action. A verdict of Accidental Death was recorded.'

What a cruel world we live in, here we have a man who was one of the very few who fought right through the war and survived only to die through an accident at work.

In addition to the 1914 Star and his Military Medal, Harry was awarded the British War Medal 1914-18 and the Victory Medal.

Andrews, Edwin Charles

When the older residents of Laindon get together and talk about old times it's not long before Andrews' post office comes up in discussion but I wonder how many are aware

Andrews' Post Office – Edwin in the doorway. *Ken Porter's Collection*

that Edwin volunteered for service in the Great War.

Edwin Charles Andrews was born in Winchester, Hampshire in July 1889. He was known by his family and friends as Charles. By 1911 he was working in Laindon Post Office in a parade of shops on east side of the High Road near the railway station as an assistant to Post Mistress Kate Collings. On 24 May 1911, although eleven years her junior, he married Kate at the Baptist Church in Langdon Hills. Kate unfortunately died early in 1935 and is buried at St Nicholas Church, Laindon. On 11 June 1936 Charles remarried; his second wife was Ethel Wicking. By now the Post Office had been relocated to the other side of the road next to the Collings hardware shop. The sorting office was accessed from Denbigh Road. At what stage Charles took over as Post Master is not known, perhaps after he returned from the First World War or after the death of his first wife.

One of the major problems experienced by the army during the war was the ability for the front line to communicate with those in the rear and supporting units. The need for telephone, telegraph lines, human runners, motorcycle despatch riders and pigeons were a necessity but were very vulnerable to enemy shellfire.

The British recognised the problem and in December 1916 'signallers' were instructed to follow close behind the attack, burying cables connected in a 'ladder' system so that one break would not disable the network. As the war continued various improvements were made but they did not completely solve the problem, although they did make it more likely that messages would get through. Charles was one of these signallers.

Charles enlisted at Warley, Brentwood on 27 October 1916, aged twenty-seven. He passed his medical (A) and his recommendation for enlistment stated:

> 'Smart, intelligent man and suitable of the branch of the service in which he desires to enlist. Brigadier General, Commandant, Signals service T Centre was willing to accept him but he would not be able to serve with his brother. He was sent to R. E. (Royal Engineers) Regiment Camp at Bletchley. Rank Private, Service number 210874.'

At the time of his enlistment they had three children Mary (3 years), Joyce (2 years) and Charley (1 year).

Approximately three months later on 10 January he embarked for France. His war record tells us that on 4 October 1917 he transferred from the 3rd Field Survey Company to the 5th, transferred back again on 2 November 1917 and on 23 January 1918 he is recorded as a Sapper and a Field Lineman, Proficient. Then on 6 February he is back with the 5th. This transferring back and forth continued throughout his stay in France. On 20 March 1918 he was promoted to acting Sergeant Corporal (paid), the same date he seems to have been promoted to Lance Corporal (paid). Promotion to Lance Corporal normally occurs during the fighting to take control of the section because the corporal has been killed or wounded. On 1 September 1918 he is promoted to 2 Corporal. The 2, I assume means that he has received a second stripe (Appendix four). Finally he was transferred on 30 March 1919 to class '2' Army Reserve on demobilization.

Charles took a well-earned fourteen-day break back in England from 28 July 1918 returning on the 10 August 1918. From this date he kept a diary, the following are extracts from it. Unfortunately we have not been able to decipher some of it, especially the various locations he found himself at but there is sufficient to understand how chaotic and gruesome war can be.

His main job was to keep the telephone lines between HQ and the troops at the front working and this must have required an amazing amount of courage, running out lines of cables, day or night with bombs dropping all around, passing injured and dead bodies whilst going about the work. It is no wonder many soldiers suffered from shell shock and had nightmares for many years afterwards.

> '10 August 1918, left home by 9pm train for Victoria, spent night at Salvation Army Hostel, St Ann's Street, Westminster.
>
> '11th Caught the 7.23am Victoria train for Folkstone, transferred to boat and arrive at Boulogne at about 3pm. Marched to camp for the night, received meal tickets.
>
> '12th Up at 4.30am and left for Boulogne at 7.40am arriving around 5pm, had tea then bathed in the river.
>
> '13th Up at 7am. Had breakfast and left by car for section arriving about 1pm, heard that the section had left Allonville ? [a small village in the Somme area in the Picardy region] and gone to another location, we followed arriving at the new location at 5pm and after tea went into the cellars for the night. We were shelled and bombed all night it was not safe to be above ground.
>
> 'Up at 5.30am on the 14th went forward to new position near HQ. In the

afternoon repaired lines 4, 5, and 6. Returning around 5pm the whole place was being heavily shelled. There were several air fights overhead and planes were destroyed. Spent night in dug-out not shrapnel proof. Boche overhead bombing and shelling but none fell within 200 yards.

'15th up at 6.30am and finished off repairing line 4 and had some narrow escapes from shells. Saw several tanks smashed and burnt out. Boche hospital in fairly good condition. Plenty of Boche rifles and ammunition lying about. Planes over again at night fairly close.

'16th went out and repaired line 4. Shells falling all about returned to camp. Shells bursting about 100 yards away. Boche over again bombing and shelling.

'17th Up at 5am, all lines destroyed, some being blown up to two miles away. Went out with a drum of cable to repair them on returning heard Hendry and O'Rourke killed in O.P. line about half mile away. Brought them in on stretchers laying them by the cemetery for the night. More bombs and shells.

'On the 18th up at 5am and ran out to check line without shell dropping within 1,000 yards "quite a treat". At 12 noon assisted in burying Hendry and O'Rourke. That night Boche fired balloon and got away, later shelling and bombing.

'19th up at 5.30am lines 4, 5, and 6 all destroyed, while repairing shells began to fall a few hundred yards away; 5 and 6 destroyed, we went out again after breakfast and repaired 5 when a shell pitched right between us, fortunately being about 30 yards away apart, both thought the other had been taken out but after the smoke cleared saw colleague scrambling back, another burst about 100 yards away. Plenty of shells dropped that night near dug-out so went deeper. Saw two planes collide and come down.

'20th up at 5.30am went out and repaired line 4, 5 and 6, left in charge of lines.

'21st, Lines 1, 2, 3 and OP lines smashed, pieces flying all round camp. Saw Mr Biggs explained situation and got orders to quit and run M4 from church to New HQ. Went back to dug-out in evening and packed up kit.

'Move out on the 22nd and run out M3 in morning and M2 in the evening.

'Following day the 23rd, went out in charge with two men in car and finished M2 testing. That night went and brought in M6 box from old position, shell dropping just in front got back to camp at 9.15pm.

'On the 24th went out by car to reel in 1 & 2 lines and on returning heard from our Sergeant that the French would be shortly taking over the base. Boche bombed that night.

'Went out again by car on the 25th and reeled in line 4 afterwards in the afternoon went for a walk and had a look at the old trenches that had been used in March. Returned about 6 pm.'

(How about that, a stroll in the middle of hostilities!)

'26th, got up at 5am to lay new line of 6,000 yards for the new base. Boche, gas shelling about 200 yards away. In the afternoon Boche came over again and set fire to the French balloons, the observers (spotters) escaping by parachute. In the evening went by car and collected in cable.

'27th, in the afternoon found that about half mile of 9th Corps line missing.

Later heard from Captain that Boche was running away.

'28th went to 9 Corps with messages and heard officially that action had ceased in the area and we started to reel in lines 1, 2, & 3.

'29th up at 5.30am and finished reeling in lines 1, 2, 3, and OP line.

'30th, had a lay in until 8am, then reeled in lines 4, 5, and 6 finishing about noon.

'On 31st went by lorry through Corbie to nearby village to collect ration returning around 5pm.

'On 1 September stay in camp and helped adjust German Exchange.

'On 2nd, went to find nearest hospital and passed through the place where two chaps were killed where lines had been blown to pieces.

'3rd, up at 6.30am had breakfast and were on our way by 8.30am. Laid line for the signal HQ Exchange, on arrival gas shell dropped about 200 yards away.

'4th, in the morning laid 5 & 6 lines, afternoon laid part of 3 & 4.

'5th, finished 3 & 4 returning at 6.30pm.

'6th, reeled in 5 & 6.

'7th, Up at 6am and reeled in 3 & 4 lines.

'10th went out scrounging for cable, reeled in 2 miles of cables, lines 5, 3, and 8.

'11th Went out in chateau grounds and picked blackberries and stewed them for tea and supper with milk pudding and custard.

'12th Had pass with Chapman for Corbie went down by lorry and had hot shower bath. Left Corbie 5.30pm and saw part of captured guns at Longeau returning to camp 7.30pm and warned for First Army.

'13th on the morning picked some blackberries and stewed them for tea with custard, afterwards made some pancakes. In the evening went to Villa's Carbonel [Villers Carbonnel] with a dispatch and at about 10pm saw Boche plane in searchlights and after a lot of firing by AA it was brought down in flames. It was like a firework display.

'14th, In the morning went on an hour's route march by Ablaincourt 9.30am till 10.30am. Afternoon had a swim in the Somme at Brie, afterwards picked some blackberries.'

(If you did not know that they were in the middle of the Somme offensive you would think they were on holiday!)

'15th In the morning did some shooting with King A.J. with German rifle getting 10 bulls out of twelve rounds 300 yards, target at twenty five yards range. Afternoon had swim in the Somme picking blackberries afterwards.

'16th In the morning went on a route march along the St Quentin road, picked some blackberries during the afternoon and did some shooting with Chapman.

'17th Another morning stroll, picking blackberries, during the afternoon and evening sports promoted by OC won needle and thread race and tournament (wrestling and piggy back) with King A J.

'18th In the morning salvaging, afternoon blackberrying and in the evening heard First Army ordered to stand by was cancelled and stand by for Bouvaincourt.

Wiring party at the trenches getting ready to go out to the lines. *Ken Porter's Collection*

'19th Morning route march, afternoon picked some blackberries.'

(We are surprised that there were any blackberries to be picked after all the bombing.) There appears to be an eight day break in his diary.

'27th Bombardment opened at about 6am. Finding two crossings down and about dozen breaks by shells pitching on the line, had to lie 'doggo' for about an hour on account of shells dropping too close to top end of M 6. Saw lots of parties of Germans, wounded and prisoners and also Yanks wounded and eight horses lying dead by the line.

'28th Day in camp and evening saw maps, going up for attack in morning, promoted 2/Corporal from 1 September, on parade.

'29th Bombardment open up at 5.45am and Hindenburg line crossed in several places. After breakfast went out with seven others to lay line from 14 Group OP to new HQ 2 Group. Laid line and stayed behind with Mussay to maintain it, at night being shelled heavily with HE gas. Saw Boche plane brought down during day and tanks in action from 14 Group OP overlooking Hindenburg Line.'

'30th Line destroyed in several places by shells getting through in about half hour from starting out, saw continual stream of wounded coming back and tanks returning. Our guns still heavily shelling and getting some back from Boche. At night mustard gas shells dropped about 200 yards away.

'1 October. Up at 6am and heard that line was destroyed and man out on it, met him about half way, line repaired. Heard Bulgaria had thrown in landing at Ostend and things going well generally. In the evening saw Boche plane bring down two balloons and get away. Observers parachuted down safely.

'2nd Bombardment opened 6am and later lots of prisoners and wounded coming in. Midday shells dropped fairly close whilst having dinner. In evening saw our plane bring down Boche balloon and another of our planes hit and brought down by one of our own shells in flight.

'3rd Several more gains and 50th Division going up. Bombardment opened about 6am and later saw 500 prisoners come in and from 14th Group OP saw thousands of Germans escaping and guns and transport moving back about 10,000 yards away. In evening 25th and 38th Divisions came in with more guns. Night shelling, about a dozen rounds falling plenty close enough. Received parcel from home with cake.

'4th Guns firing all night and more prisoners and wounded came in and another 120 brought in about 8pm. During evening heard that Turkey had thrown in.

'5th Gas masks on, troops firing long range, Boche replying, more prisoners coming in. A few bombs dropped at night not too far away. Heard through 14th Group, OP destroyed and got out on it. Heard somebody had committed suicide.

'6th Long range guns still in action. In afternoon had a stroll over to the Hindenburg line and saw several tanks. Continued walking to O section arriving 3.30pm.'

(Seems to be few days missing, probably spent time in camp, picked up his diary again on the 10th. Some abbreviated entries follow.)

'10th Day in camp and afterwards went over to POW cage and had a chat with them.

'18th Left for Premont, crossing canal by Hindenburg line and saw 500 prisoners escorted by Frenchmen. Found fine civvy billet with spring mattress and organ. Village only slightly knocked about.

'29th Went for rations to Premont Post Office for £3.5s.0d and sent home.

'1st Nov. Moved to new location had stroll through village and saw news Turkey and Austria smashed.

'2nd Arrived at R Section, billeted in farm in building next to where twelve men were blown out by 5.9 shell. Evening on M4 and OP line crossing down.

'3rd On M2 destroyed and night 4 and OP evacuated billets shelled so went down cellars.

'4th On M2 line, being shelled all day, did my line.

'5th Bombardment at dawn and heard previous day's shelling successful.

'8th Tested cable, reeled in and evening sent home £1.2s.6d postal order and 2/6d treasury note.

'9th Took charge of advance party went by car. Had a stroll by canal bank.

'10th Went and saw football match and strolled round village and saw GS Wagons collecting up dead by canal. Night of bombing.

'11th During day heard that armistice was signed. Night heard big explosion.

'12th Had a walk round and at night skylarking with the lads with Boche stick bombs and Very lights.

'13th Went away by 14th Car to Avenes? to find billets for soldiers.

'14th Went with French interpreters and found good billets afterwards going round the town and Church, a beautiful place formerly German GHQ. Night mines-continually being exploded.

'15th Heard that sections orders for moving up to Avenes? cancelled and that sections and groups were reporting to maps.

'16th Returned to R Section.

'17th Advance party left and my party left later for Domeleue Farm?

'18th Left Domeleue Farm for a new location

'19th Evening event to F.S.B club room and had a good time, later a letter card from Traffic Supt. Colchester had applied for my discharge.'

Charles survived and went on leave, arriving home in late March 1919. For his efforts in keeping the lines open he received only the standard campaign medals the 1914-15 Star, British War Medal and the Victory medal.

It is interesting to note that Charles tended to use the term 'Boche' to describe the Germans. A number of other terms were also used –'Hun' was used heavily during the First World War, a reference to the medieval Hunnic Empire of Attila the Hun; 'Fritz' was another nickname popular in both world wars; then there was 'Jerry' favoured in the Second World War although created in the First World War and believed to be derived from the German helmet or *pickelhaube* that was shaped like a chamber pot or Jeroboam. The ongoing use of Jerry is found in the term Jerrycan. There were other terms but these were classified as offensive. Tommy seems to be the most used term to describe British troops during the Great War.

He also referred to 'Very Lights'. These were flares that were often used to illuminate the fighting zone in trench warfare to be able to see what the enemy were up to in no man's land, working (wiring, digging etc) patrolling or on a raid. The lights did not burn for very long and the best thing to do was to stay still until the flare went out, any movement was easily picked up. These illuminations were named after the inventor Edward Very (an American).

The troops used to sing the following song to the tune of *When Irish Eyes are Smiling*:

When Very Lights Are Shining

When Very Lights are shining,
Sure they're like the morning light
And when the guns begin to thunder
You can hear the angel's shite,
Then the Maxims start to chatter
And trench mortars send a few,
And when Very Lights are shining
'Tis time for a rum issue.

When Very Lights are Shining
Sure 'tis like the morning dew,

And when shells begin a bursting
It makes you think your time's come too.
And when you start advancing
Five nines and gas comes through,
Sure when Very Lights are shining
'Tis rum or lead for you.'

We know that Charles's main field of action was on the Somme but we do not have a clear picture of where he actually was until 29 September 1918 when he was involved in the Battle of St. Quentin Canal. This was one of the pivotal battles of the Great War, involving British, Australian and American troops in their attack on the Hindenburg Line.

The Hindenburg Line was a German defensive position built during the winter of 1916-1917. It was named by the British after the German Commander-in-Chief, Paul von Hindenburg, and the Germans called it the Siegfried Line. It was situated several miles behind the active front line stretching from the north coast of France to Verdun, near the border of France and Belgium. There were several weak points in the line, one of them being at St. Quentin Canal. The Allies used these vulnerabilities in the so-called Hundred Days Offensive that started on 8 August just two days before Edwin Charles Andrews arrived on the scene.

The bombardment on the 29th was a marathon affair with 1,637 guns firing along a 10,000 yard long front and in the last twenty-four hours the British artillery fired a record 945,000 shells. After an eight-hour period of shelling and fighting St Quentin Canal was captured and the Hindenburg Line was breached in several places. There were heavy losses on both sides and the Germans were forced to retreat in disarray and Bulgaria, as mentioned by Charles in his diary, sued for an armistice.

The Allies continued to press home their advantage on the Western Front in the month that followed which, against all predictions, turned out to be the final month of the war.

Charles returned to Laindon to run his Post Office business, look after his family, and play football for Romford Post Masters who wore kit similar to Newcastle United. He was also a talented musician and could play the violin, viola, cello, Spanish guitar, mandolin and reed organ. He played the organ at the Baptist Church in Langdon Hills for many years.

He died on 13 February 1947 aged just 57. Although on 21 February 1919 while still in the army he had signed a statement that he was not suffering from any form of disability due to his military service, one wonders if his health was compromised by the time spent at the front with gas attacks. His obituary in the local *Laindon Recorder* read as follows:

> 'Laindon Postmaster – Mr E. C. Andrews. Many mourners, including two Post Office officials from Romford, attended the funeral of Mr Edwin Charles Andrews who was interred in St Nicholas Churchyard following a service conducted by Mr G. Fuller at the Baptist Church, Langdon Hills on Friday.
>
> 'A well known figure to Laindon residents, Mr Andrews was sub-postmaster for thirty-two years and had lived in Laindon for thirty-four years. He had been

suffering from indifferent health for the past twelve months. After five months in hospital, he died at his home, Post Office, High Road, Laindon on Tuesday of last week.

'Owing to his health he was unable to continue his duties as Postmaster. Mr Andrews leaves behind a widow, Ethel, three sons Charley, John and Brian and a daughter Mary.'

The French Family at war

French, Frank Arthur – Frank was born at Noak Bridge Farm, Laindon in 1891 to Florence Rose and Robert French. He initially went to Laindon School (now Laindon Park Junior School). On leaving school he followed the family tradition and by 1911 he was working as a farm labourer at Black Bush Farm, Lambourne, Romford. His parents at this time had now taken over Brewitts Farm, Laindon which is now part of Gloucester Park, Basildon. In 1912 he went off to farm in Australia and stayed with two sisters, Frankie and Cathy Ritchie, in a shed in their back garden in the small town of Arawata in Victoria.

He volunteered and enlisted into the Australian Imperial Force on 3 April 1916 at Korumburra, Victoria, being posted to the 57th Infantry Battalion at Broadmeadows, rank private No. 1923.

It is interesting to note the oath he had to take on enlistment:

> 'I Frank Arthur French swear that I will well and truly serve our Sovereign Lord the King in the Australian Imperial Forces from 3rd April 1916 until the end of the War and a further period of four months thereafter unless sooner lawfully discharged, dismissed, or removed therefore and that I will resist His Majesty's enemies and cause His Majesty's peace to be kept and maintained; and that I will in all matters appertaining to my sovereign faithfully discharge my duty according to Law.
>
> So Help Me, God.'

On 8 July 1916 he boarded the troop ship *Ajana* at Melbourne, arriving at Devonport on 31 August. (*Ajana* was a British motorship that belonged to the Australian Steam Shipping Co. Ltd.) He carried out a period of training at Camp 26, Larkhill, before moving on to Folkestone where he boarded the ship *Princess Henrietta*, for France on 6 December 1916. He was then posted to

Frank Arthur French.
Kind permission of Albert French

Crucifix, St. Nicholas Church – Memorial to Frank Arthur French.
Ken Porter's Collection

The small church of Arawata, Victoria, Australia where Frank Arthur French is remembered.
Kind permission of Albert French

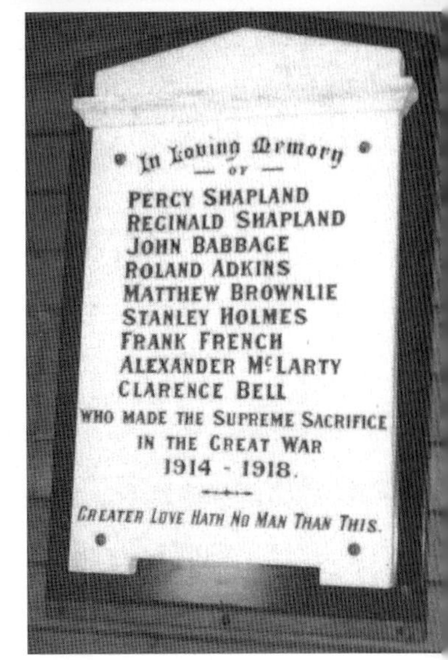

Memorial in the small church of Arawata.
Kind permission of Albert French

the 59th Battalion as reinforcement, joining the battalion at Etaples.

Unfortunately he fell ill and was out of action for nearly two months, being hospitalised for a time at St Omer. He returned to active service on 2 February 1917 and on 18 March 1917 at Bapaume he received gun shot wounds to his back and died of these wounds the following day at the 6th Australian Field Ambulance station.

He is commemorated on the war memorial in St Nicholas Church, Laindon and on a special memorial there in the form of a crucifix on the north-east wall of the vave above the pulpit:

> 'The Crucifix is in Proud and Everlasting Memory of Frank Arthur French who died of wounds received in action at Bapaume on the 19 March 1917, age 26 years, placed here by his loving parents, brother and sister.'

He is also commemorated on a plaque in the small church at Arawata, Victoria, the Shoebury War Memorial and is buried in the British Cemetery at Pozières, France.

Despite the fact that he had been away for five years in Australia a local paper reported 'WICKFORD MAN DIES OF WOUNDS' and goes on to say that this was during an attack on Deslaux Farm. His officer wrote:

'He was game and unselfish and a splendid soldier…He was killed leading the men into action and had he lived he would have risen to a higher rank.'

What is a little strange here is the reference to a 'Wickford Man'. As far as can be established he was born and brought up in Laindon, it just happened that at the time of his death his parents had moved from Brewitts Farm, Laindon to Brickhouse Farm, Wickford. His enlistment papers have Brewitts Farm as his address but later changed to the Brickhouse Farm address.

The town of Bapaume is a crossing point between Artois and the plains of Flanders on one hand and the valley of the Somme and the Paris basin on the other. Many routes passed through Bapaume, it was therefore subjected over the centuries to many battles including the Battle of Bapaume on 2/3 January 1871 during the Franco-Prussian War when the Prussian advance was halted by the French General Louis Léon César Faidherbe.

It became one of the major objectives during the various battles of the Somme and changed hands four times during the war. First it was taken by the Germans during their initial invasion in 1914; then by the British in March 1917 (the battle in which Frank was killed); then by the Germans during the 1918 Spring Offensive before finally being retaken by the British in late August 1918.

Unlike the British, the Australian records often have eyewitness reports to confirm deaths. The following are a selection from these reports.

'Saw L. Corpl. French at Delso Farm, Fremicourt nr. Bapaume on Sunday 18 March. We were attacking the German rearguard. French was kneeling to shoot and got hit in the lower part of the back. I saw him bleeding at the mouth. He was taken off by stretcher bearers. The witness was Pte. Chase who was next to him when he was hit.

'I think this must be L/Cpl. French, whom I saw badly wounded on 18 March, about 1pm at Delso Farm, which was a strongpoint of the Germans, this side of Bapaume, slightly to the right. He was hit in the stomach by bullets. I saw it happen and saw him taken to the D.S. on a stretcher but do not know of the S/B's. I heard that he died shortly afterwards. He was 21-22, a fine big chap, though not more than 5ft 8 or 9 and very popular. He was in C Company. Witness Private Neal.

'I knew him well. He was tall, fair, sturdy and about 23-25. Sergt. Facey then of C Coy, now of A, told me he had seen French killed while advancing to take a M.G. position in a crater at Delso Farm near Bapaume. He said he was sniped and died at a D/S. I have seen his grave near Bapaume and I think C. Coy made a cross for him. He was a fine fellow. Witness Private Johannecen.

'I knew Corpl. French slightly. I think he was in the 9th platoon. I saw French fall after having been sniped. We were taking a German stronghold (a successful attack) at Delso Farm on the Somme. This was on the 18 March at 2pm. I saw him taken away but cannot say if he was buried. We called him 'Frenchy', he was quite popular. I think he came over with the 3rd Reinforcements. We were all in extended order (prone position) and I was about ten yards from him. His number is correct for the 3rd Reinforcements. Witness Private Christie.

'He was a friend of mine. We come over in the 3rd to the 57th Reinforcements. He came from Gippaland. He was tall and fair and I think English, about 25 years of age. He was badly wounded through the lung by machine gun fire at Delso Farm, the first day of the advance at Bapaume. He was taken back to a dressing station and died there. One of my mates told me, forget his name. I do not know where French is buried, but no doubt it is near the dressing station. Witness Pt. Lobb.

'I knew him well, he was in C Company. He was an Englishman who had been in Korumburra, Gippeland, for three years and joined up there. Age 26. He was a tall well built man; clean shaven. He was badly wounded through the lung by a bullet on 18 March at a farm near Bapaume where we were masking a small attack during the evacuation of the Germans. I saw him hit and he was taken to the Dressing Station. He was quite conscious when they carried him away and did not seem to be very bad. Private Eastlake of the 59th Battalion told me that French died next day in a motor ambulance whilst going to the C.C.S and that the cause of death was an internal haemorrhage. Eastlake was in the same ambulance. I did not hear anything about French's funeral.'

It was nearly a month later before his family was aware that he had been killed.

The *Southend Standard* on 19 April 1917 reported the following:

'Mr and Mrs. French, of Brick House Farm, Wickford, have had notification that their second son, Private Frank A. French, Australian Contingent, has died of wounds. Deceased was 26 years of age. For five years he farmed in Australia and joined up fifteen months ago. He was in action several times previous to being wounded. Two other brothers are at the Front.'

The two other brothers were George Robert French and Albert.

His only personal effects that were eventually returned to the family were: tobacco pouch, lighter, nickel tobacco pouch, Pips 2, knife, razor, notebook, match book, Rising Sun Badge, wallet containing correspondence, photos and some francs.

French, George Robert - George was born at Noak Bridge Farm, Laindon in 1889 and at the time of his enlistment on 11 December 1915 he was working as a foreman cowman at Dagenham Park Farm, Romford.

George Robert French.
Kind permission of Albert French

He joined the Royal Garrison Artillery as a gunner, service number 86494. From that date until 26 October 1916 he was in England. He married Mary Louise Lagden on 8 February 1916 at St Nicholas Church, Laindon. His training during this time was at Bexhill. He took over the tenancy of Watch House Farm, Wash Road, Laindon and was a little concerned about going overseas. However his in-laws agreed to look after the farm for him. They were currently farming out of Laindon Farm.

He reported for duty on 17 May 1916 at Warley Brentwood and moved to Dover on 25 May to wait to go to France. He eventually arrived in France on 27 October 1916. He was soon in action at the battles of Ypres, Bapaume and on the Somme. Whether he ever met his brother Arthur while on active service we do not know.

He became a dispatch rider so was not very often called upon to work on the guns. Not only did he carry messages back and forth to the front but also between officers. He was slightly wounded on 5 October 1917 but remained on duty. On 17 January 1918 while in the field he was reported for some misdemeanour for which he received a reprimand and this is possibly why on 31 January 1918 he was demoted for a time as a gunner. At a later date he did however revert back to being a dispatch rider.

He eventually left France for home via Calais on 12 November 1919.

George became an influential member of the local community and served on the Laindon Parish Council from 1919 until 1934 and then after a thirteen year lapse was elected to Billericay Council for Laindon and Little Burstead Ward in 1947. He campaigned for the area to be designated a New Town as he was fully aware that the local council did not have the financial resources to upgrade the area's infrastructure to current required standards. He was chairman of the council in 1949 when the government chose the area to be a New Town.

Siggers, George

George was born in Kirtlington, Oxfordshire on 10 August 1879 and he moved to Langdon Hills around 1900. It is believed he worked for farmer Alfred Markham at Westley Hall, Langdon Hills as the 1901 census has him lodging on Crown Hill and occupation general labourer. Shortly afterwards he married Charlotte Mary Burr on Christmas Day 1901 at St Mary's Church, Langdon Hills.

George Siggers.
Steve Newman collection

When Markham moved to Bluehouse Farm in Laindon, George decided that it was too far to walk every day so he found himself a job on the railways. They had four children George, Leonard, Rose and Ernest (who died at only eleven months.)

George enlisted as a gunner with the Royal Horse Artillery and Field Artillery ('A' Battery, 71 Brigade) at Shoeburyness in early 1915, service number 9590. He served in France on the Western Front, in France and Flanders from 8 July 1915 until he died of his wounds. It would appear that at the time there was no major offensive by either the British or Germans taking place other than short lived skirmishes. He had taken over the role of cook becoming the officers' chef. It was outside the officers' mess that a long distance shell landed killing at least five soldiers. George was wounded and died a few days later on 8 February 1917.

He was due home for his second period of leave within a few days. The family were aware of this and when he had not arrived home became extremely worried. Charlotte received, first a letter from his captain telling her he had been wounded, and a few days later another from the nursing sister telling her that he had died. This was followed by an official letter from the War Office. George left behind his wife and three children one of whom, George Junior, was only twelve when his father enlisted and remembers quite clearly the dreadful messages his mother received some eighteen months later informing her of his death.

He is buried in St Sever Cemetery Extension, Rouen, France. Whatever his involvement was just prior to his death, he was awarded the Military Medal for bravery and the 1914-15 Star, the British War and Victory Medals. He is also commemorated on the war memorial in St Mary's Church Langdon Hills.

The Ellis Family at War

Emma Thomas has lived in Laindon all her life. Her ancestors were involved in many conflicts from India through to the Second World War.

Ellis, Richard – Her four times great grandfather Richard was born in 1823 in Tipperary, Ireland. On 20 January 1841 at the age of 18 he enlisted in the 57th Middlesex Regiment at Enniscorthy, County Wexford. Less than two months later on 7 March he boarded the troopship *General Kidd* and landed at Madras, India on 2 July.

He spent seven years in India just carrying out every day military duties. During this time he transferred to the 21st Royal North British Fusiliers following the disbandment of his regiment. Then on 14 January 1848 the regiment proceeded to Calcutta and embarked for England. On arrival he was stationed at the infantry barracks in Canterbury and while there was promoted to corporal and soon afterwards to sergeant. He celebrated this a month later in August 1848 by marrying Emma.

The regiment was then transferred to Scotland and the 1851 census has them living in Kilmallie, Inverness. A couple of years later the regiment is in Dublin where he is promoted to the rank of colour sergeant. The regiment was being prepared for the Crimean War.

They left Dublin on the *Golden Fleece* and disembarked at Eupatoria on 16 September 1853. Richard takes up the story following their embarkation:

> 'One of the heaviest night's rain that ever fell drenched us through and through. I was with my company on the outlying picket and shall never forget my experience. We had no shelter from the storm but greatcoats and blankets. It was impossible to lie down and the whole of the men kept moving about on the miserable beach to keep themselves alive and warm. No lights or watch-fires were possible. Officers and men shared alike the misery, which seemed unending. We welcomed the first streak of daylight and when the sun rose the rain ceased; but by this time many of our men were groaning with cholera and had to be re-embarked.'

Richard's memories later inform us that his company lost more men through sickness than through military action. The rest of his memoirs give a detailed outline of the battle around Sebastopol including how he saved a sergeant from being executed because he was found asleep on duty; how the French ravaged the countryside for food but the British were not allowed to; how they took rifle ammunition from dead Russians when theirs ran out and the bayoneting of dead or wounded Russians as the wounded had the tendency to shoot even if they were being treated.

Richard was wounded when a splinter from a burst of shells struck him on the head and rendered him unconscious. On recovery he found he had also received a bullet through the right arm with another embedded in his left leg. At one point it looked like they were going to amputate both arm and leg but he persuaded them not to and it was not long before he was back in the trenches.

After two years of fighting, as Richard put it 'at last I began to wear out' and was sent with others to Malta, on board the *Himalaya*. After a bout of Maltese fever he was appointed sergeant major of the 4th Division Provisional Battalion, reverting back to colour-sergeant at the end of the war, but then on 31 August 1858 re-appointed sergeant major of the 3rd Foot remaining in that regiment until his discharge.

In the meantime his wife and family had been sent out from England where his son Raphael Joseph Alphonsus was born in 1862 and on 10 June 1862 Richard took his discharge after serving nearly twenty-two years. We are not aware of what medals he was awarded other than there is a note to say he received five. The family returned to Canterbury where Richard died in 1899.

Ellis, Raphael Joseph Alphonsus – We have struggled to find out much about Emma's three times great grandfather, Raphael Joseph's military career other than, like his father, he was in the army for twenty-one years. He enlisted at Canterbury into The Buffs (Royal East Kent Regiment) in November 1881, service number 67, and the census of 1881 has him stationed at the infantry barracks in Canterbury.

The Buffs (East Kent Regiment).
Ken Porter's Collection

The Buffs were sent to South Africa when a second war against the Boers broke out in 1899 which lasted for three years. In the first four months of fighting, the Boers (Dutch) had a series of successes and successfully besieged the British garrisons at Ladysmith, Mafeking and Kimberley. British reinforcements arrived in South Africa in 1900 and relieved the garrisons and enabled the British to occupy and take control of the Boer capital Pretoria. The Boer War ended with the signing of the Treaty of Vereeniging in May 1902 with the British promising self-government which was eventually granted in 1907.

Raphael Joseph returned to Canterbury and on 21 November 1902 was discharged and his discharge form states that he was discharged in consequence of the termination of his second period of engagement. His conduct and character was stated as being very good. He had also reached the rank of sergeant.

He married Mary sometime around 1885 and had a son soon afterwards, naming him

Raphael James Ellis – on the left of the picture – the uniform could be bomb disposal clothing. *Kind permission of Emma Thomas*

Raphael James, who was born in Ireland, and it goes without saying that Raphael James was hell bent on following in his father's and grandfather's footsteps into the army. It was this Ellis who was going to end up in Laindon.

Ellis, Raphael James – Raphael James, Emma's great great grandfather, followed his father's footsteps and enlisted in The Buffs at Lamberhurst Kent, service number 5983, on 2 August 1899. He was fourteen years of age. Because of this he spent his first five years in England studying at the Royal Hibernian Military School where he was awarded a 3rd Class certificate on 13 December 1899 and 2nd Class certificate on 29 October 1905. He must have heard of his latest award in South Africa because on 2 June 1905 he embarked on SS *Dilwara*, arriving in South Africa on 27 June. On 13 November he was appointed lance corporal. He left South Africa after a three year spell on 26 October 1908 for Hong Kong.

The rocky island of Hong Kong was ceded to Britain in 1841 by the Chinese following the First Opium War as a free port with rights to trade with the mainland. In 1860 following the Second Opium War, China ceded to the British the Kowloon Peninsula and Ngon Sun on the Chinese mainland and this was to be in perpetuity. Then in 1898 Britain leased new territories including 235 Island for a period of ninety-nine years. On 1 July 1997 all leased and ceded territories were returned to China.

His records show that he was up on a charge on at least three occasions and reprimanded.

> 'Neglected duty when in charge of a room and using obscene language,
> 4 December 1903
> Overstaying his permanent pass from 1am to 6.15am, 21 September 1909
> Absent from parade, 13 November 1909.'

His medical record shows that he had three short spells in hospital. Two for minor aliments the other through a football injury on 6 August 1908, where he dislocated his shoulder and a fractured ankle.

For some reason he reverted to the rank of private in September 1906 but was reappointed lance corporal in April 1909. He returned to England in October 1910. It does not appear that he was involved in any military action while overseas. On his return to England he reverted again to a private and on 1 August 1911 was discharged. The reason given of his first period of engagement – conduct and character – very good. His record also stated that he was an intelligent, smart and hard-working man and was very good with horses.

Shortly after he was demobbed he married Eva May Jones. A daughter, Eva May, was born in 1912 at West Ham and in 1914 just before the First World War broke out they had a son named Raphael James Ellis.

Twelve years in the military and with a young wife, daughter and a baby son most would have thought enough, but no, on the outbreak of the First World War and at the age of twenty-nine he was either called up or he volunteered, rejoining the 1st Buffs at Brighton on 5 August 1914 the day after Britain had declared war on Germany. His regiment embarked from Southampton on the SS *Minneapolis* on 7 September 1914 and landed at St Nazaire, France the following day. The regiment formed part of the 6th Division.

The regiment was immediately sent to aid the British Expeditionary Force (BEF) which was in full retreat from the fierce fighting at Mons. Raphael James may not have seen any fighting in his previous twelve years in the Army but within a month of rejoining he was in the thick of it. The majority of men in this battalion were veterans of the Boer War.

On 20 September the 1st arrived at Courcelles to relieve the 1st Northumberland Fusiliers and the 4th Royal Fusiliers who had been involved in the First Battle of Aisne. They immediately had to repulse an attack and were subsequently relieved by the French. Raphael James Ellis was severely reprimanded in December 1914 for disobedience of an order.

A number of skirmishes followed at Radinghem and in the Armentières sector before Raphael James came home in April 1915. He returned to Potijze a small village in the Ypres district, a position the British held for most of the war. This again was only a short stay before returning to England in October 1915. Around this time he was transferred to the 3/5th Buffs which from time to time sent troops to 1/5th Buffs in Mesopotamia

(Iraq), where James found himself on 27 June 1916. The enemy were now the Turks and not Germans, he was to stay for the rest of the war with the Buffs who were attached to the 7th Indian Division and were involved in fighting around the Kut, Amara, Baghdad and Basra areas.

He boarded ship for home on 14 October 1918 and a letter in his file confirms that he landed at Southampton on 18 November for a twenty-eight day leave before he had to report to the 4th Buffs at Tunbridge. Soon afterwards he was demobbed. He received the 1914 Star with clasp and rose, Victory and British medals.

Around 1930 Raphael James, like many ex-soldiers, moved the family to a plotland bungalow called 'Raymor', Merrylands Road, Laindon. His daughter, Eva May married Albert Perry in 1943; Emma's great grandparents.

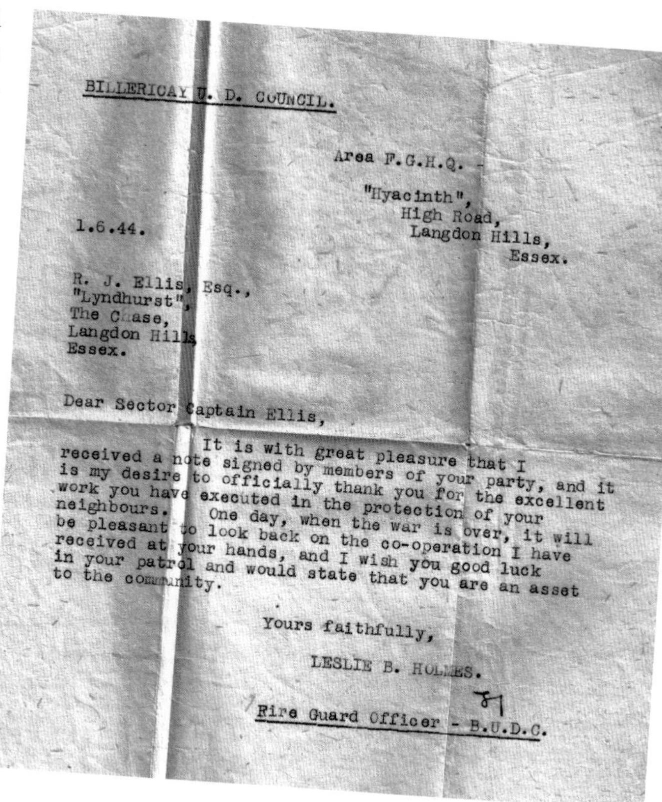

BILLERICAY U. D. COUNCIL.

Area F.G.H.Q.
"Hyacinth",
High Road,
Langdon Hills,
Essex.

1.6.44.

R. J. Ellis, Esq.,
"Lyndhurst",
The Chase,
Langdon Hills
Essex.

Dear Sector Captain Ellis,

It is with great pleasure that I received a note signed by members of your party, and it is my desire to officially thank you for the excellent work you have executed in the protection of your neighbours. One day, when the war is over, it will be pleasant to look back on the co-operation I have received at your hands, and I wish you good luck in your patrol and would state that you are an asset to the community.

Yours faithfully,

LESLIE B. HOLMES.

Fire Guard Officer - B.U.D.C.

Letter from Billericay Urban District Council Fire Guard Officer.
Kind permission of Emma Thomas

In the early 1940s Raphael James moved to a bungalow, 'Lyndhurst', The Chase, Langdon Hills, next door to a bungalow called the 'Nest' where Albert's parents lived. Albert inherited the bungalow in 1946.

Raphael James's war exploits were not over for in the Second World War when he was in his fifties he immediately signed up as a volunteer for the Fire Guard Service where he was promoted to sector captain of the 'J' Sector, Laindon. For his service in this field he received the Defence Medal. Eva May also received the Defence Medal but it is not known what volunteer service she was involved in.

The letter above states that he was an asset to the community; we would say he was an asset to the country.

The Clark family at War

Clark, John – Like many families prior to the Great War, the Clark family was a large one, five boys and three girls and at least three of the boys went to fight for their country. Their parents were Charles Edward and Elizabeth.

John was born on 17 April 1891 in 1 Railway Cottages, Laindon, though officially it was in the parish of Little Burstead. He was still living there at the time of the 1911 census and working as a railway navvy.

He married Cecilia Henty in Plumstead on 15 August 1915 and soon afterwards it appears that he received his first call up papers in November 1915. However at the time he was working at the Kynoch explosives factory, Stanford-Le-Hope and because of his work in a munitions factory, he received exemption from joining up. The regiment he would have joined was the Middlesex, rank private, service number 57023.

Then in early 1916 he received an order to rejoin the service and report to Warley Barracks at 9am on 23 October 1916. His employers Kynoch Ltd quickly responded on his behalf and sent the following letter to the Recruiting Officer, Frances Street, Woolwich on 13 April 1916:

> 'Dear Sirs,
>
> With reference to the enclosed notice calling up John Clark, to the Colours, this man is employed by us in connection with manufacture of Munitions of War for HM Government and for the present his services are indispensable.
>
> We shall be glad therefore if you will please…'

Unfortunately John's war records were badly damaged during the Second World War bombing and it is very difficult to establish exactly what happened next. He either joined the Royal West Surrey Regiment, service number 60553, or received a second reprieve, because we then find that he rejoins the service on 23 July 1917 but this time with the 9th Battalion, Border Regiment, rank private, service number 52199. On this occasion he does not get away and on 4 December 1917 he is posted to India where he spends seventy-three days before moving on to the battlefields of Macedonia.

The 9th Battalion was in fact a Pioneer Battalion that spent the duration of the Great War preparing the way for others such as making roads, bridges, trenches, wire entanglements and strongpoints that were used during the fighting. Their theatre for the period of the war was on the Macedonia Front some times referred to as the Salonika Front.

Their story is unique in as much as they spent little time in fighting, yet their skills were vital to the outcome of the various offensives and were greatly appreciated by the front line fighting regiments. The fact that they spent little time in battle does not necessarily mean that they were behind the lines, as on many occasions they would be up front and under continuous attack.

Their principal enemy was the Bulgarian Army which eventually sued for peace on 4 October 1918. The 9th Battalion's war was over but they were to stay on until January 1919. His demob came on 17 December 1919. He was awarded the British and Victory medal along with three blue chevrons. Chevron stripes were first introduced in January 1918; blue chevron stripes were worn on the right sleeve and indicated the number of years or part of years served overseas so service of one year and one day would qualify for two chevron stripes. A red stripe was awarded for being overseas prior to 31 December 1914.

On returning home he resumed his job as plate layer on the railway at Stratford, London.

Clark, Frederick – Frederick was born in 1893 at Railway Cottages, Little Burstead. The cottages were near Laindon Station and as the name infers they were for the railway workers. He enlisted on 25 October 1915 at East Ham into the 32 Battalion, Royal Fusiliers, service number 22025. The battalion had been formed on 18 October by the Mayor and Borough of East Ham and Frederick would have been one of their first recruits.

After initial training close to home they came under the command of 124 Brigade, 41st Division in December 1915 at Aldershot. On 4 May 1916 the battalion embarked and landed in France the following day. Their first real clash with the enemy came at the Battle of Flers-Courcelette in the September. This was followed in October and November with the Battle of Transloy Ridge, one of the last battles of this phase of the Battle of the Somme. Worsening weather and physical destruction of the battlefield made life hellish for both attackers and defenders. The Allies had advanced seven miles on the Somme but a large section still remained in German hands. It was Britain's costliest battle and initially it was a severe blow to the nation's confidence. A German officer, though, called the Somme the 'muddy graveyard of the German army'.

Their next involvement was at the Battle of Messines on 7 June 1917 when the British detonated nineteen underground mines beneath the German trenches. This battle was a precursor to the much larger Third Battle of Ypres, known as Paschendaele.

The bombardment had commenced on 21 May and warned the Germans of an impending attack. This loss of surprise was offset by the effect of the mines and it is understood that at least 10,000 men were killed as a result of the explosion. The infantry attack soon followed and by mid afternoon all the objectives had been taken.

Two mines did not detonate and their whereabouts were lost. On 17 June 1955 one was detonated in a thunderstorm, the only casualty being a dead cow. The second mine remains undetected although it is believed to be under a farm called La Petite Douve. Roger Mahieu is proud that he still farms the land his father and grandfather did and is not at all concerned that there could be twenty-two tons of high explosive lying eighty feet below his property.

Just before the mines were detonated General Plumer addressing his staff said: 'Gentlemen we may not make history tomorrow but we shall certainly change the geography.'

The battalion was in action throughout the rest of the summer at the Battle of Pilckem Ridge, the Battle of Menin Road and operations along the Flanders coast. It seems that Frederick received a gunshot wound to his chest and left arm some time towards the end of October 1917 and does not appear to come back into active service until 3 July 1918. The division in the meanwhile had been sent to the front line in Italy but by February 1918 is back in France.

Around this time the army was being reorganised and on 18 March the battalion was disbanded in France and the troops transferred to other brigades. Frederick was transferred to the Rifle Brigade, 33 Battalion, service number 860385.

The records show that on at least three occasions he had been in trouble, being absent from parade, his punishment was extra parades. He returned from France in late January 1919 and was demobbed on 19 February 1919. He received the British War and Victory medal and for a period of fifty-two weeks an injury payment of 7s.6d and a terminal payment of £10.

Clark, Edward – Edward was born on 2 February 1890. Unfortunately his war records cannot be located and all we know is that he returned from France suffering from shell shock and ended up in a mental home in Brentwood. He never recovered.

Burnett, George and Fischer, Carl – Neighbours

It was our intention to confine our research close to the Fenchurch, Southend Railway Line between Laindon and Pitsea but we came across one story from nearby Wickford that needed a mention. Why? Because George was a local Wickford PC and Carl a German who was living in Wickford at the outbreak of war and they were apparently both killed in the same battle.

George Burnett.
Steve Newman collection

Burnett, George – George was born William George Burnett, the son of George Burnett and was born in Chichester, Sussex in 1891. On leaving school he enlisted with the Coldstream Guards enlisting as George Burnett and indeed it would appear that this was the name he preferred to be known by. Following his discharge from the army he joined Essex Constabulary on 1 July 1911, recording his full name William George Burnett. As a Police Constable 493 serial number 2694, he served at Brentwood before being posted to Wickford where he was a keen member of the Wickford Cricket Club.

At the outbreak of war, in August 1914, he was recalled to the colours and as Lance Corporal 7591 he rejoined the 1st Battalion Coldstream Guards. The 1st Battalion Coldstream Guards was one of six battalions of Guards that went to France with the original British Expeditionary Force, crossing the Channel between 13 and 17 August, 1914. George landed at Le Havre on 14 August aboard the ship *Dunvegan Castle*. Together with the 1st Battalion Scots Guards, 1st Battalion Black Watch and the 2nd Battalion Royal Munster Fusiliers they formed 1 Guards Brigade of the 1st Division and were commanded by Brigadier General Ivor Maxse.

The 1st Battalion Coldstream Guards had little involvement in the retreat from Mons, however, they formed part of the rearguard of the division on 27 August and formed the infantry of the advanced guard of the 1st Division when the Allied armies turned and advanced on 6 September. Having crossed the rivers Petit Morin and the Marne they were not seriously engaged until 14 September, the day after crossing the Aisne. Having struggled up the wooded Vendresse valley and taken positions along the Chemin des Dames, they came under continuous artillery fire and sustained heavy losses. It is understood that one of the soldiers taken prisoner was Joseph Farmer, a former police colleague of George Burnett. Farmer was made to work in the front line on the Eastern Front and died in captivity on 15 April 1917. He is buried in Latvia.

Bayonet Charge by the Coldstream Guards. *Ken Porter's Collection*

Although the Allies had retreated from Mons they had managed to prevent Germany from encircling and seizing Paris, though they did occupy most of Belgium other than a small western section that included the town of Ypres. Over the next four years this area would see some of the heaviest fighting. The First Battle of Ypres took place between 19 October and 22 November.

On 29 October the 1st Battalion was facing the 6th Bavarian Regiment, near Gheluvelt. The War Diary of the 1st Battalion records:-

> 'Held trenches. Attack by Germans beaten off at 5.30am, in dense mist but was successful further south-east of Gheluvelt, the result being that the battalion trenches were shelled immediately afterwards from the rear. A retirement appears to have been ordered and a small portion of the battalion re-formed covering the east side of Gheluvelt village on the south side of the Ypres-Menin road covering a battery of the Royal Field Artillery. At night battalion withdrawn into Brigade Reserve between Hooge and Gheluvelt.'

The German advance could not be checked partly due to the fact that around thirty per cent of cartridges issued to the battalion were too large for their weapons. Although the Gloucesters were sent to help retrieve the situation, their counter-attack was unsuccessful and the remaining men of the Coldstreams remained cut off and low on ammunition. The Germans continued to attack until finally those men cut off were overwhelmed. The battalion lost all its eleven officers and some 180 other ranks of whom, it is believed, Burnett was one.

Only six days earlier a letter sent to Superintendent Cowell at Brentwood was printed in the *Essex Weekly News* stating 'I am well'.

George was unmarried and his mother died in October 1914 probably unaware of her son's fate. Although officially posted as missing in action on 29 October 1914 it was not confirmed until December 1918. There were at least two paper reports before the final confirmation.

Southend Telegraph 20 March 1915:

> 'The fate of PC Burnett of the Coldstream Guards is still a mystery. He was called up at the outbreak of the war and no news can be got from any source about him. The death of his mother in October caused his relatives to write to his Commanding Officer, who replied that he was missed on the 29 October and nothing has been heard of him since. The War Office has also been appealed to and they say their belief is that he was wounded about that time and is now a prisoner of war.'

Southend Standard 1 June 1916:

> 'On our photo page is a likeness of Private G. Burnett, 1st Coldstream Guards, who has been missing since 29 October 1914. He was, prior to the war, a Police Constable at Wickford, nothing has been heard of him since that date.'

Southend Standard 12 December 1918:

> 'The sad news has also reached Wickford that PC George Burnett, who was stationed at Wickford for three years before the war was killed in action in France on the 29 October 1914. He, with others, joined up soon after the outbreak and was at first reported missing and for over two years nothing further was heard until just recently. He was much esteemed at Wickford. During his stay there he was connected to the Wickford Cricket Club. He was a native of Chichester, Sussex.'

His body, however, has never been identified. When darkness fell on 29 October there only remained eighty men of the 1st Battalion Coldstream Guards. George is remembered with honour and his name recorded as Burnett G. on the Menin Gate which forms the British Memorial to the missing who fell at Ypres or in the neighbourhood. A total of 54,896 are recorded on this memorial.

Fischer, Carl – It has not been possible to establish when Carl came to Britain other than the 1911 census has him resident as a boarder at 25 Guilford Street, Russell Square, London, aged 21, occupation clerk in a shipping office.

Like many Germans living in Britain at the outbreak of war he was called up by the German High Command and left Wickford on the August Bank Holiday. His English wife remained behind. The *Southend Standard* reported on 31 December that as he made his way to the station he had tears in his eyes, so why he went or why he had not been interned is difficult to understand. He enlisted in the Bayerisches Feldartillerie infantry unit that was part of the 6th Bavarian Reserve Division. The First Battle of Ypres was the 6th Bavarians' first involvement in the war and as we know they clashed with the 1st Coldstream Guards.

Carl was killed by three bullets. His wife died a few months later, perhaps of a broken heart after receiving the news of her husband's fate. It is understood that George Burnett was killed in the same action and that they were the first men from Wickford to be killed.

Southend Standard 31 December 1914:

'News has been received in Wickford by some friends that Mr C. Fischer who was of German nationality and resided at 'Home Rest' has been killed in action in France. He was called up by the German Government in the early part of August and left Wickford on August Bank Holiday Monday, leaving behind his wife at their residence, almost his last words as he left were that he wished he did not have to go, as he felt there was going to be a fight against his friends. Tears were noticed as he bade goodbye to several on his way to the station. His first duty upon arriving in Germany was to take charge of a training school; he being a lieutenant. It wasn't until the first or second week of September he was sent into action and whilst engaged against the English on 29 September, in France, that he received bullet wounds that closed his career. His wife also left Wickford in the autumn.'

The Cottis Family

Amongst the various shops that used to stretch along the High Road, Laindon in its heyday was Cottis, the bakers. They had three shops, one in Billericay, a bakery that opened up around the turn of the twentieth century, a lock-up shop in Laindon and a bakery shop in Langdon Hills. One of these shops, probably the bakery, opened in 1908.

William Joseph Cottis the head of the family was born in Southminster in 1854 his

Langdon Hills shop – opened in 1908. *Ken Porter's Collection*

occupation at the time of the 1881 census was that of a dealer and insurance agent. By 1891 he had moved to Canewdon and is the local baker – what a career change! Then the 1901 census has him at Billericay running the family bakery along with Edwin and John. Over the next sixty years the family and bakery became extremely well known and respected.

It was William's son John Godfrey Cottis who continued the family tradition by opening up his own bakery in Langdon Hills. Although the family was well known and many Laindon people worked at the bakery, some for as long as forty years, we wonder how many of them knew that John had lost two brothers in the war, Edwin William and Cecil James. John was probably exempted because of his business, as bread was a vital commodity and he was also providing employment.

Cottis, Edwin William – Edwin enlisted at Brentwood in the Army Service Corps, service number S/256119, before transferring to The Royal Fusiliers 1/2nd London Regiment. The *Essex Weekly News* of 19 April 1918 reported under the Roll of Honour the death of Private Edwin William Cottis killed in action on Thursday, 28 March 1918, age 38.

At 3am on this date the British were woken by a terrific din of a German bombardment followed at 7am by a German infantry attack. This was the First Battle of Arras and the Germans were met with devastating fire from British artillery and well-sited machine-guns. The Germans were unable to make any effective breakthroughs and by the evening the costly assault was abandoned. It is referred to as a British defensive victory, unfortunately it was the day that the first of the Cottis brothers was killed.

Edwin is commemorated on the Pozières Memorial, France, Billericay town memorial and, with his brother Cecil, on a private memorial in St Mary Magdalen Church, Billericay, on the Great Burstead St Mary Magdalen church porch memorial and on a private headstone in the churchyard.

Cottis, Cecil James – Cecil enlisted at Brentwood on 4 October 1914 joining the Essex Regiment initially with the 4th Battalion, service number 2303, and later transferring to the 9th. He first saw action in the disastrous Gallipoli campaign against the Turks landing at C Beach, Suvla Bay after leaving Devonport on the SS *Marquette* on 21 July 1915.

The *Essex Weekly News* 4 October 1918 reported 'that he took part in the second

J.G. Cottis, horse and bread delivery cart – pre 1920.
Ken Porter's Collection

landing at Suvla Bay in August 1915, where he received severe wounds. He was three months in the military hospital at Devonport.'

The battalion had a difficult time in Gallipoli, making little progress against the Turkish army. Following the failure of the campaign, the battalion was withdrawn from the peninsula on 1 December 1915 but by this time Cecil was back in Devonport. It is understood that he returned to France in June and was killed on 18 September 1918 at the Battle of Epehy. This was against German outpost positions in front of the Hindenburg Line. This offensive was not a great success but the British realised that the Germans were weakening and the offensive continued into the Battle of Saint Quentin Canal. His death was a month after his twenty-third birthday.

Cecil was awarded the 1914-15 Star, British and Victory Medals. He has no known grave but is commemorated on the Vis-en-Artois Memorial, France, and the memorials previously mentioned for his brother.

Garnish, Thomas

Thomas was born in 1884, Laindon and married Martha Bird from Little Burstead in 1905. By the time of the 1911 census they were living at 21 Maldon Road, Southend-on-Sea and with them is his five-year-old daughter Charlotte and Martha's father, James William Bird. Thomas's parents, Francis and Mary were living at Friern Manor Cottage, Dunton.

Thomas volunteered at the start of the war, enlisting in Southend with the Royal Fusiliers (City of London), 24th Battalion, 7th Platoon, service number G/51222. It is possible he may have initially enlisted with the Middlesex Regiment, service number 29910. Unfortunately his war records have been lost but from the limited knowledge we have, he was part of the British Expeditionary Force that went to France in the first few months of the war. He was wounded and reported missing on 29 April 1917.

Working on this date, it would appear that Thomas was involved in the Battle of Arras, a British offensive that raged from 20 March to 16 May 1917 when British and Empire troops attacked German defences near the French city of Arras on the Western Front. Until this point the various armies on the Western Front were at a stalemate with a continuous line of trenches stretching from the Belgium coast to the Swiss border. The British objective was to break through the German defences into open ground and, though they made significant advances, they were unable to achieve a complete breakthrough.

The battle started with the bombardment of Vimy Ridge on 20 March, with the rest of the front being bombarded on 4 April. More than 2,600,000 shells were used, over one million more than used previously at the Somme. In the last ten hours of the bombardment gas shells were also used.

Infantry attacks started on 9 April with the First Battle of the Scarpe (9 – 14 April). In fact the Battle of Arras was a series of smaller battles, Battle of Vimy Ridge (9 – 12 April), Battle of Bullecourt (10 – 11 April), Battle of Lagnicourt (15 April), Second Battle of the Scarpe (23 – 24 April), Battle of Arleux (28 – 29 April) and the third Battle of the Scarpe (3 – 4 May), followed by skirmishes until 16 May.

Whether Thomas was involved in a number of these short battles is unknown but it would appear that the one in which he lost his life was the Battle of Arleux. The Canadian troops had taken Vimy Ridge, but they were having difficulties in securing their south-eastern flank. To try and rectify this, British and Canadian troops launched an attack towards Arleux-en-Gohelle on 28 April. The village of Arleux was captured by the Canadians with relative ease but the British troops' advance on the nearby village of Gaurelle met stiffer resistance. They eventually managed to secure the village by early evening but a German counter-attack forced a brief retreat until reinforcements arrived. Further attacks by the Germans on the 29th were repulsed but casualties were high and one of them was Thomas.

Thomas is commemorated on the Arras Memorial at Faubourg-d'Amiens, Arras. He would have been entitled to the 1914 Star, British and Victory medals; whether his family ever received them we do not know.

What is a little surprising is the 24th Battalion was a Sportsman's battalion, one that well known sportsmen joined. The question that remains unanswered is whether Thomas was a well known sportsman, if not how did he manage to enlist into the battalion?

The Garnish family go back a long way in Laindon, probably as far back as the late 1700s and an interesting footnote is that Thomas's uncles Walter and George went to Puckles Charity School in the last couple of years of its existence. Like many families around this time it was a large one so it is possible many went to this school.

Puckles was a local farmer who farmed just off Wash Road, Laindon. On his death in 1617 he gave the farm to St Nicholas Church, Laindon to pay for a school master and other than for a short period of time during the 1700s, the school was held in the Priest House which is the wooden building attached to the western end of the church. The school closed down in 1877 when a new board school was opened nearby, now known as Laindon Park. The minute book informs us that Walter (12 years old) and George (9 years old) left the school in May 1877 a few months before it closed down. They both first appear in the register in November of 1875 so it would seem that they only had a couple of years schooling. Descendants of Walter and George still live in the area and are very proud of their Laindon past.

Monk, Percy James

Percy was born on 7 July 1896 in 8 Railway Cottages, Laindon Station. His father, Thomas, was a railway signalman and before the war Percy was a railway clerk. He belonged to St Mary's Church, Langdon Hills and was one of their bell ringers. We are not sure when he enlisted other than he was initially in A Company, 24th Battalion, London Regiment, 47th Division, service number 684166. His memoirs inform us that his first taste of action was in early 1917 near Rocquigny (north-east France).

Percy James Monk.
Kind permission of Tom Monk

The following is his report of his first year in France:

'We went to Rocquigny by light railway, then went across country and landed in some very deep dugouts where we stayed a few days before going up to reserve. Our packs, greatcoats, etc were left behind to be collected by transport. It was fairly quiet where we were. It turned bitterly cold so a number of us were detailed to return and collect as many greatcoats as possible but what a shambles! Jerry had evidently spotted the transport column and blown the lot sky high. We tried to get into our dug outs but could not owing to it being blocked by dead horses, etc, so no greatcoats.

Surviving trenches, with duck boards.
Ken Porter's Collection

'Back at the front line it rained and rained. The duckboards were floating on about a foot of water and mud. It was about this time we saw our first tank and were scared stiff not knowing what they were but got used to them and blessed them many times. Ideal for hiding behind when going over. As far as I can make out the huge "mother" tanks also supplied the little ones – "Whippets" – with fuel. I suppose they would be armoured carriers of today.

'On one occasion we were in a trench and I could see the Commune (village) of Albert in the distance and what struck us was a statue of Virgin Mary and infant Jesus at an angle of about 45 degrees on a large building, and one dawn it was gone, it either fell or was blown off. (See Appendix 5).

'We saw very little real village life. Most villages had been evacuated and smashed up. The strange thing was that around the pulverised countryside there were larks singing. Some shells would go screaming over, then a lull and off they would go again as much as to say "ah missed me".

'We were sent to rest at a place called Allouagne (a farming village). We were billeted on a farm which was run by women. There was grandma, two women of about thirty-five, two little lads and a girl of about nineteen. We understood the men had been conscripted to work in the mines at Lens.

'My mate "Jellicho", nicknamed "Admiral" which got shortened to "Ad" had shocking colds and had reported sick. We were given two days off and spent it in the farm's cowshed.

'On the second day, when all was quiet (most blokes being on fatigues) an angel in the guise of the nineteen-year-old girl appeared at the door with two steaming hot mugs of red wine and made Ad and I drink it while she waited. I think it must have made us real drunk. Whatever it was we were as fit as a fiddle the next day.

'We learned that the family name was Delpouf, not sure of the spelling, and the girl was Jeanne. We had slight contact with the family for a few days and then back to hell.

'On another occasion , around Christmas 1917, the family treated Ad and I as part of the family and we were invited into the house a few times. I think they were strict Catholics, crucifixes were all around the room. We had some good laughs over language but we got by near enough with signs. I remember they warned us against going to Madam of the rouge lamp.

'Jeanne's one ambition was to go to London. Wonder if it was realised? Once or twice they gave us some black bread and lard and stewed coffee, was that powerful! They were really good to us two. I'm sure they could ill afford to give us anything because they were harshly rationed.

'We never saw them again and soon afterwards Ad went back down the line and I never saw him again.'

It would appear that in early 1918 Percy took a well earned rest and was sent back home on leave. We then picked his diary up again from 5 March 1918:

'5 March – left Chiseldon 9.15am. Arrived Southampton 1.05pm. March to rest camp. Went to Hippodrome in evening. Wilkie Baird's first appearance there.

'6 March – Still resting

'7 March – Left Camp at pm. Arrived docks 6pm. Boarded about 8pm. Sailed 10.20 pm.

'8 March – Arrived le Havre 6am. Marched to Honfleur camp six miles.

'9 March – Left camp 8pm. Enter Havre about 8.30pm. Arrived Rouen about 6am.

'10 March – Rest and looked around town. Left about 8.30pm. Arrived Rouen about 6am.

'11 March – Arrived Achiet-le-Grand about 6.30am. No sleep, too draughty. Left 2pm. Arrived Puchevillers about 6pm. And marched to Mirvaux, six miles.

'12 March – Billeted in barn, fairly comfy – went through gas.

'13 March – Parade, had drill etc

'14 March – Reported sick – diarrhoea.

'15 March – parade, route march, musketry

'16 March – Reported sick, Quarter stores fatigues

'17 March – Left Mirvax 7.30am, arrived Puchevillers 9.05am. (Marched, moved on to Achiet-le-Grand 12.30pm. Left 2.30 pm., arrived Bourgogne 11.30 pm. Marched about six miles, whacked some sleep under canvas.

'18 March – Good breakfast, transferred to platoon company, did nothing all day, heavily shelled twice from aircraft.

'19 March – Wet, no parade, left for Metz by light railway.

'20 March – left dugouts for line. Heavily shelled and gassed.

'21 March – retreat, no time for this, trust memory.'

This was the day the German Army launched their Spring Offensive, Operation Michael or *Kaiserschlacht*. Percy takes up his story again from here.

'Am 21 March 1918. In front line, an air of anticipation and rumours galore, we

Dug-outs created by British shelling. *Ken Porter's Collection*

were not in doubt for long. About noon Jerry started softening up with everything he had, or so it seemed. It went on nearly all day. Eventually word came through that the battalions were withdrawing and that a holding platoon would remain "to hold the fort" of which I was one.

'You can guess the feelings of us; the battalions cleared off that night and there we were in miles of empty trench. However our lieutenant ordered us to man the fire step at the top of the trench called Shaftesbury Avenue which was to be our

Our chaps going over the top.
Ken Porter's Collection

bolt hole and to keep our eyes skinned. Around dawn the barrage increased and soon after Jerry came over on the right at about 500-600 yards away but nothing in front. The lieutenant guessed at a pincer move, which turned out to be correct.

'We let Jerry have all we had, Lewis and rapid, we could do no good and the lieutenant said 'run for it boys' which we did. Along Shaftesbury Avenue which seemed twenty miles long, because Jerry had busted it up. I think it was about a mile. It ended in a valley, after that open ground and plenty of stuff coming down. We could see chaps in trenches on the right and left ridges beckoning us on. From their high positions they could see Jerry coming. The lieutenant said, "what's it to be boys, right or left?" We chose left and belted across and bundled in. It was a shallow trench and well overcrowded and all mixed up with umpteen different units.

'We were told the 24th were on the right ridge and the Lieutenant decided, owing to the overcrowding, we should try and make it. This meant another dash across the open but we made it. Then we could not get into the trench again due to overcrowding so had to make do with shell holes. At that time Jerry was about 1000-1500 yards away but coming in their thousands. We were pumping every bit of small arms fire at them without much effect.

'Where were our guns? Not a sound from them. A Very SOS went up and soon after they opened up but the tragedy was it was on us and not on Jerry. It was hell let loose. There was nothing else for it but to make another dash back. What a nightmare, ammunition dumps going up and stuff coming down left, right, centre and behind. We were all shaken in having to leave badly wounded behind but it was everybody for himself.

'The store dumps were also going up and where possible these were raided for "grub". All we could get was some tins (cardboard) and some iron biscuits and jam. Rations were out of the question.

'Late that night we got somewhere and after a while were ordered to dig in. You can guess what we looked like when daylight came. We were laying in our hole at dawn when Jerry opened up again with really big stuff and to our surprise there was a line of our guns about 500 yards in front of us. I do not know how they got there. They were letting loose with all they had but Jerry had their range and horses, guns and chaps were going sky high and we were getting the strays. We were ordered out and back. How far we went and where, heaven knows. I'm sure the officers were as lost as we were but so long as we kept going back apparently it was all right. Orders came through anyone dropping out would be left behind. Some did due to exhaustion and lack of food and water. Also anyone dumping full Lewis panniers would be for it. Imagine two of these round your neck when you were nearly on your knees; it was killing.

'That night we came to a hamlet. News leaked that Jerry was thereabouts. A patrol was sent out and in the meantime the majority of the chaps flopped to the ground to snatch forty winks, very soon after we were all kicked awake and moved on, which we did more like machines than anything else, where to I haven't the slightest idea now'.

This was the first day of the last major German offensive on the battlefield of the Somme a little further east of the area of the 1916 fighting.

The Germans had been strengthened by 500,000 troops from the Russian Front and the German commander, Ludendorf was confident of success but he knew that he had to strike before the Americans, who were now in the war, could bring their numbers into play.

He was confident that if they could beat the British the French would sue for peace. The main attack against the British was code named Operation Michael and in terms of land gained was successful but the necessary supply lines could not keep up with their storm troops. Unlike soldiers burdened with weighty kit, the storm troopers carried little except weaponry. On this day 21,000 British soldiers had been taken prisoner. The German Kaiser, William II declared 24 March a national holiday giving the Germans the idea that the war was nearly over in their favour.

This was obviously not the case and by late April the German thrust slowly petered out and by July the Germans had lost one million men. By now the Americans were pouring men on to the front line and in August 1918 the Allies began their final counter offensive which resulted in the Germans retreating or being driven from all the ground they had achieved, the collapse of the Hindenburg line and the capitulation of the German Empire in November.

To read the account of somebody who was in the thick of it gives one a much better perspective of what it was really like but Percy's story does not end here, there were still several months to go before the end.

> 'After the March retreat we found ourselves at Etaples. I have forgotten how and when we got there but we had a good time in the great camp. We must have been there about three weeks or more, replacements arriving all the time to make up depletions. We eventually left and I really don't know where to. We knew things were moving, rumours flying about all sorts of wonderful things such as home next month etc, wishful thinking.
>
> 'Eventually we were told that Jerry was on the run so when we moved up to where Jerry had been, everything was in reverse, fire steps the wrong way round and the devil had laid booby traps everywhere.
>
> 'When all was quiet we reverted to the usual routine up the line for two hours on fire step and four off in dugout. Those four hours were used for fatigues, lugging rations from dump up to the line, cans of water, bags of bread and anything else that was needed and that was hard work because we were in fighting order along with rifle etc, and up to our backsides in mud, it was no picnic. If you were not on fatigues you were usually delousing yourself and others. The method was to strip out and get a mate to hold one end of your shirt vest and pants while you ran a lighted candle up and down all the seams and burn them off. This lasted about a week and the devils returned again; where from heaven knows. As soon as you got warm they would start to appear, they drove you up the wall, just another of those trials we had to suffer.
>
> 'The other thing was to try and boil a mess tin of water over a candle for a cup

of tea. That would take three hours of your four hours off and if some careless clot happened to knock your tin over you were not too pleased and the air would turn blue.

'I suppose it must have been October time when we started to advance in earnest. We gradually edged our way forward in open echelon, occasionally held up by machine-gun fire. Eventually we came to a river or canal about thirty yards wide and we had to cross this by duckboards lashed to oil drums and a guide rope to hang on to. It took ages to cross one at a time but at last we were over and away again. If Jerry had been about he could have had the lot of us on a plate.

'It must have been somewhere about 6-8 November we came to a place near Lille. Four of us were billeted with an elderly couple. The dear old lady was concerned because she had nothing to offer us. Evidently Jerry had pinched everything he could lay his hands on. They had taken all the metal out of the place, door handles, locks etc. We were lying in the empty room asleep when we were roused by an old gentleman. He had a dish of boiled potatoes for us and they were smashing. I'm sure they could ill afford it but they seemed so thankful that we had come.

'We entered Lille on 10 November and had to clean up as much as we could as we were to march past GOC next day. We marched through a big square and I think it was General Slim that took the salute. There were crowds of people and posters were appearing everywhere. I managed to scrounge one; it read "Honour and Glory to 47th Division, our Deliverers".

'That same day we were on our way back. That was 11 November. As regards the Armistice we were too tired and weary to appreciate what it meant. On the way out of Lille we saw a chap from home, called to him and we had a natter for about five minutes; the first person I had seen from home since I had joined up. How long and how far we marched back I don't know but we came to Tournai or what was left of it – not much.

'There are lots of minor happenings I haven't mentioned as they do not seem to be important, such as my first rum ration, which nearly strangled me but I soon got used to it, and the frightening experience of patrols and raids. On one occasion at night our lieutenant was doing his rounds, we were on the fire steps as usual "everything all right chaps" then he spotted me and said "Hello Monk, heard you were killed." Quick as a flash I said "No, not yet". Doesn't sound much but it made us laugh, silly little things like that seemed to help our state of mind.

'We often wondered what day it was as they were all the same to us, just day and night. When any of us received a letter from back home with a date on it we would spend time working out what day it was, it passed the time.

'After leaving Tournai, a number of us were kitted out with topee and drill as we had been detailed for the Middle East. We arrived after four days at Marseilles and shipped to Alexandria.'

Percy had survived some of the worst fighting, saw terrible things and instead of being sent home like many of his compatriots he was sent to the Middle East where he was going to spend another year. We will pick up this part of his story in the next chapter.

British loading a trench mortar or, as they called it, 'flying pig'. *Ken Porter's Collection*

Glading, Arthur

Arthur was born in Basildon in 1883 to George and Maria. The family had originated from Great Clacton, George being an agricultural labourer. At the time of the 1901 census Arthur was living with his brother William at Great Clacton, his occupation being a coalman. It was from here that he enlisted into the 2/4th Duke of Wellington's Regiment (West Riding) as a private, service number 26376 on 10 May 1915. They were an infantry unit and part of the Territorial Force and were assigned with others to the 62nd (2nd West Riding) Division.

What records we were able to find state that his theatre of war was France and during his time there he transferred to the 186th Trench Mortar Battery attached to the Duke of Wellington's Regiment and for a time he was with the Royal Army Service Corps, service number 4/094280. At some time during these last two assignments he was awarded the Military Medal.

It was not until late 1915 that the British obtained trench mortars. Light mortar units were manned by the infantry; medium and heavy trench mortars were manned by the Royal Field Artillery.

The infantry units were not always happy with the fire from the trench mortar batteries as they tended to draw the enemy fire. However, they did play an important part in helping to gain the upper hand in either attack or defence by attacking machine-gun, sniper posts or other local features also by co-ordinating with the firing of the large guns by the field artillery. The large mortars were often used for cutting through the barbed wire, especially when the field artillery large guns could not be used.

One of the major offensives that the regiment, and we assume Arthur, was involved in was the Marne Offensive (20 July – 2 August 1918) and in particular the Battle of Tardenois (20 July – 31 July 1918). The net result of the operation from 8am on 20 July to 10pm on 31 July had been the advance of about four miles commencing on a frontage of 7,000 yards reducing to 4,000. In an order of the day the French General Berthelot specially thanked XXII Corps who were involved in heavy fighting for their success in extremely difficult country.

The 62nd (2nd West Riding) Division had been assigned to the XXII Corps and placed at the disposal of the French Fifth Army for the Marne Offensive. Perhaps it was during this battle that Arthur won his Military Medal.

Arthur was discharged on 19 June 1919 and married Ellen Parsdons from Vange at Clacton on 30 May 1931. He died 18 July 1950 and is buried at All Saints Church, Vange. In addition to the Military Medal he was awarded the 1914-15 Star, the Victory and British Medals.

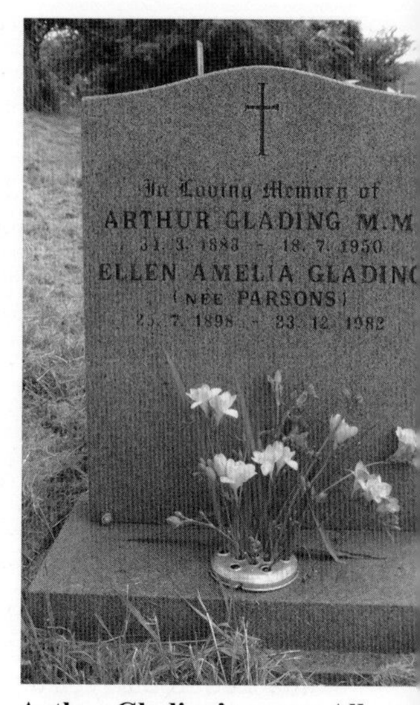

Arthur Glading's grave, All Saints Church, Vange.
Ken Porter's Collection

The Brown family at War

Brown, William Henry – William was born in Rochford in 1883 and he enlisted at Pitsea into the Suffolk Regiment, 12th Battalion, rank private, service number 43060. He was one of ten children to Alfred and Mary Brown, seven boys and three girls. Three of his brothers were in the army; his elder brother Alfred J. Brown was in the Royal Marines and a younger brother, Ernest Arthur Brown was with the 2nd Battalion, Grenadier Guards, service number 19460. We have not been able to establish who the third brother was.

William Henry Brown.
Steve Newman collection

Unfortunately we have not been able to locate William's war records. However, it would appear that his battalion had been involved in the Second Battle of Arras and at the time of his death, 16 June 1917 they were carrying out a holding operation on the Arras front, which included several flanking operations along the Hindenburg Line.

He had been assigned duties of stretcher bearer and his company commander wrote to the family following his death saying that:

> 'Private Brown was carrying out his duties as a stretcher bearer and carrying a wounded comrade to safety with great coolness and courage when he was hit by a piece of shell and died instantly without pain. He was reverently buried and a cross erected to his memory. He was one of the cheeriest, most willing and promising soldiers it has been my good fortune to command and please accept the deepest sympathy from all ranks of the company.'

His wife Florence and his two children, William and Florence, were living at St Mary's Lodge, Vange at the time of his death. He was initially buried in Fins Churchyard extension but later moved to Fins New British Cemetery, France. He was awarded the Victory and British War medals and is commemorated on the Vange War Memorial and also has an entry in the Southend-on-Sea Roll of Honour.

Brown, Ernest Arthur – Unlike William, Ernest does not appear to have any connection with the Vange area, although we believe that his parents Alfred and Mary did move to the area at a later date. Ernest was killed on 15 September 1916 while the Guards were attacking the village of Les Boeufs. The battle was part of the 1916 Somme offensive and it was the day, as already mention in Frederick Pitts' story, that the British used tanks.

In the war records of the 3rd Battalion of the Grenadier Guards we came across the following report:

> 'In the centre a party of men of 2 Guards Brigade under Major Rocke went forward and established themselves just short of the second line in T.9.B but as that party was only 100 strong and had two open flanks it was impossible to assault the second line. It appeared that Les Boeufs would have fallen into our hands without opposition, or at any rate with only ill-organised resistance, if more troops could have been packed on. This was not done doubtless owing to the threat to the right flank of the division – a threat which would have become more acute with every additional yard forward.
>
> 'The position was therefore consolidated but the advance party under Major Rocke, after withstanding one counter-attack had both flanks enveloped and being attacked frontally had to fall back on to the first objective.
>
> 'On the evening of the 15th therefore this battalion held a small frontage on the right of the first objective. This flank was subjected to bombing attacks and the Germans also attempted to work riflemen round it. Fire steps had to be dug in both sides of the trench and bombing parties organised to resist the enemy bombing down. Fighting on a small scale therefore continued throughout the night of the 15/16 and resulted in all counter-attacks being repulsed. The enemy drove us back at one time about seventy yards but his success was momentary only and the ground was immediately re-taken and one machine-gun captured.'

Ernest is commemorated on the Thiepval Memorial to those missing on the Somme. It bears the names of 72,000 officers and men of the United Kingdom and South African forces who died on the Somme, pre 20 March 1918 and have no known grave. Ninety per cent of these died between July 1916 and November 1916.

Brown, Alfred John – Little is known about Alfred other than the 1911 census records him as being a Royal Marine. Hopefully, along with his unknown brother, he returned home safely.

The film *Saving Private Ryan* was based on a true story of the Second World War in which two brothers had been killed and the American Army was trying to get the third home before he was killed in accordance with their 'sole surviving son' policy. At the time of the First World War families were much larger, meaning that several brothers could be at the front at one time during the war. Our stories so far have revealed four occasions where brothers have served: the French family where one was killed and we believe the other two survived; the Clark family, where all three returned home safely, albeit one ended up in a mental home; the Cottis family, where both brothers died and the Brown family, where two brothers were killed and two, we believe, survived.

Our research found many other families who lost more than one son.

Basildon: Harold David Cornish Pean, killed 30 November 1917, aged 26 and P.D.F. Pean, killed 26 June 1916, aged 29, the sons of David and Ada Jane Pean of Southview,

Basildon. George Edwin Revening, killed 9 September 1917, aged 22 and William Revening, killed 3 August 1916, aged 24 the sons of Henry and Louisa Revening of Woodford Cottage, Oak Road, Basildon.

Dunton: Arthur George Beatwell, killed 18 November 1914, aged 28 and Ernest Beatwell, killed 3 May 1916, aged 21, the sons of George and Emma Beatwell of Stock Road, West Hanningfield.

Langdon Hills: George Robert Jay, killed 22 April 1917, aged 33 and Walter Arthur Jay, killed 13 April 1918, aged 20, the sons of Mrs Ellen Cubberley (formally Jay) of Eagle Cottage, Langdon Hills and the late Robert Jay.

Pitsea: Ernest Hills, killed 3 May 1915, aged 21 and Henry Hills, killed 24 October 1917, aged 32, the sons of Henry and Eliza Hills of Vange Road. Francis Albert Howard, killed 23 April 1917, aged 24 and Reginald Douglas Howard, killed 4 October 1915, aged 22, the sons of Archibald and Emma Howard of 1 Agamemnon Road, West Hampstead. They were also nephews of Harold G. Howard of Blue House Farm, Pitsea and previously Bowers Hall, Bowers Gifford. Howard, of whom more later, was one of Pitsea's main benefactors.

Bowers Gifford: Clifford Payne, killed 13 April 1916, aged 18 and Victor George Payne, killed 14 November 1915, aged 20, the sons of George Henry Payne, 6 Gun Hill, Bowers Gifford.

Laindon: Alfred Sydney Douglas, killed 22 September 1914, aged 26 and Arthur George Douglas, killed 20 April 1916, aged 25, the sons of Alexander James and Emily Douglas of 60 Selwyn Road, Upton Manor, Plaistow. Edward Bright, aged 32, killed 2 August 1916 and Frederick Bright, aged 24, killed 12 June 1915, the sons of Alfred and Rachel Bright of Laindon. Frederick Brockwell, killed 7 July 1916, aged 27 and William John Brockwell, killed 25 May 1917, aged 24, the sons of George and Caroline Brockwell of York House, Laindon. John Charles Fowler, killed 6 March 1919, aged 29 and William George Fowler, killed 13 March 1915, aged 39, the sons of J.J. Fowler of 'Fairoak', New Century Road, Laindon. Arthur Jones, date unknown and Leonard Jones, killed 23 March 1918, aged 31, the sons of Frederick and Ellen Jones of 'Oakden' Worthing Road, Laindon. Arthur Edward Stewart, killed 14 April 1917, aged 36 and James Arthur Stewart, killed 31 October 1916, aged 25, the sons of William and Clara Stewart of Laindon Common.

So at least thirteen families in the district lost at least two sons, and one can imagine how many families countrywide lost more than one son and possibly even daughters working as nurses or in munitions factories.

However, the four sons of Thomas and Mary James of Laindon went to war and survived. Thomas served with the 24th London Regiment; George Henry, with the Royal Field Artillery; Albert Charles, with the 9th Lancers and Leonard, with the Army Service Corps. They all were awarded the usual medals but Albert also won the Military Medal. George Henry was killed by enemy action in the Second World War in London and was buried at St Nicholas Church on 31 May 1940, aged 50.

Garrod, (Jarrod) William Edward

William was born in 1899 at Aveley, Essex. The 1911 census has him living with his parents, Ernest and Kate Elizabeth, at Hall Cottages, Old Church Hill. His father, Ernest, worked on the Langdon Hall Farm as cowman. William was aged 11 and presumably went to the Langdon Hills School opposite St Mary's Church, the building we now know as the Old School House, and at a later date to the new school further downhill in the High Road opposite St Mary's Church Hall. William's parents, eighteen years later, moved to 1 Well Green Cottage in Dry Street.

He enlisted at Romford and it would appear that he had previously served with the Bedfordshire Regiment as a private, service number 11764, before transferring to the 10th Battalion of the Essex Regiment, service number 44030. The 10th was a service battalion, a fighting unit that one voluntarily enlisted into for a period of three years or for the duration. It was attached to the K2 Army Group; short for Kitchener's Army sometimes known as Kitchener's mob. Horatio Kitchener was Secretary of State for War and one of the few who believed the war would be a long and bloody one. Other service battalions were attached to K1, K3 and K4 Armies.

William was killed on 24 August 1918, aged 19 possibly at the Third Battle of Picardy or Battle of Amiens which was part of the last hundred days of the war. The CWGC record that he is buried in Becourt Military Cemetery, Picardy, France, grave 11 B 17.

He was awarded the British and Victory medals and is commemorated locally on the St Mary's Church, Langdon Hills Memorial, Bulphan St Mary's Church Memorial, Great Eastern Railway Memorial at Liverpool Street and in the *Men of Essex Volume 8 – the 10th Service Battalion The Essex Regiment* published by the Essex Branch of the Western Front Association.

Markquick, Arthur Christian

We must not forget the part played in the First World War by the Royal Navy and at the outbreak of the war it was recognised that Britain had the largest and best navy in the world. It was to play a major role in the downfall of Germany by keeping us supplied in food, arms and raw materials while starving Germany of these things by blockading the ports of the Central Powers. International waters were mined to prevent any ships from entering entire sections of sea. Germany's response was unrestricted submarine warfare in attempt to cut our supply lines. This was brought under control until convoys were introduced in 1917. Until then, merchant shipping experienced heavy losses.

By blockading the German ports the Royal Navy was also trying to draw the German Navy (Hochseeflotte – High Seas Fleet) into an engagement where a decisive victory could be gained. There was no decisive battle but there were several engagements, the most notable being the Battle of the Falkland Islands, the Battle of Dogger Bank and the Battle of Jutland. Here the Royal Navy suffered severe losses but succeeded in its goal of ensuring that the German Fleet never again put to sea, other than to scuttle itself after the end of the war at Scapa Flow.

The Royal Navy's manpower expanded from 250,000 men at the start to 450,000 men by the end of the war. The Women's Royal Naval Services (Wrens) was set up in 1917 and numbered 7,000 by the end of the war. They were involved in administration, transport, logistics and communications work.

One of the heroic naval stories of the First World War that of Boy Seaman 1st Class Jack Cornwell, who at the age of sixteen, was killed at the Battle of Jutland and was posthumously awarded the Victoria Cross for staying at his post mortally wounded while men were dying around him. He was born in Leyton, Essex.

This area had its own young hero in Arthur Christian Markquick from Pitsea who died on 15 October 1914 at the age of seventeen. He was also born in Leyton and at the time of the 1911 census living with his parents, John and Ellen Markquick, at Chestnut House, Chestnut Road, Pitsea.

His rank in the Royal Navy was the same as Jack's, Boy Seaman 1st Class, and he was aboard HMS *Hawke* which was patrolling just above Aberdeen in the North Sea when it was hit by a torpedo from the German U-boat U9. The torpedo ignited a magazine and caused a tremendous explosion which ripped the ship apart. *Hawke*, a cruiser, sank within a few minutes with the loss of her captain, 26 officers and 497 men. Destroyers *Swift* and *Modesta* rushed to their rescue but only managed to pick up seventy-one men. Arthur's body was never recovered. He is commemorated on the Chatham Naval Memorial.

The Royal Navy was to lose nearly 45,000 personnel, through either military action or disease.

Shields, John

John was born on 23 December 1891 at Walworth, London to Robert and Elizabeth Shields. In 1895 the family moved to Laindon where Robert and family built their own brick bungalow 'Cleve Cottage' in Basildon Road, one of Laindon's first wave of pioneers.

The 1911 census has John's occupation as wire weaver, following in the footsteps of his father who had his own business in London. Wire weaving was a form of wire netting. John enlisted at Southend on 14 November 1914 into the Royal Regiment of Artillery (RH & RFA), RH being Royal Horse and RFA being the Royal Field Artillery, service number 17540. He was initially attached to the 13th Reserve Battery and later to 109 Brigade.

John spent approximately ten months training at Portslade, Brighton before being

Cleve Cottage, Basildon Road, Laindon – 1895. *Kind permission of Robbie Shields*

John Shields, standing – 1919.
Kind permission of Robbie Shields

transferred to France landing at Le Havre on 29 August 1915. His records are a little confusing as it appears that he was promoted to the rank of bombardier on 7 January 1915 and again on 1 July 1915. Could it be that he had been demoted following a reprimand for an improper reply to a senior NCO (Warrant Officer) on 15 May?

Over the next twelve months John was to see a considerable amount of action on the battlefields of the Somme. He received two wounds, one in the leg and another in the head but they only required short spells in hospitals. In December of 1915 he is in trouble again and this time he requested that he be reverted back to a gunner so as to avoid a court martial. Unfortunately his records do not indicate what his offence was.

Towards the end of 1916 he is transferred to 107 Brigade and in December of that year is granted two weeks leave to go home. We then find in May 1917 he has a couple of spells in hospital due to sickness. Then on 20 November 1917 he is transferred again, this time to the Labour Corps, reason given 'Benefit of Services' or does this mean that the military authorities believed he had seen enough action up front and needed a rest? The Labour Corps was formed in 1917 because there was an urgent need of men to ensure that the huge network of roads, railways, canals, buildings, camps, telegraph and telephone systems, etc, were maintained. By the end of the war approximately 700,000 men were engaged in this labour intensive work. This did not mean that they were away from the fighting because the enemy would often target these particular areas and it certainly was no rest.

John was again granted leave in December 1917 so that he could go home and get married to Sarah Solomon. The wedding took place on 12 December at Lambeth.

John eventually returned home and was demobbed on 31 May 1919 and is transferred to Class Z Army Reserve. This appears to have been the normal route out of the Army and you could stay on this reserve list for a year. He was awarded the British, Victory and the 1914-15 Star. John and Sarah returned to Laindon in 1920. During the Second World War he joined the Laindon Home Guard that was stationed at the New Fortune of War, Laindon and was awarded the Defence Medal.

He died on 7 October 1965 and is buried at St Nicholas Church, Laindon. Members of the family still live in the Basildon area.

Ansell, Lieutenant Arnold Edward

Very little has been said about the role of the Royal Flying Corps (RFC) and the Royal Air Force (RAF) during the war, possibly due to the fact that flight was still in its infancy. Because of this pilots became popular figures of mythic proportions, partly because of the sheer romantic improbability of flight but also because they restored an element of single combat to the anonymous slaughter of modern war. Pilots with five 'kills' became aces and their chivalric image survived long after air tactics slid into deadly routine. One such observer/gunner/pilot was Laindon's Arnold Edward Ansell.

Arnold Edward Ansell was born at St Paul, Minnesota, USA on 23 August 1896 to Alice (born Esher, Surrey) and Walter Ansell (born Tottenham, Middlesex). By 1911 the family were back in England, living at Ware, Hertfordshire.

On leaving school Arnold underwent training to become an electrical engineer, working for his father's company. By 1914 the family had moved yet again to Belle Vue, Laindon and at the outbreak of war he signed up, serving with the 1/24th Battalion of the London Regiment. He attended courses as a bombardier, in trench mortar and Lewis machine-gun firing, plus sniper training.

He saw service in France during 1916 but then in 1917 he volunteered to transfer to the Royal Flying Corps. His training experience was to prove beneficial when he became a RAF observer/gunner.

Ironically, the risk of serious injury to aircrew at the time was probably greater than being in the trenches. Not only was there a risk of being shot down by hostile aeroplanes but also the risk from anti-aircraft and rifle and machine-gun fire from the ground. There was also the unreliability of engines and air frames; we must remember that powered flight in Great Britain had only existed for around nine years. Parachutes were not issued other than to balloon observers as the High Command believed this could lead to aeroplanes being abandoned rather than airmen facing hostile combatants.

During his period of training with the Royal Flying Corps he took leave to get married at St Nicholas Church, Laindon on 2 February 1918 to Nellie Augusta Targett from Woburn Square, London.

At the end of his basic training as an observer/gunner, Arnold joined the 48 Squadron, based at Bertangles on the River Somme near Amiens. The squadron was the first to be equipped with the new Bristol Fighters F2A and F2B; these aircraft became to be known affectionately as the 'Biff' or 'Brisfit'. By the end of the war they had become a highly efficient machine, much loved by the crews who flew them. Within a few days, 7 July 1918, Arnold was in the thick of the action. He was on escort duty in Bristol Fighter F2B – D7909 piloted by Captain C.R. Steele. They were assigned to escort DH4 light bombers on a mission near Proyart.

As the mission proceeded the British formation was intercepted by eight Pfalz Scouts and in the general melee that followed Captain Steele managed to engage one of them, firing a long burst from his forward Vickers machine-gun. The gun jammed but Steele managed to manoeuvre the Bristol into position to allow Arnold, in the rear seat, to bring his machine-gun to bear. Arnold fired 100 rounds into the Pfalz, causing it to go into a steep dive from which there was no recovery. It crashed in flames on the Amiens to St Quentin Road.

This was one of five victories achieved by Arnold. They included three direct successes and two victories shared with his pilot, who shot two planes down. Five victories, the benchmark, entitled Arnold to achieve the status of 'ace'. Arnold's operational flying was not without incident and on one occasion, whilst being piloted by Second Lieutenant. T.G. Jackson their Bristol Fighter was shot up and both men were fortunate to land without injury. Even on the ground Arnold was still not safe. On 24 August 1918 after dinner at Bertangles airfield, 48 Squadron was attacked by six hostile planes. Their bombs dropped onto hangers destroying a number of aeroplanes. Such was the ferocity of the attack that four men were killed and thirty wounded. The airfield descended into chaos and was a place of horror with screaming wounded men and fiercely burning hangers. Arnold was fortunate to escape unscathed.

On 7 November 1918 he transferred to 84 Squadron with a view to piloting single seat SE5A fighter scouts and four days later the war was over and Arnold had survived. The cessation of hostilities led to massive cut backs in the number of RAF personnel and he was demobbed on 3 March 1919.

After the war Arnold moved to Winchester, Hants, but he continued his RAF service in the Volunteer Reserve which required him to attend annual training and refresher camp for two weeks each year until 1925. Just after the outbreak of the Second World War he was promoted from Pilot Officer to Flying Officer and then in December 1939 he was transferred to Administrative and Special Duties Branch as an Air Force Officer Reservist. Following the end of the Second World War he moved to Southampton where he lived until his death in September 1982, aged 86.

He was awarded the First World War Victory and British War Medal.

Partmenter, Astor Gilbert

Astor was born on 31 August 1891, Holloway, Middlesex to Alice and John Parmenter. By the time of the 1901 census they had moved to Basildon. Astor joined the Navy in 1910, service number M2960(po). His parents at the time of the 1911 census were living at Basildon Lodge, Rectory Road, Basildon.

He was initially stationed at Gosport where he was engaged in submarines, he then became a cook's mate (baker) on board ship for about three years before he lost his life on HMS *Queen Mary* at the Battle of Jutland on 31 May 1916, a few months short of his twenty-fifth birthday.

Astor Gilbert Parmenter.
Steve Newman collection

HMS *Queen Mary* was launched in 1913 being the last battleship to be built before the outbreak of war. She spent all her time in the North Sea as part of the 1st Battle-cruiser Squadron and was involved in the Battle of Heligoland Bight in 1914. She was refitted in 1915 and missed the Battle of Dogger Bank.

There were other skirmishes before she came to a violent end at the Battle of Jutland, the largest and last major sea battle of the First World War. She had opened fire on the German battle-cruiser SMS *Seydlitz* hitting her four times in the exchange of fire. The *Seydlitz* managed a couple of hits but it was the German battle-cruiser *Derfflinger* that hit her twice, with one shell hitting her magazines which exploded, sinking the ship; 1,266 officers and men were lost, there were only twenty survivors.

Germany's plan was to break the British stranglehold on the German ports so as allow their mercantile shipping to operate. They did not succeed – the battle was more or less a stalemate. The British lost fourteen ships and 6,000 sailors compared to Germany's eleven ships and 2,500 sailors. Britain continued to blockade the ports and Germany's Navy turned its efforts and resources to unrestricted submarine warfare, which by April 1917 triggered America's declaration of war.

Meredith, Richard

Richard was born on 10 September 1892 at Walthamstow to James and Mary. By the time of the 1911 census the family had moved to Station Estate, Pitsea. This is where the local plotland era first started in 1891.

Richard enlisted at the beginning of the war at Gravesend, Kent into the Royal Horse and Royal Field Artillery, 81st battery 5 Brigade, service number 70252. At the time of his death on 29 September 1917 he had been promoted to acting bombardier.

According to his great nephew, Tony Hamilton, his main responsibility was leading the front horse of four that pulled the gun carriages. Like many men he had been used to handling horses back home.

By mid 1917, following mutinies in the overstretched French Army, the British forces assumed an even greater role than previously on the Western Front. This gave Field Marshall Sir Douglas Haig the opportunity he had been waiting for to unleash his great attack on the ridges in the Ypres area that the Germans were dominating. The attack started on 31 July 1917 until November often in appalling conditions. The offensive eventually came to an inconclusive close with both armies stuck in muddy fields churned up by artillery fire. Although the battle is referred to as the Battle of Passchendaele (Third Ypres) it was actually a series of battles, often named after the village that had become the last objective.

It would have been in one of these battles that Richard lost his life. He was awarded the 1914 Star, Victory and British War medal and is buried and commemorated at the Divisional Collecting Post Cemetery near the village of Ieper (Ypres), West-Vlaanderen, Belgium.

British troops getting ready for another offensive. *Ken Porter's Collection*

Wilson, William Walter

We have made reference to the Scottish farmers moving into the area and changing the face of the farming environment from sheep and arable to dairy cattle and arable. One such family from Kilmarnock were the Wilsons. They moved to Upper Dunton Hall, Dunton in the 1890s.

William was born at the hall in 1894. His parents were William (senior) and Ellen Wilson (nee Dove). William senior died of epilepsy and was buried at St Mary's Church, Dunton on 18 March 1898. The family were split and William Walter found himself in an orphanage at Wanstead, Essex. Then at the age of sixteen he went to Australia, where on 28 October 1914 he enlisted into the Australian Imperial Force, joining the 1st Battalion (Infantry), service number 1728. He rose to the rank of sergeant.

In April 1915 he was with the Australian Expeditionary Force in the Dardanelles and Gallipoli, where the British and Empire along with the French initially launched a naval campaign against the Turks to force a passage through the Dardanelles. The idea was to secure a sea passage to Russia. A land invasion on the Gallipoli peninsula followed again with the idea to take control of the strategically vital strait separating Europe from Asia.

The campaign was a disaster, resulting in one of the greatest victories for the Ottoman (Turks) Empire of the war. Winston Churchill, the British First Lord of the Admiralty, who was one of the main instigators of the campaign, was forced to resign. He then took himself off to the front and became battalion commander of the 6th Battalion Royal Scots Fusliers, returning to his parliamentary duty in 1916.

The *Chelmsford Chronicle* 8 August 1916 reports William's death:

> 'Corp. Wm. Walter killed in action was the son of the late Mr and Mrs Wilson, formerly of Dunton Hall, Essex and well known in the Brentwood district. Corp Wilson was just twenty-two and was born at Dunton Hall. At the age of sixteen he went to Australia. He joined the Australian Expeditionary Force and went through the Dardanelles campaign, subsequently going to France.'

Interesting to note the paper refers to 'corporal' whereas in fact he is commemorated at Villers-Bretonneux memorial, France (Somme) with the rank of sergeant.

Australia and New Zealand commemorate those who died in the Gallipoli campaign on 25 April every year. It is known as Anzac Day and it is now a national holiday, a day of remembrance in these two countries, plus the Cook Islands, Niue, Pitcairn Islands and Tonga in respect of those that served and died in all wars, conflicts and peacekeeping operations.

Two of William Walter's cousins also died in the war. Edward Alfred Dove, born Dunton Wayletts in 1873 also also emigrated to Australia and enlisted at Goulburn, New South Wales into the Australian infantry, 34th Battalion, service number 3250, in September 1916. He was killed on 10 May 1918, aged 44 and is remembered with honour at Brookwood Military Cemetery, Surrey, England. It would appear that William Walter was following him out there.

We were surprised to find that he was buried in England but with help from Allen Seymour, a descendant of the Wilson and Dove family, we have located the following letters from the Australian Red Cross Society files, which describes exactly what happened to him.

'34th Battalion, A.I.F – Dove, E. A. No. 3250 – Died 10 May1918.

'This man Pt. Dove E.A. died in this the 3rd A.A.H. Dartford (Australian Auxiliary Hospital) on 10 May 1918 about 10.30am and was buried in the Brookwood Cemetery on 16 May 1918. His grave would be in the Australian portion of that cemetery and would be properly marked by a cross having full details thereon. He enlisted on 28 September 1916 at Goulburn, NSW, and was forty-four years of age. He was hit by a piece of shell in the forearm and a nerve to the hand muscles was divided. It was necessary to stitch the ends together, which is but a simple operation and most necessary for the future use of the hand. Unfortunately the patient collapsed while taking the anaesthetic before coming in for the operation, owing to weakness of heart muscles. Next of kin: Mrs E.A. Dove. Dated 14 August 1918.

'34th Battalion, A.I.F (late 55th Battalion) – Dove, E.A. Private No. 3250 – Died of Wounds, 10 May 1918.

'Informant described Dove as about 5ft 6ins high, medium build, dark complexion, aged about thirty to thirty-five. Had been transferred to the 34th from the 54th or 55th Battalion.

'Informant states that they both belonged to 'D' Company and Dove was on the same Lewis gun as informant. On 4 April 1918 the battalion was alongside Villers-Bretonneux preparing for a counter-attack against the Germans. About 1.30am they were at their gun digging themselves in when one of the shells wounded Dove in the arm. It appeared to be a severe wound. Informant was alongside him when he was hit. Dove spoke to him and said that his arm was very painful and that he wanted to get away to have it attended to. He walked away with some stretcher bearers about a quarter of an hour afterwards and the informant never saw him again. In fact he was surprised to learn from me that he was dead. He evidently lived for some weeks after being wounded. According to the informant Dove was very well liked by his mates.

'Informant: Private J. Davies, No. 1659 – "D" Company, 34th battalion – dated 23 September 1918 – Verdict: Heart failure under anaesthetic.'

The other cousin was, Dove, Bernard Joseph, born Great Burstead, Essex in 1893, the son of Joseph and Jane Gray Dove (nee Wilson). Jane was the sister of William Walter's father William Wilson. He enlisted with the Essex Regiment 2nd Battalion, service number 40171. He was killed on 23 October 1916, age twenty-three and is buried in the Guards' Cemetery, Lesboeufs, France.

The Dove family, through Charles Dove, moved to the Laindon and Dunton area sometime prior to 1850 from Suffolk. Over the next fifty years the family occupied several farms in the area: White House Farm, Laindon; Dunton Wayletts, Dunton; Salmons Farm, Pound Lane, Laindon and Dove's Farm, Pound Lane, Laindon. Dove's farmhouse is still there. It is a Grade II, eighteenth century, weather-boarded house with a modern addition on the

Dove's Farm, Pound Lane, Laindon.
Ken Porter's Collection

south side. Pound Lane at one time was known as Doves Lane and the grass track leading up to St Nicholas Church is known as Doves Hill. The farmhouse at Dunton Wayletts is also still there, also Grade II listed. The Doves were mainly cereal farmers but with the influence of marrying into the Wilsons in the latter part of the 1800s they became dairy farmers.

Buckham, Robert Charles

Robert was born in 1889 and, as previously mentioned, was accused with his brother, Richard, of the murders of Albert and Emma Watson in August 1906. He was acquitted and set free in November of that year.

He enlisted in the 1st (Royal) Dragoons C Squadron. The 1911 census has him living with his parents and three sisters in Basildon, his occupation being a poultry farmer, but it is understood that he joined up prior to the outbreak of the war. Perhaps he wanted to make a break from his past which must have been haunting him.

We know that he was in France and Flanders from October 1914 to January 1919 other than a short break in August 1918 to get married. He saw a considerable amount of fighting and was involved in some of the greatest battles of the war. These included Ypres, 1914-1915, Frezenberg, Loos 1915, Arras, 1917, the Somme, Amiens, Hindenburg Line, Cambrai and the pursuit to Mons, 1918. He was obviously a fearless, courageous leader of men as can be seen from the following comments made by the various commanding officers under whom he served. In the progress of the war he was promoted to lance corporal, June 1915; corporal, February 1917; acting lance sergeant, December 1917; lance sergeant, May 1918; acting sergeant, June 1918 and finally sergeant, October 1918.

He was wounded in his left hand in January 1916 but soon rejoined the regiment. He received the 1914 Star, British, Victory medals and the Silver War Badge. In addition he was also awarded the Military Medal.

Major Leahy, adjutant in charge of supplies for the 3rd Cavalry Division of the Third Army commanded by Sir John French records in his book that 'C' Squadron had left British waters about 9pm on Wednesday 7 October and arrived at dawn at Zeebrugge and by 4.30pm 'C' Squadron of the Royals were out on the road. He goes on to say: 'Needing to join my Service Corps post haste, I travelled with them, accompanied by some of their officers – Captain Miles, Lieutenant de Trafford and Edwards and we were well looked after by Private Buckham.'

Lieutenant William Edwards served as an officer in the 1st (Royal) Dragoons and commanded a troop from Robert Buckham's regiment. In a very long letter to his father 28 December 1914 he had this to say about Buckham:

> 'When I was waiting for the boat to take me home, I saw large gangs of English prisoners – men sent back for cowardice, sleeping on duty, looting and robbery. They were doing the most degrading work bareheaded in the rain, under command of officers with loaded revolvers. One of our men made an attempt to give tobacco to one of them but I stopped him just in time. He was horrified to learn he could have been given twelve months' hard labour or detention for such a deed. I should have disciplined him myself but I was unexpectedly touched by his compassion. We got talking. He was a slightly built fellow from a farming background in Essex – not the physical quality of recruit you were used to in your day when the

minimum height for the Royals was 5ft 10in. He was in the first batch of privates to be given leave for seventy-two hours until 1 January. He was intensely proud of serving with the Royals and of sharing his good fortune with his family. There was nothing, he said, he would ever do to dishonour them. Quite the contrary, he would "rise like the morning dew" and gain his stripes. He will too, if he survives – 6650 Private Buckham R. – the man who reminded me of pride.'

Lieutenant William Oswald Berryman served with the 'C' Squadron of the 1st (Royal) Dragoons and following a reconnaissance into enemy territory on the 28 September 1915 he was awarded the Military Cross. This is what his Squadron Leader Strutt-Irwin had to say in the citation for his Military Cross:

'On Tuesday 28 September at 4.30am, Lieutenant Berryman and three men made a reconnaissance to find out the exact line held by the enemy from Hill 70 to Chalk Pits about a mile east of Loos. Lieutenant Berryman, Lance Corporal Buckham, Private Purves and Private Duff returned about six hours later with very valuable information. They had crawled along a great portion of the line in broad daylight and at one point actually penetrated a German trench. Lieutenant Berryman's success in this assignment is highly to be commended, both for the quality of the intelligence

British soldiers in a German dug-out. *Ken Porter collection*

> gained and for the effectiveness of his command in the safe return of all the men.'

Later, when Lieutenant Berryman thought back on his actions and award of the Military Cross he thought that it was both a farce and an injustice. Explaining he said:

> 'The farce was when we penetrated the German trench it was because we thought the occupants were Guardsmen with Smoke Helmets on. It was only due to Buckham's swiftness with his revolver that none of us was killed by them. He has always had the uncanny impulse to fire first, to kill before being killed – one of the reasons I chose him for the mission. If anything will win this war for us, it is his calibre of instinct for survival. I would not be alive but for him and this is the injustice. Both Buckham and Purves saved my life – Purves got a sniper on the way back – yet they have no rewards. If there's nothing else I can do in this blessed war, I will do everything I can to right that wrong.'

Then in a letter back home Lance Corporal Kettle refers to a chat he had with Buckham that followed a football match when C Squadron beat A Squadron 4-1 with Buckham scoring two goals.

> 'He was made Lance Corporal the same time as me and should be up for a medal, the sergeant says, for his reconnaissance work in Loos last month. All the chaps had a fine old sing-song after the match and Buckham and me had a good talk. He comes from Basildon, you know, where my Uncle Arthur was a policeman. I asked him if he knew him and he thought he did. I told him I thought my uncle had a cushy job there. He only had a few thefts to deal with and just one murder case in the last ten years, not like London. Buckham said he knew about the murder although it was a long time ago.'

One of the first policemen to arrive at the murder scene was a PC Kettle, it would be an amazing coincidence if he was Lance Corporal Kettle's uncle. A further letter refers to him and Buckham being injured on 16 January 1916 during the Battle of Hohenzollern Redoubt:

> 'Then in the evening, the Boche threw everything at us – trench mortars, rifle grenades, hand grenades, as well as the guns. Four of our men were killed and thirty-nine wounded – including me and Buckham.'

They were in fact both hit in the left hand but Buckham had rejoined the regiment by 21 January.

Captain Francis Wilson-Fitzgerald DSO MC in his personal log states:

> 'Lastly, I am delighted to report to you that 6650 Lance Corporal Buckham has indeed been awarded the Military Medal and will be gazetted on 22 January 1917. Our warmest congratulations to him, it is well deserved.'

We wonder how his family felt back home, one son hanged for murder and another awarded the Military Medal for bravery, hopefully it brought pride back to his parents.

Captain Thomas Strutt-Irwin's letter had this to say about Buckham…

> 'especially Buckham who seems totally without fear. I've observed him going over the top with no more regard than if he were going on a Sunday afternoon stroll. We all find our own ways to cope with this war.'

We are nearing the end of Buckham's story; we have left out a number of his heroic moments but possibly his most difficult time came when he was talking about his family to his mate Sergeant Elliot who had also been awarded a Military Medal for his involvement in the Battle of Amiens in March 1916. Elliot tells us of their conservation:

> 'He had two brothers, one called James who died before he was three months old and an elder brother, Richard. The family moved to a farm in Basildon when Buckham was fifteen. His brother looked after it when his dad went back to work in London at Watson's Wharf, Wapping. Buckham went quiet for a time before he told me that he and his brother were charged with murder. They'd had a problem getting water one summer and the people who tried to pinch some from their pond got killed. Apparently, his brother got attacked with a bucket by the old man and it broke his gun-stock and somehow the man and the woman got shot.
>
> 'But the worst of it was, Buckham said, was having to go to court and testify. He said giving evidence was the worst thing he'd ever had to do. He'd never felt so frightened and he'd never felt so bad about speaking out against his own brother. So every time he got worried about going over the top, he'd make himself live through it again. He said he knew nothing could ever be so bad.
>
> 'Elliot responded, "It's been a sort of good luck charm?". "Yes", he said, "but I've got a new one now, I've got a girl. I'll get through this for her."'

Then a short time afterwards in August 1918, Buckham's father died, he did not want compassionate leave but did request seventy-two hours leave to get married. Lieutenant Lithgow in his report says:

> 'His request, from a man who seems to be made for our ghastly war and its killing, was so unexpected I said, "Great heavens – where did this lucky lady spring from?" His answer was equally unexpected – fulsome and fervent:
>
> "She's pretty," he said. "She's really pretty. I met her when I got injured at Hulloch two years ago. She was a nurse, just sent over, didn't think I'd ever see her again. Thought I wouldn't care. Then last spring, after the charge at Collezy, after we used our sabres, she was there, nursing the German prisoners we'd cut up, but she saw me, she smiled at me, she'd remembered, after all that time.
>
> "She's waiting for me now in lodgings near Wimbledon barracks. I've got to get back to her. That's it, sir."

The final word comes from Lady Agnes Pia de Trafford, youngest daughter of Rudolph Fielding, 8th Earl of Denbigh, who was present at the victory march on Monday, 14 July 1919 in Paris.

> 'I met this slightly built man, perhaps thirty years of age, with a taut wiry look about him. I wondered why he had been singled out. I was told he had served throughout the war and won the Military Medal. I asked him to explain his other medals. "This is the 1914 Star for serving in the first part of the war," he said; "This the British War medal because I served in France; and this is the Victory Medal because of the battles I've been in" and with his delicious smile he said, "We call them Pip, Squeak and Wilfred."
>
> 'Your parents must be very proud of you", I said, "My father is dead, ma'am,

but I think my mother is pleased and my sisters. My wife too."

"You have children?" I asked him. "My wife is with child," he said, "due in a few months."

"Then you will have much to celebrate on the anniversary of the Armistice this autumn", I said.

"Yes", he said. "It is the beginning of my new life."

"And where will your new life be, Sergeant?"

"In Canada ma'am, where my wife was born, she is my family now."

'We smiled at each other for a moment. I said, "what a wonderful culmination to all these awful years! His face was suffused with pride. Then touchingly inappropriately, he said, "Thank you, milady."

What an amazing story, a young boy of seventeen sees his brother kill two old people over water, turns his life round by going to war, wins the Military Medal for bravery, finds love and goes off to Canada to start a new life. We hope he found it. With this story it is time to leave the battlefield of France and Flanders but before we do we should have a look at the poor old war horse.

War Horse

In the chapter on civilian life we mention briefly the effect the requisitioning of horses for the war effort had on civilian life, but what about their story at the front? The horse was one of the real forgotten heroes of the war.

In the opening shots of the war the British Army only had eighty motor vehicles. The only answer was the horse. Anyone who has seen the film *War Horse* will have an idea of the appalling conditions that the horse, pony and mule had to deal with. Their story begins with the mass call up of horses from every farm and country estate in the land and between 1914 and 1918 the British Army took over a million horses to war. The first clash between horse and the machine-gun was terrible. Although the horses, and the men that rode them, had gone through a period of training, no form of training could prepare them for the devastating fire power of the machine-gun and artillery shells. It was chaotic, horses and men were tumbling and falling in every direction. It is bad enough witnessing the death of a loved one but is it strange to be extremely upset at the death of an animal comrade? In most cases man and horse become one and this was certainly the case in this war and it was not long before the public back home were getting very concerned about their welfare,

It is understood that many of the horses conscripted in Essex were dispatched to the front from the quayside at Wat Tyler Park, Pitsea.

As early as November 1914 the Royal Society for the Prevention of Cruelty to Animals sent the editor of the *Chelmsford Chronicle* the following letter:

'Sirs – In spite of the excellent arrangements and splendid work carried out by the Army Veterinary Corps for the care of the sick and wounded horses of the British forces at the front, the public has long felt a desire to co-operate in the humane and economic work of this department. It is interesting here to mention that already some 23,000 horses have been drafted into hospital and tended with such care that large numbers have returned fit to the front. The Army Veterinary

> Corps has already availed itself of the assistance of the RSPCA by drafting a large number of its inspectors into the ranks of the Corps.'

By the end of the war there were twenty horse hospitals behind the lines. The military were aware that the war could not be won without them. However, following their initial engagements they realised cavalry charges were not the most effective use of horse power. The cavalry soldier for the next eighteen months joined his fellow infantry soldiers in the trenches.

The horse, pony and mule during this period were therefore mainly used for logistical support as pack animals or for pulling the wagons, gun carriages, ammunitions, stores, ambulances, reconnaissance and for carrying messages. This did not keep them out of the firing lines as the transport routes were frequently shelled by the Germans. Although many of them were killed in this way the majority died of exhaustion or due to the appalling weather conditions.

Every soldier that had the responsibility of looking after a horse had in his pocket a book entitled: *'The Drivers', Gunners' and Mounted Soldiers' Handbook to management and care of Horse and Harness'* written by 'Two Officers'. It was a step by step guide of how to care for your horse and one short paragraph epitomises the care that was expected:

> 'When a horse is tired or cold pull his ears and hand rub his legs, it refreshes him and he will appreciate it.'

Brigadier-General Frank Percy Crozier who took part in the various battles of the Western Front had this to say:

> 'If the times are hard for human beings, on account of the mud and misery which they endure with astounding fortitude, the same may be said of the animals. My heart bleeds for the horses and mules.'

On 30 June 1916 the Battle of the Somme commenced with a massive bombardment of one and a half million shells that were meant to destroy the enemy's fortifications. The plan was for the infantry to follow up the bombardment and then the cavalry regiments of the British and Empire with their 50,000 men were to sweep round and rout the enemy. But this did not happen, the bombardment was unsuccessful and almost 20,000 were killed, the worst day in British military history. On the following day, to the frustration of the cavalry, they were stood down and with few exceptions, this was the situation until March 1918 when their day at last came.

It was 30 March 1918 at the Battle of Moreuil Wood near Amiens where the Germans, over the previous few days, had commenced their Spring Offensive, broken through the British lines and were holding Moreuil Wood. General Jack Seely on his beloved and famous horse 'Warrior' was commanding the Canadian Cavalry Brigade and was ordered to attack and capture the wood. As they poured into the woods they took the Germans by surprise but the enemy retaliated furiously, requiring the cavalrymen to dismount and fight hand-to-hand on foot. The Germans were slowly forced out of the wood. It was a turning point and in the last months of the war the cavalry at last come into its own as they helped push the Germans back. Their only disappointment was that they did not push them all the way back to Germany. (Appendix 6)

It was not only the British that used horses – all the other armies in the field did, so you can image the millions that were killed. It was the Allied blockade that prevented

Germany and her partners from importing horses to replace those lost, which contributed to Germany's defeat.

At the end of the war 85,000 were sold for horse meat and half a million were sold to French farmers to help rebuild the countryside. Only 60,000 made it back to Britain. Amongst them were six black horses that survived the war together and, fittingly, these pulled the body of the Unknown Warrior to its lasting resting place in Westminster Abbey.

These are just a few of the many amazing stories of those that either survived or died in this devastating war. In Appendix 7, we have listed at least 188 military personnel who were killed from the district – excluding Billericay and Wickford as they are covered in previous publications.

Chapter 8

The War's End and Aftermath

BY EARLY 1918, following Russia's withdrawal after the 1917 revolution, it looked like the war was turning in favour of the Germans as they could now throw all their efforts in to the Western Front. At this point the Americans had barely entered the war but the Germans had managed to get within forty miles of Paris. However behind the front line, Germany was far from strong. Port blockades by the Allies had helped cause food and other major supplies shortages. Their railway systems were collapsing and the German people were going on strike, along with mutinies within the German military.

Then, on 29 September 1918, Bulgaria sued for an armistice followed by the Ottoman Empire on 31 August 1918. The Italians, who came into the war late, on the side of the Allies, scored a decisive victory against Austria-Hungary. The Americans by now had deployed over two million troops in the field.

So by early November Germany was on its own which led to a German delegation on 7 November crossing the front line to discuss peace terms. Then at 11am on the 11th day of the 11th month of 1918 the guns fell silent and the fighting stopped.

Although Germany had not actually surrendered, her soldiers were surrendering in their thousands and their Navy had mutinied. Our allies, in particular the French, wanted to ensure that the German people never went to war again.

The Treaty of Versailles, the peace treaty between Germany and the Allies, was signed on 28 June 1919, followed with peace treaties between the Allies and Austria in September 1919, Bulgaria in November, Turkey (Ottoman Empire) in April 1920 and Hungary in June 1920. By this time a new map of Europe and the Balkans had emerged.

As we know today, the terms of the Treaty of Versailles were met with great resentment by the German speaking people and instead of being a war to end all world wars, the treaty had become the catalyst for the Second World War twenty years later.

But for the time being, after four years of fighting, there was peace – but at what a cost in human lives. Over sixty-five million men had been mobilised, eight million had been killed, two million died of disease, twenty-one million were wounded, eight million taken prisoner or missing and nearly six million civilians perished (one million through military action).

Of these numbers the British Empire lost just over one million military personnel and 2,000 civilians due to military action.

Peace – but did we celebrate? Certainly, in the cities people gathered but there were mixed feelings, some cheered and waved banners but families who had lost loved ones, though grateful that the war was over, had other emotions to deal with. The 11 November Armistice was only a cease fire – the peace treaty was not signed until June the following year with others not until 1920. Peace day was therefore officially set for 19 July 1919.

The French celebrated their day on Bastille Day 14 July 1919. Ours was held on 19

Victory march of Allied troops in London – 19 July 1919. *Ken Porter's Collection*

July, the day in 1588 that a chain of beacons had blazed across the country to warn of the coming of the Spanish Armada, so it was planned for nationwide bonfires to be lit as night fell.

The parade in London was a success with nearly 15,000 troops taking part, followed later in the day with various forms of entertainment and ending in a lavish firework display in the evening.

Out in the country it seemed a different story, some areas involved themselves in the celebration, others did not.

A report in the *Chelmsford Chronicle* on 27 June 1919:

> 'A meeting of the committee appointed to arrange a Peace celebration for the Brentwood and Billericay districts was held at the Town Hall, Brentwood. The Chairman said the Executive Committee had received reports from outlying parishes which led to some doubt as to the ultimate fate of the proposed united celebration at Brentwood. The Secretary read letters disapproving of the proposal to hold united entertainments at Brentwood, from Bowers Gifford, Pitsea, Dunton, Nevendon, Laindon, Basildon, Billericay etc. It was stated that there was no enthusiasm for the proposal among the local Old Comrades' Associations.'

However in the end Billericay, and we assume the surrounding districts, decided to go it alone. They held a united service outside the parish church. This was followed by a decorated procession of farm vehicles with prizes valued at £1 and 10s. There were also prizes for the best turned out tradesman, smartest horse (not decorated), motor vehicle, cycles and farm vehicle driven by a lady, fancy dress competition for ladies, gentlemen and children and best decorated house on route.

There were the usual children's sports as well as bell ringing, a Fire Brigade demonstration and a celebratory cricket match – the country's national sport. The only difference was that it was a mixed ladies and gentleman's match. The day finished with a sing-song by comrades of the First World War followed by a bonfire built by the local Boy Scouts.

Whether Pitsea were involved or not is not known as the Pitsea Parish Council had decided to celebrate the declaration of peace with tea and sports for the school children but there is little real evidence of celebration in the Laindon/Pitsea districts.

Although it would appear from reports in the *Chelmsford Chronicle* that the County of Essex generally rose to the great occasion and rejoiced whole heartedly in marking the conclusion of the greatest war that has ever taken place in the world, it went on to state:

> 'This nation of ours can breathe again and if it sets itself to the task of peace in a constructive spirit all will go well with it. It is understood that Sir David Beatty and Sir Douglas Haig are to be made Earls and receive a grant of a £100,000 each. These grants will certainly not be in excess of the services which have made their names prominent in the great constellation of British heroes.'

Maybe, but we have to remember that there was hardly a family in the country that did not lose a loved one or have someone returning so badly affected by the war they were never the same again. Many returning soldiers were still looking for jobs and homes and probably did not feel like celebrating because they did not have anything to celebrate – they had been through an ugly war and all they had to come back to was poverty. The jobs and homes that were promised were not there, so these were our real heroes.

David Cameron, our current Prime Minister, reported that only fifty parishes in Britain were fortunate enough to have all the men who went to war returned unscathed.

Although the war was over and on the home front things were trying to get back to normal, the Middle East was still very unstable and many of our men did not come back home immediately as they were sent there to help stabilise the area. Percy Monk was one of them. How must he have felt in early 1919 as he boarded the Hospital Ship SS *Assaye* at Marseilles for Palestine. This is his continuing story:

> 'There were about twenty of us who had missed going back home owing to various causes, mine seemed to be because I

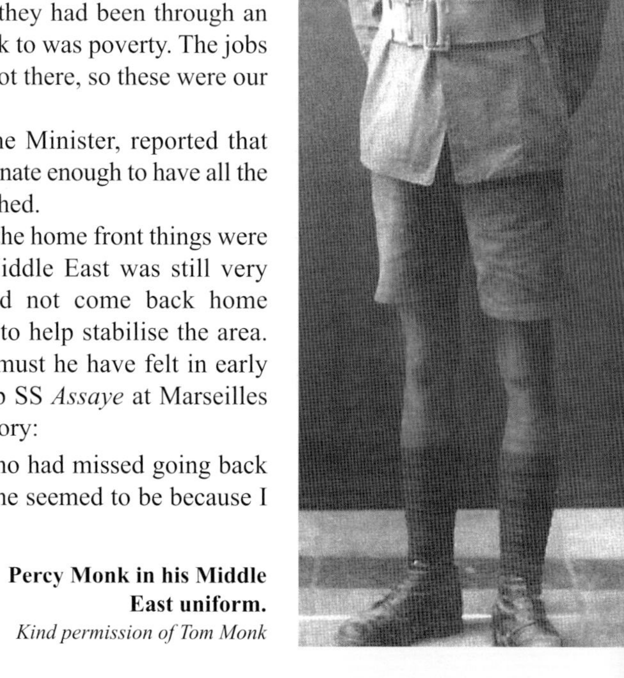

Percy Monk in his Middle East uniform.
Kind permission of Tom Monk

cut my arm badly with a broken knife and had two weeks in hospital. However, we had a smashing time on the ship – it turned out to be a real Mediterranean cruise. We had lovely quarters and plenty of food. Lazed and played deck games but we had to keep our quarters spick and span.

'One exciting time was when we went through the Straits of Messina. On one side was the town or city of Messina, the other side the volcano Stromboli towering up and belching smoke or steam from craters. A wonderful sight!

'At last our cruise came to an end when we docked at Alexandria, where we took the train to Kantara, a long but interesting journey. The line ran for miles alongside a river, whether this was the Nile or a tributary I do not know. At intervals there were small villages, mud huts covered with round slabs which turned out to be camel and cow dung made into rounds and stuck on the huts to dry out to be used as fuel. The women were doing the washing at the water's edge.

'At other places there were crude waterwheels worked by oxen going round and round, collecting water into a sort of bucket and tipping it into a dyke. This ran away into small channels which irrigated the cotton fields. The cotton wasn't out but we could see the green rows.

'We eventually arrived at Kantara, a vast camp and railway marshalling yard. Kantara is very near the Suez Canal. After settling in, our duties there were patrolling the marshalling yards, in pairs. The Egyptians and Bedouins were such a thieving lot and with half a chance would raid a train. We were ordered to shoot to kill, luckily that didn't happen to me.

'On one occasion I, with others, had the job of guarding a goods train from Kantara to Port Suez, eastern end of the Canal, a long journey. Half the train was open trucks, in which we travelled – it was baking hot. We could not touch the ironwork it was far too hot. Not very interesting country, only Ismalia seemed to be civilised, otherwise sand, sand, and more sand till it shimmered in the distance, save some salt lakes, sheets of water surrounded by salt. Return journey the same.

'We used to swim nearly daily in the Canal, it was very buoyant. The big ships passing through appeared huge, being so close. There were many hundreds of Egyptian Labour Corps working in the yards. They seemed to be very low intellect. They worked in gangs under an overseer who was usually a great big Nubian who carried a great whip and often used it. The "slaves" fought among themselves. I saw one hit another over the head with a pickaxe and nobody took any notice. The victim was just carted off. At knocking off time hundreds were herded together like cattle and were driven by their Nubian guard, cracking and slashing their whips, not a pleasant sight.

'Eventually we were moved onto Jerusalem. We crossed the Canal into Palestine. Kantara is in Egypt. We more or less followed the east coast of the Mediterranean to Ludd. Half this journey was what is now called the Gaza Strip. We turned inland at Ludd and headed for Jerusalem. This was a long, slow journey and very hot until we got to the Judean Hills. It was a military railway so there were no intermediate stops, only every so often for water. Eventually we arrived at Jerusalem and were taken to a rest camp to be sorted out. Since leaving

Marseilles I had been transferred to the Royal Sussex. There were two parts to Jerusalem, the old and the new, the old [part] being walled. We moved into some old Turkish barracks and soon settled into general duties and guarding. Our chief guard was St David's Gate or Jaffa Gate. This was a tiring job and very hot. We had a shade made out of a straw mat on a frame fixed to a pole which we could tip according to the sun. It was interesting to see the mixture of people and donkey trains loaded down with fruit and vegetables. No other traffic could enter as inside it was too narrow.

'Inside Jaffa Gate was St David's Hotel, HQ Eastern Command. NCOs and other ranks were not allowed in the old city on their own and only in company with a YMCA guide who arranged tours of the Holy City. The YMCA were a great boon and helped in lots of ways and were well patronised. I went on lots of tours, visiting many places mentioned in the New Testament. The only traffic in the Holy City was donkeys and pedestrians. It is so narrow, more like a tunnel with various offshoots of alleys where there were food shops. There were million of flies, they were a real menace.

'It sounds if all we did was sightseeing, not the case we had daily parades, fatigues and guard duties. Then out of the blue I had orders to report for duty with the 3rd Lahore (Indian) Division at a place called Bir Salem. Got the train to Ludd and then by road. By the way, roads in this part were wire netting over the sand about twelve feet wide, very effective until it broke. Bir Salem was just inside the Sinai Desert.

'On arrival I reported to HQ. I was taken to a tent on the outskirts and there I met A.G. Orr (Ago), J. Bishop (Bish) and E. Barnett (Barney). It appears that HQ had been through my records and discovered I was a clerk in civilian life so I had landed a clerical job in the demobilisation department along with Ago and Bish, a real cushy number. Barney was batman to a major who we referred to as a mad Irishman.

'Nothing very exciting here other than being pestered by jackals and occasionally hyenas – all scavengers. We could hear them at night sniffing around and cocking their legs on the tent. We used to bash the tent to scare them off. Also there were thousands of small lizards about four inches long, sand coloured with a red belly. Couldn't see them until they moved, little devils used to run over us during the night, you could feel them on the blanket. One day Bish found a chameleon, we had fun with it making it change colour but it eventually got away.

'The heat was very oppressive although very cold at night. There were very sharp electrical storms which seemed to rage for hours but not a drop of rain. I remember one sand storm, an almighty wind and at a distance a great spiral of sand. We hung for dear life on to the centre pole of the tent. It blew the tent over but not away, very frightening. After it passed the whole landscape had altered. Where there had been hills there were holes and vice versa. The desert is far from flat.

'Eventually, Barney was put on demob and went down to Kantara to be transferred to Alexandria to catch a boat. I followed about a month later and found

> him still there stuck in Kantara. He was going berserk. Within a week though, hundreds of us embarked on the SS *Czaritza*. It was not a pleasant trip, the weather was vile and conditions were cramped, poor old Barney was terribly seasick. We eventually passed Gibraltar and into the Bay of Biscay. Was it rough! Up and down, rolling at all angles. On occasions the propellers came out of the water and made a real screaming noise. I though Barney was going to die, so did he, poor old boy, wanted to, but he survived.
>
> 'The question on everyone's lips was where are we going to end up – London, Southampton, Plymouth but no, it was Liverpool. When we got ashore we were sorted into counties. In the meantime we were showered with eats and drinks by the locals. Eventually I caught a train, arriving at Purfleet where my final demob took place and I arrived home rather tired at Laindon on 31 December 1919.'

What a war Percy had, he had been in some of the fiercest fighting then sent off to the Middle East for nearly a year. His family must have wondered if he was ever coming home. He was awarded the Victory and British War medals. On 14 July 1923 he married Beatrice Alice Clarke at St Nicholas Church, Laindon. Beatrice also lived in the Railway Cottages, at number 7 and they had obviously known each other from childhood. Percy returned to work on the railway and when the railway cottages were compulsorily purchased in the 1970s they moved to Shelley Avenue, Langdon Hills. They were very well known in the community, both regular members of St Mary's Church where Percy was the bell ringer for many years.

What was happening in the area and the country while Percy was spending that further year away from home?

It would appear that every generation over the centuries has been infected by some form of deadly disease. Many come to mind immediately, the Old Testament stories, the Black Death of 1347/8, the Great Plague of 1664/66 and in more modern times the 'flu pandemic of 1918.

So there we were in the middle of an indescribably deadly war and the world gets hit by an unusually deadly influenza pandemic which was to become known as Spanish 'Flu. The war did not help the situation because it was impossible to isolate the disease. The close quarters and massive troop movements helped to transfer the influenza virus across the continents. Many soldiers died of the 'flu probably because their immune systems had been weakened by malnourishment as well as the stresses of combat and chemical attacks.

Wartime censorship tended to minimise early reports but with Spain being neutral there was no censorship and papers were free to report on the effects it was having there. This created a false impression of Spain being particularly hard hit which resulted in the nickname Spanish 'Flu.

The pandemic lasted for two years, January 1918 to December 1920 and it is believed to have infected around five hundred million people worldwide and killed between fifty and a hundred million. In London eighteen thousand people died of the 'flu and with London only twenty miles away from our area we wonder how many of the local people succumbed to it. Unfortunately we have not been able to locate any records that might reveal how many died, but living in the country with a low population unlike London where people lived close together in slum conditions, must have made a difference. It was poor conditions and their effect on health which caused so many in the years that followed to move to the countryside.

While the country was getting over initial peace celebrations and struggling with the 'flu epidemic the major concern was to get our prisoners back home. At the end of the war there were some 2,400,000 prisoners being held by Germany but British prisoners amounted to only approximately 200,000 and 25,000 Empire soldiers.

This report from the *Chelmsford Chronicle* two days after Christmas 1918 gives us an idea of the efforts being made to get our men back home.

> 'Returning Prisoners – The number of British prisoners actually repatriated, including those from Turkey, Bulgaria and Austria, amounts at present to about eighty thousand and there are nearly as many still in Germany but on their way home. A careful record of prisoners has been kept and all possible measures will be taken to trace any who may be found not to have returned home. The Inter-Departmental Committee on prisoners of war says that although railway communications are in a disordered state, many of the British prisoners are already safe in camps on the Rhine, while others are being sent to Copenhagen for ports in the Baltic. Large stores of food and medical supplies are available at Rotterdam and Copenhagen and there are depots at the chief Baltic ports. The German Government have been warned of their responsibility for the treatment of prisoners pending repatriation and it is reported that no British prisoners are now employed in any salt or coal mine. The number of French and other allied prisoners to be provided for is very great but it is hoped that all British prisoners in the enemy countries will be home in a few weeks.'

It turned out as hoped and all prisoners were back home within a few weeks but a number of Russian prisoners did not return home until 1922. There do not appear to be any complete records of British prisoners but one local man did return a few months before the end of the war.

The *Essex Newsman* on 22 June 1918 reported that Private W. Murray from Nevendon, who had been with the Royal West Kent Regiment, was returned home after nearly two years as a prisoner of war. He had been wounded and his left leg had to be amputated near the thigh.

At the end of the war there were approximately 116,000 German prisoners in Britain, comprising 94,428 military and 24,522 civilians most of whom were men.

Ivy Powell tells us that when going and coming home from school her mother told her not to speak to the men with patches on their clothes who were helping to clear the scrub land around Laindon Station on the Langdon Hills side. The presence of these Germans was confirmed by Percy and Beatrice Monk in their memories of the time. The question is where was their camp? It is understood that there was a German PoW camp in Nevendon Road, Nevendon opposite today's Fire Station.

Early in the war *The Daily Telegraph* reported that three bombs fell on the beach at Southend-on-Sea and one was picked up a short distance from a prison ship moored near the pier which was housing 1,200 interned German civilians.

The *Chelmsford Chronicle* on 8 February reported that the authorities agreed to house forty German prisoners along with ten to twelve guards in various buildings on the workhouse site in Billericay. These small groups were known as 'plough man's camps' as the prisoners were employed to work on the local farms.

One of the clauses of the Treaty of Versailles was very clear: prisoners were to be returned as soon as possible. As far as we can establish all German prisoners had been sent back home by mid 1919 and all internees released.

To help to explain what life was like for the returning soldiers and the civilian population in the years following the war it is sometimes easier to reflect on individual experiences.

Laindon Postman – One of our heroes was Edwin Andrews who ran the Laindon Post Office on the corner of Denbigh Road and Laindon High Road, known locally as Andrews Post Office. We wonder if he realised that one of his postmen for twenty-five years from 1927 to 1952, Henry Richard Devine was also a war hero.

Henry was born on 12 July 1892, Bethnal Green. In 1913 he married Jessica Clements and their first child Jessica was born in June 1914 and soon after the outbreak of war he volunteered for the Royal Fusiliers. Unfortunately his war records had succumbed to the bombing of the Second World War however, we know that he spent the next two years in the trenches where he got shot twice, patched up both times in hospital and sent straight back into the fray. A third bullet fractured his skull and this time he was invalided out, sent home with a metal plate in his head and suffering from severe shell shock.

On returning to civilian life he initially had no recollection that back home he had a two-year-old daughter. This was obviously very disconcerting for the family and if he was distracted by a noise such as catching a tram he would start shaking violently and uncontrollably, terrifying his young daughter. The family were informed that it might take up to ten years for shell shock traumas to subside.

His granddaughter, Nina Humphrey (nee Burton) takes up the family story which reveals what family life was like during this period and possibly why the family eventually moved to Laindon.

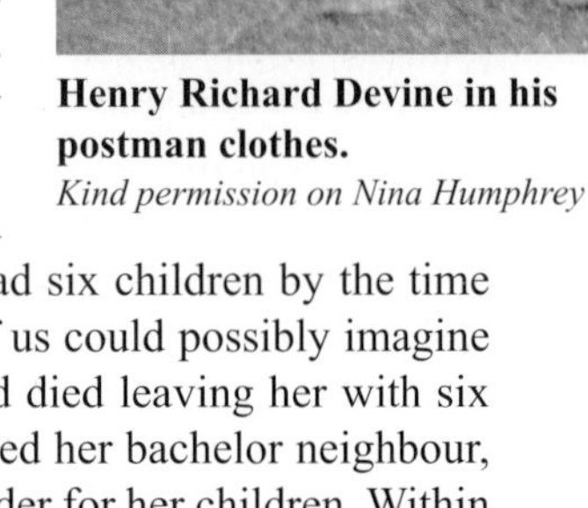

Henry Richard Devine in his postman clothes.
Kind permission on Nina Humphrey

'Henry was the first son of his mother Selina's second marriage. Selina Jane had married at eighteen and had six children by the time she was twenty-five. Times were harder than most of us could possibly imagine but 1891 was a horrid year for her. Her first husband died leaving her with six young children but within four months she had married her bachelor neighbour, Henry Devine senior, mainly I would guess as a provider for her children. Within two months she was pregnant with my grandfather. Before the end of the year, her youngest son, not yet a year old, died. My grandfather was born in July 1892 and named after his father. Selina went on to have another seven children, only three of whom survived. In fact of her fourteen children, five of them died at around six or seven months due mainly to poor nutrition after weaning.

'Selina and Henry sometimes used the surname "Gardner" instead of Devine. According to the programme *Who Do You Think You Are* using an alternative name was not unusual in those times, mainly due to not wanting to be traced due to debt.

'On Christmas Day 1911, when my grandfather was eighteen, his mother Selina, aged 47, took her own life by drinking household disinfectant. I have a copy of her death certificate which states 'suicide temporary insanity'. I will never agree with that, she was a sane woman living in poverty in intolerable conditions and had reached desperation point.

'On returning from the war Henry Richard Junior and Jessica had two further children. Richard Henry was born in 1917. Apparently Jessica had wanted him named after his father and grandfather but somehow my grandfather managed to get the names the wrong way round when registering him. When the second son was born in 1919 he was simply named 'Henry' without a second name, possibly to avoid a similar mistake. However, young Henry became known as "Harry".

'In 1923 the family eventually moved to Laindon to get away from the slums of Bethnal Green and some horrible memories. It must have felt like heaven, fresh air and green fields which made up for the lack of amenities. Initially he had little work and would often cycle many miles looking for a day's work. Eventually in 1928 he joined the Post Office attached to Andrews. His route, in addition to delivering around Laindon, included Langdon Hills as far as the West Ham TB Sanatorium off Dry Street, where the staff often gave him cucumbers and other fresh produce from their extensive greenhouses.

'In the meantime Jessica was able to grow vegetables in the garden and raise chickens, a dozen at a time which she would sell to friends and neighbours, especially at Christmas time. When the chickens were ready, she would prepare them herself and making them ready for the oven, by wringing their necks, cleaning and plucking them.

'Tragedy struck in 1928 when young Harry aged eight, contracted polio. He was taken ill at Dunton School with 'flu-like symptoms and my mother was told to take her little brother home. He was obviously very poorly and started to collapse, so she had to carry him 'fireman lift' style across the fields. The doctor was called but he didn't know the cause. An ambulance took Harry to an isolation hospital in Buttsbury Road, Billericay, where he died the following day. A diagnosis of polio was given and Harry was buried at St Nicholas Church on 10 May. Obviously the family were grief stricken.

'My mother married George Burton, also of Alexandra Road. Her brother Richard Devine went on to become a teacher at Markhams Chase School after spending four years in France as a prisoner of war in the Second World War. He was one of Ken's teachers and possibly the one who showed him how to hold a cricket bat properly.

'Family and friends who still lived in Bethnal Green and South Hackney loved to spend days and even their holidays with my grandparents in Laindon as it was such a hospitable place and in summer, always beautiful. I can remember happy summer days in their garden, laughing and singing with family members while shelling peas, each of them reluctant to leave Laindon and return to their homes and jobs in London at the end of their stay. They would be counting the days until their next visit. It certainly wasn't an easy life as times were still hard throughout the fifties but Laindon in those times had a charm of its own.

'Grandfather once told me that the husband of his older half-sister Selina survived the war but didn't return to her, leaving her without an income with a very young child to support. She needed to get a job but the only one available was 'swimming pool attendant' at the local pool (Bethnal Green I assume). At the interview she was required to show that she could swim one length of the swimming pool. Selina couldn't swim. She mustered all her courage and threw herself into the pool, throwing her arms out in front of her and kicking her legs while chanting "swim or starve, swim or starve" she somehow managed to reach the far end and haul herself out. She was given the job and spent the next few years at the pool working seven days a week to make ends meet as the small wage she received was her only income. There were no pensions or benefits in those days.

'After years of suffering from bronchitis probably caused by being exposed to gas attacks in the war Henry died at Colchester age 68 in January 1961 and is buried at Colchester. He had moved there a few years earlier because of ill heath and was struggling to cope with the unmade roads of Laindon.'

Researcher John Devine explains that during the unsuccessful search for Henry's war records, we found those of his younger brother, John. He in fact joined up in three consecutive years, the first occasion at the age of eighteen.

On 22 August 1914 he enlisted with the Special Reserves, King's Royal Rifle Corps at Shoreditch. He gave his next of kin as his father, Henry Richard Devine of 12 Moss Street, Bethnal Green and older brother Henry Richard Devine of the Royal Fusiliers (who by then was married with a one-month-old daughter). John, who was described as 5ft 2ins tall, 126lbs with a 34in chest, was discharged as unfit on 24 November 1914 due to deafness.

On 23 March 1915, John, now 'a driver' aged nineteen, enlisted again in London, for Short Service with the Royal Regiment of Artillery. He was discharged on 22 July 1915 as 'not likely to become an efficient soldier' due to deafness.

On 22 January 1916 John now 'a carman' aged twenty, enlisted at Finsbury Barracks with the Royal Dublin Fusiliers. Posted to Cork on 29th January, he eventually attended hospital where he was found to be deaf in both ears with occasional episodes of vertigo. He was discharged on 17 April 1916.

This shows not only John's enthusiasm to join the army right from the start, but the fact that the army didn't immediately detect his health problem. It took up to four months to diagnose his deafness each time. John's persistence in trying to gain acceptance as a soldier proves he was a hero in his own right.

Newman, Edith Rose – Mrs Edith Rose Newman, who moved with her family to Laindon just after the war, gave her memories of those early years to the Basildon Heritage Group in 1985:

'We lived in East London and my father had bought a small sweet shop but at the age of thirty-six he was called up for the army. We stayed working the shop during the war while he was away but in the meantime we got to know a neighbour who owned two or three plots of land in Laindon with a rough shed on one of them, in fact you would call it a little shack. Everything in this little shack was home made, the rugs, the blankets were all home made. Everything was made and taken down to this little place and you know it was heaven. Laindon was such a country place it was just like heaven you could hear the birds singing – not a sound of anything and it was beautiful. He invited us down there for the several weekends and we thoroughly enjoyed it.

'My mother absolutely adored it and she said how lovely to be able to live down here away from the bustle of London. So after the war Father sold the business and bought some land next to the little chapel in Wash Road and that little chapel is still there today, built in 1905. We used to get the steam train from Barking to come down to Laindon which was a tiny station with oil lamps. We'd walk along the old muddy track all the way there 'cos you never had any conveyance. There used to be a woman called Daisy Russell, an old lady and she had a pony and trap. Now if Daisy Russell was anywhere near the station and anyone had come off the train and they wanted a lift she would give you one. Otherwise it meant just Shanks's Pony, walking, and I might tell you for a Londoner that was a dickens of a long walk from Laindon Station right down the Wash but we loved it.

'All the hedges used to grow over the path and the smell of the may was terrific and in the fields there were all these dog-daisies and cuckoo flowers, marguerites everything you do not see today; cornflowers and poppies you don't see either but it was like a little bit of heaven. We used to bring a child's pram to carry our coal in, so that in the evenings when it got cold we could light a little bit of fire. Mainly the fires consisted of chopping the hedgerows and collecting bits of twigs that used to lie around – the fire had a beautiful smell. It was the children's job to collect the twigs and we loved doing it.

'My father, Bert, built his first bungalow in wood next to the chapel. It had two rooms and we got it looking lovely and really nice and we were looking forward to coming down to live in it but unfortunately the Council said it was too near the chapel and being in wood we had to demolish it. Father was not happy but complied and being of determined mind, built a two-room brick bungalow at the back of the garden. He dug a deep well, a filter so that we could have drinking water. We had no gas or electricity only oil lamps and oil stoves to cook on and the oven to the fire place when you had a fire. No bathroom, you just brought the tub in from the garden and everybody had to clear out the living room while you had a bath. It was quite a performance to live there but we all loved it, really loved it.'

The Wash in Wash Road, Laindon, tributary of the River Crouch. *Ken Porter's Collection*

There is no doubt that Edith loved Laindon. She got married in 1927 at the age of twenty-two at St Nicholas Church, Laindon and her husband, Percy, was the local blacksmith in Dunton Road.

What Edith's recollections show is that in the first decade after the end of the war very little changed other than more people were moving out of the cities to enjoy the healthy country life.

The population in the area just before the beginning of the war was approximately 3,000. By 1921 it had risen to approximately 6,000 and by 1931 to 18,500. The villages of Laindon and Pitsea, west and east of the area in question, were slowly becoming small towns, where you could shop for anything.

Soldiers returning home had gained an independence of mind and wanted to control their own lives and people were expecting a fairer and better Britain 'a land fit for heroes'. Our area was ripe for another wave of pioneers wanting to own their own homes and have a better life. If they were not initially moving to the area permanently they were certainly spending weekends and holidays here. The next twenty years was the period when we see the greatest growth in the plotland type of development that had started back in the early 1890s. You could call it the 'Golden Years of Plotlands'.

Plotlanders

From London to Dunton they came, a trickle then a rush
Seeking respite from overcrowded, noisy, smoky city crush.
They came to stake their claim to farms gone to seed.
Times were hard, soil poor and there were mouths to feed.

So whole families wanting a weekend retreat or holiday home
Came to the countryside where it was clean and free to roam.

The available land was divided into small lots
And for only Ten Pounds you could buy two plots.

The Land Company hoped to make a killing
Using techniques worthy of time-sharing billing.
Many were caught, believing their tales,
Carried away in the 'Champagne Sales'.
Some maybe went beyond their means
To finally own the plot of their dreams.

Travelling from London at the weekend,
Tools in hand and chores to attend.
The land having none of the normal utilities
They had confidence in their normal abilities.

Desirable plots were near Laindon Station
But dwellings sprang up in every location
Tents, shacks, if they kept out of the rain,
Even the carriages of an old railway train,
Proper huts and chalets later would come
And for many these were 'home from home'.

In the 50s Londoners descended again
On Basildon. Coming by car, bus or train
To new homes being built in a new town
On land that the 'Plotlanders' used to own.
These former residents selling out one by one
Brought an end to an era whose time was gone.

Andrew Summers

This independence of mind was further encouraged by the Representation of the Peoples Act 1918 which gave the vote to every man over the age of twenty-one and to women in certain circumstances over the age of thirty. This increased the voting population from just under eight per cent to over twenty-one per cent and changed the political scene. Prior to the war Liberal and Conservatives were the main political parties but the election of 1918 changed all this. The Liberals started to lose their way and a new Labour party came to the fore, although Lloyd George leader of the Liberal Coalition became Prime Minister. The election of 1924 saw the country's first Labour Prime Minister, Ramsey McDonald.

There was an increase in strikes in the early years of the 1920s followed by the Great Depression of the early 1930s. By the 1940s, Laindon and Langdon Hills alone had well over a hundred shops stretching along its main road. Pitsea and Vange were also seeing a similar increase in activity. Basildon, Bowers Gifford, North Benfleet, Nevendon, Dunton, Lee Chapel also experienced a large increase in new residents but relied on the towns of Laindon and Pitsea for shopping.

A new main road from London to Southend, running through the centre of Laindon and the Basildon area, was officially opened in 1925 by Prince Henry and by the mid 1930s it had been widened into a dual carriageway. It was built to help relieve some of the unemployment problems created by the depression and also helped to encourage more people to move to the area.

One of the noticeable changes was that women emerged from the war with more confidence in their own abilities and wanted to play a greater role in determining their lives and socialising with men on equal terms.

The change in the farming environment was continuing, mechanisation was slowly beginning to have an effect, sheep were around but disappearing as more and more farms were moving over to dairy cattle.

By the end of the 1930s Laindon and Pitsea were well established towns rivalling those of Billericay and Wickford and the majority of people were relaxed, friendly and enjoying life. There was a tremendous community spirit but the Second World War was going to dramatically change all that.

Tucked away in the Basildon Heritage archive is someone's memory of Laindon from 1916 to 1928.

> 'My family moved to Laindon in 1916. I was thirteen years of age and the war was by now becoming truly frightening. I had two brothers in the Navy and my father was in the army. Soldiers were being drafted into private homes in Laindon. Mother still had three children at home so we were not required to house any soldiers. However we soon became friendly with some of them. All the ones I knew had been wounded and were therefore convalescing. They were all gentlemen.
>
> 'It was an exciting time for us young ones. Mrs Fothergill was our headmistress (Langdon Hills School). She managed the school and taught the Top Class herself. All the men teachers were in the forces. I remember the hole in the school roof where shrapnel had fallen through one night.
>
> 'We were asked to dig up some of the playground to grow vegetables. That was jolly, because the boys were allowed to come into the girls' playground to help with the digging. We grew some really large cabbages. We were also allowed some days off from school to go blackberry picking. The teachers came with us – to our amusement one teacher, Mrs Hill, always picked the low down ones.
>
> 'I never forgot the night when the Zeppelin was brought down. It caught fire right over Laindon, drifting away with flames soaring into the sky; it came down to earth at Great Burstead. Early next morning we rode our bicycles over to the scene but the site was being guarded by a regiment of Irish Guards with fixed bayonets. We were therefore prevented from getting close to the wreckage. However we could see the bodies of the German crew covered with sheeting being taken into nearby farm buildings. There were twenty-one men and the captain (Peterson). They were buried in Great Burstead churchyard in one grave with the captain in a separate grave.
>
> 'So many people tried hard to make life bearable in those difficult times. Our Rector, Reverend Carpenter (St Nicholas Church, Laindon) had a good girls' choir (the first in the country), and was himself an excellent bass singer. His choir was

augmented by Dorothy and Lynette, two girls sent by the Land Army to work for John Markham at Bluehouse farm. Our organist was Sergeant Fletcher who was stationed at Basildon with a gun crew. Sometimes the girls from the Langdon Hills choir came to join the St Nicholas choir. Services on Sunday were a musical joy.

'The 'Mud' has to be mentioned. At the end of the war the main road was in a dreadful state, mud almost up to the kerb – the pathway was treated with sand. The side roads were just tracks of mud. Everyone had Wellingtons to get to the station. Galoshes were usually lost in the mud.

'In Langdon Hills there was much musical talent – we had Professor Le Brun, a very familiar figure going to the station each morning in his Inverness cape and carrying his gold headed umbrella and briefcase. There was Madame Edith Spencer and her husband who sang tenor solos with a good finish. Madame also formed the Laindon Ladies Glee Party to which many of us belonged. We sang our glees and madrigals remarkably well. Mr Green and his daughter Rosie were responsible for The Crescent Singers later augmented by Harold Curtis and his Orchestra. Mr Lammin was responsible for the "Kum and See Us" concert party, a very spirited and go ahead group who never kept their audience waiting.

'Important dances were held in the school hall. These dances were often augmented towards the end by folk from whist drive sessions taking place in an adjoining classroom. A little dance was held every week in the Institute (Women's Institute hall in Samuel Road, Langdon Hills – The Hut) for which we had to pay 4d. The school hall affairs had a violin and piano but the institute dances only a piano.

'Our doctor was an unusual Irishman who had a charming wife and a family of young children. He possessed a car, a Trojan and later a Singer. Both were always in a dilapidated condition, with broken trailing hoods, often breaking down and needing assistance.

'Our first district nurse was introduced I believe in the early 1920s to everybody's pleasure. The train service seemed very adequate and the return fare to Southend was less than 2d. Tickets were obtained from Percy Monk who was in the ticket office for many years. There was also a Finlays Tobacco Kiosk on the platform.

'The house "Hiawatha" was a landmark at the corner of St. Nicholas Lane and

'Hiawatha' on the corner of St Nicholas Lane and the High Road – 1920s. *Ken Porter's Collection*

> the High Road. It had a good weathercock until a storm dismantled it. The hotel was the most imposing building in the High Road. After the war we acquired the Memorial Hall and the British Legion Hall as places of entertainment. The field adjoining the hotel was used by the pupils of Langdon Hills School for their football matches, there being no field for such activity nearer the school.
>
> By 1928 the population had increased considerably and Langdon Hills School became very overcrowded. The new senior school in the High Road, Laindon had to take the overflow from the school until a new infants and junior school was built in Markhams Chase.'

Although by the end of the war Laindon and Pitsea had developed into small towns there was a tremendous growth in the next twenty years,. There was a mixture of planned housing and plotland type development either for permanent occupation or as holiday homes. Both areas and the surrounding areas became recognised as a holiday resort.

There was, however, still a lot of hardship and heartache about but somehow people found ways to enjoy themselves. They were going to show the same resolve during and after the Second World War until one battle descended on them in 1949 that they could not defeat - The New Towns Act. Basildon was to become one of eight new towns to help house those unfortunate people who had lost their homes during the Second World War. For those who lived in the Laindon to Pitsea area it was to destroy their environment and their way of life forever.

Chapter 9

Remembering the War

PLANS FOR COMMEMORATING the victims of the First World War commenced as early as 1915. Agreements were signed with both France and Belgium for the granting of land 'in perpetuity' for British Empire war graves and cemeteries. The Imperial War Graves Commission, later the Commonwealth War Graves Commission, was created by Royal Charter on 21 May 1917.

Britain's allies, France and Belgium led the way on the continent in establishing national memorials:

Menin Gate at Ypres in Belguim – 1927
La Ferté-sous-Jouarre in France – 1928
Ossuary of Douaumont in France – 1932
Vimy Ridge – constructed by the Canadians
Tannenberg Memorial – constructed for the Germans – 1927

It was however, not until the inter-war period that official commemorative war memorials started to appear in the various villages, towns and cities around Britain. The same was happening on the continent. The King of Belgium remarked in 1931 that the unveiling of war memorials was the only job left for his profession.

In Britain permanent national memorials to the war dead such as the Cenotaph in Whitehall and the Tomb of the Unknown Soldier in Westminster Abbey were in place by 1920. The Imperial War Museum was formally opened in 1920 and the organisation The British Legion was established in 1921.

Menin Gate, Ypres.
Ken Porter's Collection

Dead Man's Penny

Although it was in October 1916 that the government came up with the idea of a 'Next of Kin Memorial Plaque and Scroll' it was not going to be until after the war ended that the next of kin received them.

A competition was held and there were more than 800 entries from within the United Kingdom, from countries in the British Empire and from all the theatres of war. The results of the competition were announced in *The Times* on the day the German Army launched a massive surprise attack on several miles of the British front on the Somme battlefield, so by the end of the day there were another several thousand names added to the list.

The winning design was by Edward Carter Preston. The design incorporated the figure of Britannia facing to the left and holding a laurel wreath in her left hand, over the box where the commemorated serviceman's name was to be placed. In her right hand she is holding a trident. Representing Britain's sea power are two dolphins facing Britannia on either side. By Britannia's feet, facing left is a lion with a menacing growl and beneath him a smaller lion facing right biting the winged creature representing the German Imperial eagle. Around the outside are the words 'He Died for Freedom and Honour' and for women casualties, 'She Died for Freedom and Honour'.

The scroll that accompanied it read:

> 'He whom this scroll commemorates was numbered among those who at the call of King and Country, left all that was dear to them, endured hardness, faced danger and finally passed out of the sight of men by the path of duty and self-sacrifice, giving up their own lives that others might live in freedom. Let those who come after see to it that his name be not forgotten.'

The covering letter that was sent with them read: 'I join with my grateful people in sending you this memorial of a brave life given for others in the Great War,' signed by George V.

The relative named as next of kin in the serviceman's service record was sent a form to complete. In all, from 1919 and for several years afterwards over one million plaques and scrolls were sent out, including around 600 for women, who died between 4 August 1915 and 30 April 1919 whilst in military service and those who died as a result of sickness, suicide, accidents or wounds in home establishments.

However, the next of kin of the 306 British and Commonwealth military

Dead Man's Penny – William Charles Mott.
Kind permission of Edna Baldes (nee Mott)

personnel who were executed following a court martial did not receive a plaque. The plaques became widely known as 'Dead Man's Penny', 'Death Penny', 'Death Plaque' or 'Widow's Penny'.

The photograph is of the plaque commemorating William Charles Henry Mott, uncle to Edna Baldes (nee Mott), and is still in the family's possession. Edna's father, Edward James Mott, also enlisted in the King's Royal Rifle Corps. Unfortunately we have not been able to trace William or Edward's war records. Edna and her father moved to Dunton at the beginning of the Second World War.

The family still have the original letter that William sent to his brother in 1915 more or less telling him not to sign up but look after his mother – 'The war is not what you think it is'. William was killed a few months later.

Also written on a piece of paper in the family archive is a song the soldiers of the King's Royal Rifle regiment used to sing as they marched to war.

It's here where Tommy once stood
In a place just outside Swanson's wood
Though Jerry's bin shelling all day
His wiz bangs all sent to say:

Chorus

This war will soon be over
It's now all over France
It cannot last for ever
So I think we stand a chance
The Kaiser he will regret it
He's lot to answer for
But all we hope
They'll hand him to
The King's Royal Rifle Corps.'

The District War Memorials

Laindon

The Remembrance Day service in Laindon, unlike others, is held at 3pm. This dates back to the first ever memorial service, a tradition believed to have started because when the war memorial was unveiled on the 19 September 1935 the vicar of Laindon cum Basildon, the Reverend Lake could not officiate until the afternoon because he had a morning service. The following is the *Laindon Recorder*'s report on its unveiling:

'On Saturday the memorial to those who fell in the Great War was unveiled. It is a simple column of blue pearl Aberdeen granite, surmounted by a cross of the same stone and stands outside the hall of the

Laindon War Memorial outside Laindon Shopping centre.
Ken Porter's Collection

British Legion in the High Road. It is the gift of Mr A.E. Symes, of Brentwood and Stratford. Twenty branches of the British Legion from different parts of Essex were represented at the unveiling, each with its standard. The ceremony was to have been performed by Mrs Symes but she was called away to a daughter who had been taken ill and Mrs J. McLachlan, another daughter, took her place.

'The gathering sang "O God, our Help in Ages Past", and there was a Scripture reading by Mr J. Tourie. Mrs Mclachan, releasing the Union flag that veiled the column, said: "To the memory of the Glorious Dead I unveil this memorial." All the standard bearers dipped their flags until after the dedication by the Rector of Laindon (the Reverend M.N. Lake) chaplain to the branch. Prayers were offered by the Reverend T.W. Shepherd, of the Langdon Hills Baptist Church and "The Supreme Sacrifice" was sung.

'Buglers from Warley Barracks sounded the "Last Post" and after two minutes' silence, the "Reveille". Captain F. Cornish said although some people might remark upon the memorial being unveiled at such a late hour, he, personally, could think of no more fitting or opportune moment. The memorial did not belong to the Legion but to everybody in the district. Mrs McLachlan laid a wreath on the memorial and there were wreaths from the women's section and a number of private ones. Visitors were entertained to tea by the branch and at night the memorial was floodlit.'

The memorial is inscribed as commemorating the two world wars: 'TO THE GLORIOUS DEAD 1914 – 1918 LAINDON AND DISTRICT 1939 – 1945. AT THE GOING DOWN OF THE SUN, AND IN THE MORNING, WE WILL REMEMBER THEM.' It is non-denominational and there are no individual names inscribed.

Although the war memorial does not list the names of those who died in the district, St Nicholas Church, Laindon and St Mary's Langdon Hills have tablet memorials in their churches and the Baptist church has engraved stones in their external walls in remembrance of some of the fallen.

Laindon War Memorial originally stood in a prominent position in front of the British Legion Hall facing the High Road. The hall itself was built in the early 1920s and stood next to Laindon High Road School until it was sold and finally demolished in 1975. The memorial then languished in a store house near Pitsea tip until it was rescued and relocated to its current position in front of the Laindon shopping centre. With the pending redevelopment of the

Garden of Roses, Laindon – 1930s.
Ken Porter's Collection

shopping centre it will be once more be relocated, hopefully in a more permanent position.

For many years this was not the only memorial in Laindon in remembrance of those who died in the Great War. A 'Garden of Roses' was laid out just after the war in memory of the local men who gave their lives. The garden was triangular in shape with a wall of white painted clinkered brick and chain linked black timber posts. It was on the junction of St Nicholas Lane and Basildon Drive.

In the early years it was the responsibility of the local roadman, a Mr Pratt who lived in Green Lane, now Markhams Chase, to maintain the garden. Unfortunately during the Second World War the chains from around the garden were taken, as were all metal fences and posts in the area, to be used in the war effort. From that day on it gradually deteriorated and eventually disappeared under the road.

A Memorial Hall was also built in Laindon by voluntary labour. It stood more or less where the Laindon Community Centre is today until it was demolished in 1967. This building nearly became the village cinema but the plans fell through and the following year in 1929 Mr L. Silverman had the Laindon Picture House built, later best known as the Radion or 'the flea pit' to the locals. During the Second World War the hall doubled up as a British Restaurant.

During that war and for many years afterwards the Radion Cinema in the High Road was used for the Remembrance Day service. Representatives from the British Legion, Home Guard, ATC, ARP, Youth Training organisation, St Nicholas Church Lads' Brigade, members of the Urban District Council and many other local bodies, attended, often marching along the High Road to the service, where the Manor Mission Band, on many occasions, accompanied the singing of hymns.

Prior to the Second War and the building of the cinema, the Remembrance Day service was held at St Nicholas Church following a parade that started at the Laindon Hotel past the British Legion Hall to the church. It was normally led by the Manor Mission Band. Wreaths and flowers were placed before the altar. Afterwards the procession re-formed and marched back to the Laindon Hotel.

The cinema, British Legion Hall, and Laindon Hotel are no longer. The ATC, ARP, Home Guard, Church Lads' Brigade also no longer exist so the Remembrance Day service at 3pm is held in front of the memorial.

Pitsea

The Pitsea War Memorial is one of the most impressive in the form of a Greek maiden representing life, holding a torch of truth in her right hand high above her head and an olive branch in her left hand. At night the torch would illuminate.

At a meeting on 23 August the Pitsea Parish council had discussed the possibility of a monument in memory of the men of Pitsea and Bowers Gifford who had lost their lives. There were several suggestions on what form the memorial should take, in particular from Harold George Howard, a local prominent farmer and business man who owned Howard's Dairy with 1,000 employees and lived at Bluehouse Farm, Pitsea.

The unveiling ceremony and dedication service took place on Sunday 18 November 1928 and was performed by guest of honour Sir Ernest Beachcroft Towse VC KCVO CBE and the Rector of Pitsea, the Reverend Ernest William Grevatt, the Reverend

Joseph Brightman and Mr H. Stevens.

It was originally sited on its own island in the centre of Station Lane at its junction with the High Road. In 1969 due to various road realignments in the Pitsea area it was moved to its present position in Howard Park. The memorial commemorates both world wars:

'TO THE GLORIOUS MEMORY OF THE MEN OF PITSEA AND BOWERS GIFFORD WHO FELL IN THE GREAT WAR 1914 – 1918.

'AT THE GOING DOWN OF THE SUN AND IN THE MORNING WE WILL REMEMBER THEM.

'THEIR NAME LIVETH FOR EVERMORE.

'IN REMEMBRANCE OF LOCAL COMRADES WHO FELL IN THE 1939 – 45 CONFLICT.'

Pitsea War Memorial. *Basildon Heritage collection*

In 1925 Harold Howard had a vision of recreating the town of Pitsea on a Tudor Theme. Pitsea Railway Hotel was built on land he sold to the brewery and this was followed by the Broadway Shops and cinema opposite and then the building on the same side as the inn which is now Lloyds Bank. The Second World War and the coming of Basildon Corporation spoilt his plans. The Railway Hotel has just been demolished to make way for the regeneration of Pitsea (May 2013).

Harold died in 1961 and is buried at St. Margaret's Church, Bowers Gifford; his wife Rose died ten years later.

Vange

At a meeting held on 14 November 1919 it was reported that the Vange War Memorial Fund had raised £105.8s by voluntary subscriptions. Previously the Metropolitan Drinking Fountain Association had agreed to bear the cost of the trough and fountain. The meeting agreed that the tribute to the twenty men who had fallen should take the form of a wayside cross of Cornish granite. The cross was eventually erected on the side of the road along Paynters Hill, Vange. Next to it was a horse trough, the one that fell off the barge and seriously injured Edward Baker (see Our Heroes).

It was also agreed to have a bronze tablet on an oak mount placed in All Saint's Church.

The memorial engraving on the base of the cross read:

'TO THE HONOURED MEMORY OF THE MEN OF THIS PARISH WHO FELL IN THE GREAT WAR 1914-1919'

This is followed by twenty-one names of those of the parish who had lost their lives. We have since established that thirty-five lost their lives.

'THEIR NAME LIVETH FOR EVERMORE'

A further engraving on the plinth reads:

'IN MEMORY OF ALL THOSE WHO HAVE FALLEN IN THE SERVICE OF THEIR COUNTRY'

Vange area saw a considerable amount of development in the years following the Second World War. This resulted in various roads being realigned and because of this the Memorial Cross was relocated in the early 1960s and now stands in front of St Chads, Clay Hill Road, minus the horse trough.

Vange War Memorial outside St Chads, Vange. *Ken Porter's Collection*

Nevendon

There is no memorial in Nevendon in regard to the First World War however in the Church of St Peter's on a choir stall is the carved inscription 'In memory of Lt. T.A Turner RFA Churchwarden of Nevendon killed in action April 29 1917'.

Turner, Thomas Alfred - Thomas was born on 18 August 1878 and enlisted into the Royal Horse Artillery, D Battalion, 50 Brigade, service number 152166, on 18 September 1914. At the time of his enlistment he had been living with his wife at Summerhill Cottages, Basildon. His parents were living at Milestone Cottage, Wickford. He was commissioned lieutenant in the Royal Field Artillery on 16 August 1915.

He was a lay preacher and churchwarden at St Peter's Church, Nevendon. In Appendix 7 is a letter dated 4 February 1916 he sent to Reverend A.W. Hands for inclusion in the parish magazine barely a month after he left England. It gives a fascinating insight into what trench life was like. The fact that he had only been at the front for about a month is probably why he sounds so buoyant and we wonder what he would have written a year later just a few months before he was killed.

Working on the date of his death, 29 April 1917, it would appear that he was involved

Memorial to Lieutenant A. Turner on the choir stall in St Peter's Church, Nevendon.
Kind permission of the Rector of St Peters.

in the Battle of Arleux, part of the Arras offensive (9 April to 16 May 1916). The objective was to secure the south-eastern flank of Vimy Ridge that the Canadian Corps had taken a few days earlier. The attack started on 28 April and the Canadians managed to capture the village of Arleux but the British found stiffer resistance in trying to take Gavrelle. The British managed to capture the village early in the evening but the German counter-attack pushed the British back before reinforcements helped them to secure the village. Subsequent attacks by the Germans on 29 April were repulsed but it appears that in one of these attacks Thomas was killed.

He was awarded the 1914 Star, Victory and British War medals and is buried at Sainte Catherine British Cemetery, France.

Wickford

After the end of the war Wickford lost no time in planning for a memorial to commemorate their dead. A meeting was held on 13 February 1919 where various suggestions were put forward – a water fountain, meeting centre for young men, a plaque at the church or an institute of some kind. It was eventually decided to purchase a piece of land to build a Nurses' Home to provide local care to the population, where a district nurse could live for free. For various reason this proposal to build a home did not

Wickford War Memorial Nurses' Home. *Basildon Heritage collction*

materialise and instead a cottage named 'Emscott' on Church Hills, Southend Road was purchased for the same purpose.

A memorial plaque with names of the fallen was affixed to the building and a grand opening took place on Thursday, 19 July 1922 with the unveiling of the tablets by Lord Lambourne, the Lord Lieutenant of Essex, in an emotional service attended by many of those who had served and many of the families who had lost someone.

The building was now ready as a 'loving memorial' and outside was a flag pole with large letters stating 'Wickford War Memorial Nursing Home'. The Nurses' Home became the central location for Wickford Remembrance Day Parades, where the parade would lay wreaths in the porch under the tablets with the names of those lost.

In the 1970s the home was demolished to make way for a bypass, the tablets were relocated to the Second World War Memorial Park off Runwell Road. Due to vandalism and deterioration the War Memorial aspect of the Memorial Park has been going through various stages of refurbishment since 2004 which are now nearing completion.

The following parish churches have memorial plaques: All Saints, Vange; Holy Cross, Basildon; St Mary's, Langdon Hills; St Nicholas, Laindon; All Saints, North Benfleet and, in St Peters, Nevendon, there are individual commemoration plaques on the backs of furniture. Unfortunately these plaques do not include all the names of those who died, the problem being there was no accurate recording of names of those who had died and should have been included. There were many reasons for this; some families would have moved away and were no longer in touch, other soldiers might have grown up in their various parishes but moved away before enlisting. Some families were illiterate and had no idea they needed to subscribe the name of their loved ones, others even refused to accept their missing were actually dead. Lastly there were those who simply had no family to subscribe them and were thus forgotten.

This situation is slowly being corrected. Steve Newman in 2007 produced the book *Wickford's Heroes* where he has listed all those with a connection to Wickford and Runwell who lost their lives.

On the first page is a poem that appeared in the Wickford and Runwell, welcome home dinner programme, 28 October 1919.

'Our fallen Comrades, we miss you all,
Your courage has not been in vain.
'twas God's wish that you answered this call;
Oh! could we but see you again,
The greatest of honours to you we would give;
But, alas! you died that England may live.'

Karen Dennis has also produced a similar book covering the Billericay and surrounding district. *A Book of Remembrance Billericay & District.*

A roll of honour for the rest of the Basildon borough is being produced by Basildon Heritage in loose leaf binder format. Hopefully those that lost their lives in the First World War and had a connection to the Basildon Borough will be recorded and therefore remembered forever.

British Legion

Lance Bombardier Tom Lister was concerned that the government was not doing enough to improve the lives of ex-service men who had fought so gallantly and for the wives, children, widows and orphans as well as the parents who had lost sons in the war, on whom they were often financially dependent. He decided to do something about it and this resulted in the British Legion being formed on 15 May 1921. It brought together four national organisations of ex-service men that had been established just after the war.

The legion was granted Royal status in 1971 and extended its membership to serving members of the armed forces and men and women whether they served in the armed forces or not.

Basildon borough has four branches – Laindon and Basildon, Pitsea and Vange, Wickford and Billericay.

Remembrance Day

Finally every year on 11 November at 11am the people of all Commonwealth countries commemorate members of the armed forces who died in the line of duty and a two minute silence is observed. There are a few exceptions and Laindon, as explained, is one which holds the commemoration service on Remembrance Sunday (nearest Sunday to the 11th) at 3pm.

To many it also known as Armistice Day or Poppy Day. The red poppy has become the familiar emblem of remembrance due to the poem 'In Flanders Fields' by Lieutenant Colonel John McCrae.

In Flanders fields the poppies blow
Between the crosses, row on row,
That mark our place and in the sky
The larks, still bravely singing, fly
Scarce heard amid the guns below.
We are Dead, short days ago
We lived, felt dawn, saw sunset glow,
Loved and were loved and now we lie
In Flanders Fields.

Take up our quarrel with the foe
To you from failing hands we throw
The torch; be yours to hold it high.
If ye break faith with us who die
We shall not sleep, though poppies grow
In Flanders fields.

The first Remembrance Day was held in the grounds of Buckingham Palace on the morning of 11 November 1919.

The First World War has almost deserted living memory so why has it stayed firmly in the modern mind? The Second World War is rightly prominent too but it still has thousands of surviving veterans to remind us. The Boer wars that ended in 1902 have virtually been forgotten. Part of the reason must be because of the sheer scale of the slaughter and as we come up to the 100th anniversary of the beginning of the war, the need to remember gets stronger and stronger. More than 300,000 people each year still visit the battlefields of Northern France and many more visit the Menin Gate at Ypres at 8pm every evening and experience the buglers playing the 'Last Post' which has been played uninterrupted since 2 July 1918, except during the Second World War when the country was occupied by Germany (see appendix 8).

The First World War marked the beginning of the modern age, its shock waves are still being felt today in our political and social structures and our economy and technology.

Finally the 'Ode of Remembrance' taken from Laurence Binyon's poem, 'For the Fallen'.

They shall grow not old, as we that are left grow old;
Age shall not weary them, nor the years condemn.
At the going down of sun and in the morning
We will remember them.

Appendices

Appendix 1

Wootton Farm, Dry Street, Langdon Hills was purchased by West Ham Council in 1911 with the intention of converting it into an isolation hospital for smallpox. Local opposition and the pending war put pay to this idea. After the war the council built around the farmhouse a purpose built sanatorium for children suffering from tuberculosis. It was opened on 26 October 1927. When the National Health Service was introduced they took over the site and had the buildings converted for male patients. It eventually closed in December 1957. It was sold and became a privately run dog kennels, a service it still provides today.

Appendix 2

Ted's great grandson, John, is a geo-cacher, a form of treasure hunting, whereby you navigate to a specific set of GPS co-ordinates and then attempt to find the geocache (container) hidden on the location. (See www.geocaching.com) John has developed a tour round the Pitsea Explosive factory site named 'The Devil's Porridge'.

Appendix 3

Stow Maries, Essex First World War Aerodrome was a front line home defence airfield and the home of the 37 (Home Defence) Squadron, Royal Flying Corps. Restoration of the site has been going on since 2009 and it is well worth a visit. www.stowmaries.com

Appendix 4

Second (2) Corporal was a rank in the Royal Engineers and Army Ordnance Corps. They wore one rank chevron but unlike Lance Corporals they held full non-commissioned officer rank. They were the equivalent to Bombardiers in the Royal Artillery. The rank was abolished in 1920.

Appendix 5

The statue of the Virgin Mary and Infant Jesus which had been designed by sculptor Albert Roze and dubbed the 'Golden Virgin', was situated on top of the Basilica of Notre Dame de Brebières. It was damaged by a British shell on 15 January 1915, falling horizontally to one side; there it stayed until further shelling by the British in April 1918 destroyed the tower. The statue was never located.

It had become a familiar sight to the thousands of British soldiers who fought at the battle of the Somme in 1916. The Germans said whoever made the statue fall would lose the war – they got that wrong.

The village of Albert and the basilica were completely reconstructed after the war, with a replica of the statue.

Appendix 6

Warrior was foaled on the Isle of Wight in 1908, he went to war with his owner General Jack Seely (Lord Mottistone) in 1914. He was involved in many of the famous battles of the Great War including the charge at Moreuil Wood on 30 March 1918. The men of the Canadian Cavalry were aware that they had a special fearless horse in their midst and made him their mascot. He survived the war, returning to the Isle of Wight and died at the grand old age of 32. His obituary in the *Evening Standard* in 1941 read as follows:

> 'HORSE THE GERMANS COULD NOT KILL'
>
> Lord Mottistone's famous old warhorse Warrior, which he and Sir John French (Lord Ypres) rode during the last war, has died at Mottistone Manor, Isle of Wight at the age of 32. Warrior had so many narrow escapes from death in the last war that the Canadian Cavalry, who Lord Mottistone commanded in France, used to call him 'the horse the Germans could not kill'.

Appendix 7

Letter from Alfred Thomas Turner sent to the Rector of St Peter's, Nevendon.

Kind permission of the Rector of St Peter's Nevendon

Friday, 4th Feb., 1916,

"SOMEWHERE IN FRANCE."

Dear Mr. Hands and Parishioners,

What a strange mixture of civilization and brutality war as waged in this campaign is. It seems almost incredible that so short a time ago as Christmas I was with you all.

And here I am now at the front, most of you have friends and dear ones here as well, so my attempt to give you in a few brief lines some idea of the life we lead may be of interest.

Our "home," where I write this, consists of a little hut built of trees and bags filled with earth, and is in a large wood, which no doubt may be quite a nice place in the summer when the Boches do not send us any compliments in way of shells, but just now it is little more than a lake of mud. From here a walk of about a mile over shell-torn desolate country takes one into the fire trenches. You must not imagine them as anything resembling any you may have seen in your neighbourhood.

Try to picture what a rabbit warren would look like if it were left undisturbed for months, only substitute men for the rabbits, and it may give you some idea of the life we lead. Holes burrowed into the earth provide kitchens, bedrooms and parlours, whilst here and there the sound of a gramaphone can be heard reeling off some well-known popular refrain.

During the day things are usually more or less quiet, but when dusk comes activity on all sides is noticeable. Huns are by no means the only creatures to be killed, for rats then come out in their hundreds. A sergeant of a certain famous regiment proudly shewed me yesterday a bag of twenty which he had made with the aid of a little terrier he possesses. I wish it were as easy to kill our larger enemy, but of course one has to be careful that he does not kill you first.

Another interesting excavation is the T.P. or trench post office, carefully protected by hundreds of sand bags, here letters and parcels are sorted, and then distributed to the eager recipients. Life would be indeed dull without these messages of home to cheer the men in their monotonous vigil. I will now say good-bye.

Always yours,

THOS. A. TURNER.

Appendix 8 Basildon Borough Roll of Honour

Name	Date killed
Basildon	
Bates, Percy John	26 Aug. 1914
Bridge, Henry James	9 April 1917
Brown, William Edwin	3 July 1916
English, John	3 Sept. 1916
Hawton, Leo Victor	23 Oct. 1918
McMahon, Arthur	26 Aug. 1914
Mockford, Joseph	8 April 1917
Moores, Frank	30 Nov. 1917
Parmenter, Astor Gilbert	31 May 1916
Pean, Harold David Cornish	30 Nov. 1917
Pean, P.D.F.	26 June 1916
Revening, George Edwin	9 Sept. 1917
Revening, William	3 Aug. 1916
Strong, Edward George	27 May 1918
Dunton	
Beatwell, Arthur George	18 Nov. 1914
Beatwell, Ernest	31 May 1916
Dove, Edward Alfred	10 May 1918
Ellis, Charles	27 Nov. 1918
Gigg, Henry	6 Aug. 1915
Jiggens, Arthur Thomas	6 Oct. 1917
Lincoln, Harry	23 Mar. 1917
Smith, Thomas	21 Feb. 1917
Willis, Frederick	26 Sept. 1918
Wilson, William Walter	20 Aug. 1916
Laindon	
Ackers, Alfred William	22 April 1918
Andrew, John	29 April 1916
Barker, Benjamin	22 Nov. 1914
Branch, William John	13 June 1918
Bright, Edward	2 Aug. 1916
Bright, Frederick	12 June 1915
Brockwell, Frederick	7 July 1916
Brockwell, William John	25 May 1916
Brooks, William	Unknown
Bruce, Bemjamin	9 Sept. 1914
Curtis, Alfred James	12 May 1917
Danzig, George	25 Sept. 1915
Douglas, Alfred Sydney	22 Sept. 1914

Douglas, Arthur George	20 April 1916
Dove, Bernard	23 Oct. 1916
Fowler, John Charles	6 Mar. 1919
Fowler, William George	13 Mar.1915
Francis, Harry George	2 Dec. 1917
French, Frank Arthur	19 Mar. 1917
Garnish, Thomas	29 April 1917
Hazell, Rowland Herbert	24 Jan. 1918
Hornsey, Edwin William	9 Oct. 1917
Jarvis, William	1 Oct. 1916
Jones, Arthur	Unknown
Jones, Leonard	23 Mar. 1918
Kerby, James John	28 Sept.1916
Larkin, Harry John Leslie	25 Nov. 1918
Lockwood, Arthur Charles	14 April 1918
Mead, Herbert Arthur	9 July 1917
Moulder, John Silvanus	19 July 1916
Nicklin, Herbert Hudson	15 Nov. 1916
Palmer, William Watson	1 Aug. 1918
Price, Robert Edward	14 July 1916
Smith, Stanley	26 Dec. 1916
Stewart, Arthur Edward	14 April 1917
Stewart, James Arthur	31 Oct. 1916
Stockwell, James	14 Nov. 1915
Stuart, A	19 May 1917
Walshe, James D	6 April 1918

Langdon Hills

Tavener, Harold Tait	12 April 1918
Bassford, Harold Edwin	10 Nov. 1918
Bruce, Benjamin	9 Sept. 1914
Clayton, Harold Robert	4 June 1915
Denton, George Clarke	9 Oct. 1916
Faux, Gregory Christopher	21 Feb. 1917
Flack, Frank Edward	6 Aug. 1916
Franks, Charles Frederick	13 Oct. 1914
Garrod, William Edward	24 Aug. 1918
Grant, Herbert Samuel	20 May 1916
Hammond, Reginald Ernest	10 Aug. 1917
Hollowbread, Ernest John	6 Aug. 1915
Jay, George Robert	22 Apr. 1917
Jay, Walter Arthur	13 April 1918
Laws, Thomas	18 April 1918
Love, F Brunton	8 June 1918

Miller, Ernest Vivian	25 Sept. 1915
Pavitt, Ernest Charles	30 Nov. 1917
Rogerson, Thomas William	24 Aug. 1918
Siggers, George	8 Feb. 1917
Stephens, John Hay	21 April 1917
Stratton, Harry Charles	31 May 1919
Swan, Henry George	22 Nov. 1914

Vange

Avery, Frederick William	11 Oct. 1918
Blake, Thomas	20 Feb. 1916
Blanks, Charles	15 April 1917
Brown, William	3 July 1916
Brown, W. H.	6 June 1917
Brownjohn, Frederick	9 July 1917
Carter, Joseph	26 Sept. 1916
Cheshire, Albert Edward	27 Mar. 1917
Clark, John	3 July 1916
Cranfield, Reginald	31 July 1917
Derrick, Tom	30 June 1915
Doe, Leonard William	5 May 1918
Edwards, William	3 May 1917
Garrod, Albert William	3 July 1916
Grey, Arthur	31 Mar. 1918
Hadlow, William Thomas	27 Mar. 1918
Harris, Emmanuel	5 July 1915
Hiscox, Frederick Herbert	15 Sept. 1916
Hooker, James	20 Jan. 1917
Hull, Luke Alban	28 Aug. 1918
Jiggins, Edward James	20 Aug. 1916
Johnson, Frederick William	5 Apr. 1918
Johnson, James	26 Sept. 1917
Kroenig-Ryann, Alexander Charles	24 Oct. 1915
Little, Thomas Scott	21 Aug. 1916
Main, Bert Albert	8 Mar. 1916
Mclachlan, Sidney James	8 Nov. 1918
Methuen, St John Arthur Paul	20 July 1918
Moore, Herbert	14 June 1917
Mottant, Henry	28 Aug. 1918
Ockenden, Albert Ernest	4 June 1915
Rust, Frederick Charles	26 Oct. 1916
Snoswell, Arthur Cecil	11 Mar. 1917
Spurgeon, Ernest Arthur	23 Aug. 1914
Thurgood, Frederick George	24 Apr. 1918

Pitsea

Annall, James A.T	3 Oct. 1918
Collins, Alfred John	29 Sept. 1918
Crouch, James George	15 Aug. 1918
Davis, William	18 Oct. 1916
Farrant, William	12 Jan. 1917
Gray, Sidney Benjamin	11 April 1917
Hawkins, Charles	4 Mar. 1917
Hills, Ernest	3 May. 1915
Hills, Henry	24 Oct. 191
Hills, Vincent	4 May 1917
Hopper, Joseph Henry	27 June 1918
Howard, Francis Albert	23 April 1917
Howard, Reginald Douglas	4 Oct. 1915
Keene, Hector Conway	11 July 1918
Lawton, Sidney	14 Oct. 1917
Leeks, Arthur Ernest	1 Oct. 1915
Lewsey, Arthur Henry	2 June 1917
Little, William Scott	22 June 1917
Lodge, Albert	23 Nov. 1914
Lord, Arthur Malcolm	23 July 1916
Lovett, Clarence	8 Nov. 1918
Markquick, Arthur Christian	15 Oct. 1914
Markquick, John Alfred	3 May 1917
Meredith, Richard	28 Sept.1917
Moore, James Henry	9 Nov.1918
Muggleton, Frank Ronald	23 Mar. 1918
Pinnock, William	23 April 1915
Robertson, Amos	8 Oct, 1918
Smith, Leonard George	1 July 1916
Steele, William	13 Jan. 1915
Street, Thomas	21 April 1918
Strong, Robert Abraham	1 Dec. 1918
Swan, Henry George	22 Nov. 1914
Thompson, Frederick	2 Nov. 1919
Turner, William Henry	21 Oct. 1914
Wedlock, Ernest William	13 Sept. 1918
Welford, James William	10 Feb. 1917
Willsmer, Reginald Claude	27 Oct. 1918
Wood, Thomas Frederick	17 Sept. 1916
Yarwood, Albert	18 May 1916

Bowers Gifford

Franklin, James	25 Oct. 1915

Gallant, William	13 Nov. 1916
Harrison, Wilfred Ernest	10 April 1918
Key, William Samuel	2 Oct. 1918
Lucas, Frank	23 Feb. 1919
Newman, Herbert Henry	25 Mar. 1919
Neville, Ernest George	9 Oct. 1917
Ockendon, Wilfred	28 Sept. 1915
Payne, Clifford	13 April 1916
Payne, Victor George	14 Nov. 1915
Polley, Charles	4 Aug. 1917
Reed, George	25 May 1918
Willis, Alfred	18 Nov. 1918
Wootten, Joseph Henry	30 Oct. 1914

Nevendon

Hart, Percy	30 Nov. 1917
Harvey, William	8 Oct. 1918
Harvis, Albert	16 April 1917
Key, William	13 Oct. 1915
Kimberley, Frederick John	20 April 1918
Letch, Percy	7 Nov. 1917
Love, F. Brunton	8 June 1918
Masters, Harry	6 April 1915
Ruggles, Albert Walter	7 July 1917
Turner, Thomas Alfred	29 April 1917
West, Charles	6 Aug. 1915
Wright, Sydney Reginald	28 July 1917

North Benfleet

Burrells, William John	10 Oct. 1917
Parslow, Joseph Henry	6 May 1918
Peacock, William David	24 Sept. 1916
Porter, Reuben	27 April 1915
Stribling, John	31 May 1916
Watson, Henry	31 Dec. 1916

This roll of honour does not include the parishes of Wickford, Billericay or their surrounding districts as they have already been published. The information has been gathered by the Basildon Heritage Group, there could be other names that have not come to light.

Appendix 9

Menin Gate – during the period of the Second World War when Ypres was occupied by the Germans the daily service was conducted at Brookwood Military Cemetery in Surrey.

References

Australian Red Cross Society Files
John Williams. *From Corn to Cordite*
Basildon Heritage Group, Green Centre, Wat Tyler, Pitsea – www.basildonheritage.org.uk
John Barfoot. *Essex Airmen* 1910 – 1918
Essex Police Museum, Chelmsford.
Andrew Summers and John Debenham. *The Essex Hundred*
R.A. Beckett. *Romantic Essex*
E. Milton Small. *Told From the Ranks*
Stow Maries, Essex WWI Aerodrome Museum - www.stowmaries.com
Fiona Waters. *A Corner of a Foreign Field*
Steve Newman. *Wickford Heroes*
Karen J. Dennis. *A Book of Remembrance Billericay & District*
C.T. Atkinson. *The Queen's Own Royal West Kent Regiment*
Captain E.G. Godfrey *The Cast Iron Sixth*
Cross and Cockade International Publications
Kelly's Directories
Chelmsford Chronicle
Essex Newsman
Southend Standard
Laindon Recorder
Marion Hill, *The Honeypot Killers*
National Archives
Essex Record Office (SEAX) – www.seax.essexcc.gov.uk
Commonwealth War Graves Commission – www.cwgc.org
Find my Past – www.findmypast.co.uk
Ancestry – www.ancestry.co.uk

INDEX